Oz Clarke's
Australian
Wine Companion

An essential guide for all lovers of Australian wine

Harcourt, Inc.

Orlando   Austin   New York   San Diego   Toronto   London

www.HarcourtBooks.com

Created and designed by
Websters International Publishers Limited
Axe and Bottle Court
70 Newcomen Street
London SE1 1YT
www.websters.co.uk
www.ozclarke.com

Library of Congress Cataloging-in-Publication
Data available upon request

ISBN 0-15-603025-X

GFEDCB

Color separations by PT Repro,
Multi Warna, Indonesia
Printed and bound in China
Phoenix Offset/The Hanway Press Ltd.

Editorial Director/Chief Editor Fiona Holman
Art Director Nigel O'Gorman
Editorial Assistant Davina Russell
Maps Andrew Thompson
Indexer Angie Hipkin
Production Sara Granger, Jo Fillingham
Regional Consultant Peter Forrestal

*Pages 1, 2: Oz in the Barossa Valley, South
Australia*
*Page 3: Lindemans' Karadoc winery tank farm at
night, Victoria*
*Page 4 McWilliam's Barwang Vineyard in the
Hilltops region, New South Wales*
*Page 176 Oz taking a break at Seppeltsfield in the
Barossa Valley*

Readers' note
The producer entries are organized
alphabetically state by state. Within these A–Z
sections producers with their own entries
elsewhere in the text are indicated by SMALL
CAPITALS.

Contents

Why Australia Matters

Y NAME IS OZ. True or false? I am Australian. True or false? Well, both are false. Let's deal with this Australia thing first. Because I like Australia and have been a great supporter of Australian wine over the years – and I sport the name 'Oz' – a lot of people have just assumed I am an Aussie. A few seconds spent listening to my ludicrous Dame Edna-inspired Aussie accent would rapidly convince them otherwise, but there you go. I'm a merry Anglo-Welsh-Irish concoction – mostly Irish – but then quite a lot of Australians would say they fitted that bill too.

And 'Oz'. Well, my mum christened me Owen – there's Welsh for you. That did me pretty well until I took up cricket, a game similar enough to baseball to interest Americans but sufficiently different to bemuse them! My heroes were the entire Kent County First team – and the Australians. They used to come over to England and flay our bowlers, whose best efforts were dispatched either to the boundary rope or well over it with brutal power. So that's how I played, furiously belting any ball that came within reach. Which caused my extremely conservative cricket master at school to regard me as a contagion, an ebola that would lay waste to his precious team if we were allowed to mingle. But my fellow juvenile cricketers loved it. And one day, in the showers, as the Australians were thrashing us at Lords, I was solemnly dubbed Oz. Simple as that. Because I played cricket like an Australian.

Which is all very well, but are we going to get on to wine soon? Yes, right away. My first communion. When I asked where the communion wine came from – Australia was the reply. Lovely, it was. All rich and gooey. It made eight o'clock on a cold Sunday morning positively inviting. Then at university I won half a barrel of Burgundy in a blind tasting by guessing that a wine was Australian. Why did I choose Australia? Because it tasted like nothing I'd ever experienced before. Since I'd never tried Australian wine, it seemed like a fair bet – with a dozen cases of Burgundy dangling before my eyes. I don't know where the organizers had got it from, but it was a Seaview Cabernet 1968! And I liked it.

And I really *don't* know where they got it from. Australian wine in Britain was simple in those far-off 1970s: 'Port', 'Sherry', some Emu sweeties – and communion wine. Actually there was a red – Kanga Rouge. Again, I thought it was pretty good but the quality was immaterial as programmes like Monty Python mercilessly pilloried such grog as Chateau Chunder and Australia was condemned to The Ministry of Silly Wines. I've just got out a couple of wine lists from leading British merchants. Summer 1979. *No* Australian wines. By then, even the 'ports' and 'sherries' were on the slide. In Europe the world of wine was stiflingly conservative. Even such countries as Italy, Spain and Portugal were likely to be consigned to the 'Other Wines' section at the end of the list with, if you were lucky, perhaps a token Chilean or South African.

> '…I found in Australia a soulmate. And I sometimes feel as though purely by chance we've both been beating the same path to the same destination at the same time. Good wine; enjoyable, approachable wine available to all, affordable by all. Sometimes seeking to provide the greatest pleasure for the greatest number and achieving it. Sometimes saying, 'We're not frightened, we can equal those old-timers from Europe'. But more often saying, 'We're Australian, we don't copy anyone. Take us for what we are. And enjoy it.'

This is what I dream about as I sit through a winter's day in dull ol' London town. A valley of vines and paddocks roasted by the heat of a sun that finally relents and drifts away towards the west, leaving trails of red and gold to be slowly lapped up by the shadows. Distant hills reaching up into a sky of the deepest, purest blue. And a wise old eucalyptus tree, older than any of us, standing thoughtful guard over this unique and addictive landscape. These are the Porongurup Hills near Mount Barker in Western Australia.

But I knew things were changing. I'd joined the Royal Shakespeare Company as a budding actor and headed off to the USA and Australia to perform *Hedda Gabler* with Glenda Jackson. Now, actors didn't earn much, and so I'd become something of an expert in Britain at ferreting out half-decent bargain basement booze. But, by God it was hard work. No fruit. No freshness. Rarely even any cleanness. Just flat, stale muck from the rump end of the ancient, exhausted vinelands of France, Spain, Italy and wherever. And never ripeness. It's as though Britain had been starved of ripeness in its wines for a thousand years.

And then I hit the streets of Sydney and Melbourne. I'd buy the cheapest wine in the shop. It would be bursting with fruit, with ripeness, with a cheery 'grab me and drink me' personality that was a revelation. And the way wine was drunk was a revelation. You didn't have to get out your best crystal and order a three-course dinner to drink wine of any level. Wherever you were, whoever you were with, whatever you felt like drinking from, whether a tooth mug or a tumbler or an heirloom, or whether you were at a picnic or a barbecue – or neither – you just drank it for the sheer pleasure of the thing. And I returned to Britain bursting with excitement about the 'New World' of wine – its flavours, its styles, and its drinkers – that I'd just discovered.

Well, for years, my zealous pronouncements fell on deaf ears. The establishment still had an iron grip on our wine world and didn't want young whippersnappers like me upsetting their cosy cart. But this 'New World' freedom that I had experienced was based on several phenomena. First, social liberalization. The long post-World War Two slumber was over. Worldwide the 1960s had witnessed a new generation demanding change. America was in the thick of it, but Australia didn't take long to catch on and young Australians began travelling the world and questioning how things were at home. And one of the things they questioned was that none of the Anglo-Saxon side of their society seemed to be interested in table wine as an everyday beverage, whereas all over Europe these Aussies found people drinking wines with their meals with as little fuss as if it were water. But it rarely tasted good. And that's where the second phenomenon came in. Technological change. Beginning in the 1960s and rapidly spreading through the '70s and '80s, Australians and Californians became fired by a desire to prove they could match and then master the traditional wine gods of Europe. At the top end of the market, the battle is still joined, every vintage, as the Old Countries learn from the New and the New from the Old. Barossa Shiraz versus French Hermitage? Margaret River Cabernet versus Bordeaux? The rivalry is intense and largely beneficial to both parties.

However, it's the lower end that I see as crucial – the area populatedby such brands as [yellowtail] [sic], Jacob's Creek, Banrock Station and Lindemans Bin 65. Northern Europe had no popular wine-drinking culture, because it had almost no enjoyable popular wine. More than any other 'New World' country,

The Yarra Valley just near Melbourne is a beautiful place – calm, almost enchanted in its tranquillity, strewn with meadows, bedecked with vines and ringed by blue-hazed hills. Hoddles Creek vineyard is way up in the forested hillsides, far removed from the pressures and tensions of life. A place to sit in the sun, listen to the birdsong, and gain a little heartsease. Unless you're the grape-grower. Because this is the coolest, highest part of the Valley, and you'll be fretting about whether you can get those darned grapes ripe before the first winter frosts snatch your harvest from your grasp.

Australia provided this. Small amounts of fine table wine had been made in Australia throughout the twentieth century but it wasn't until the 1960s that the mood which now characterizes the Aussie wine world became at all widespread. My friend and colleague Michael Broadbent once described the bush fire that raged through the nascent Australian wine community as massive enthusiasm, but also a burning desire to learn, to understand and to excel. At every level. The Aussies don't like being topped by anybody, or anything. This may get up your nose on the sports field, but this 'you gotta have a go' attitude was just what the whole world of wine needed 20, 30, 40 years ago. Australia led the way in pioneering the use of stainless steel and temperature control in winemaking – absolutely fundamental in a hot country if you're going to produce fresh easy-drinking styles in large quantities. Advances in filtration and hygiene allowed commercial wines to keep a bit of sugar in them – sugar tastes nice – without starting to re-ferment or go sour. The 'bag in box' or cask – or bladder pack as some Aussies touchingly term it – revolutionized wine drinking, sweeping away snobbery and welcoming hordes of first-time drinkers to the wine world. And the development of yeast technology and winemaking 'tricks' such as oak chip flavourings have given a large winery producing millions of litres of wine a year the kind of control that used to be only possible for the handcrafted products of tiny estates.

And we all benefited. 'Sunshine in a bottle' is what Australia offered in the 1980s. Lovely, ripe, affordable grog, labelled simply according to its grape variety as you'd label an apple in a supermarket. And an array of images winging northwards from the Southern Seas – from *Crocodile Dundee*, to the America's Cup sailing triumph, to their bicentennial in 1988 which must have been one of the most joyous national celebrations ever – until the Sydney 2000 Olympics showed that the Aussies were champions at celebrating almost anything so long as you gave them an excuse. And an outdoors life. Sunshine, beaches, barbies, a cheery bonhomie that seemed like paradise in the far frozen north of Europe.

And my good fortune has been to be there right through the rollercoaster ride. I wasn't intending to make a career in wine when I first visited Australia as an actor. My first 'serious' wine trip was to Australia when I got a week off from singing General Perón in *Evita* during the 1980s. But both trips fired me with some of the passion that was so evident down under. They made me want to democratize wine, to push back the barriers of elitism, to swipe away the cobwebs of snobbery and start to preach the simple, classless, open-to-all joys that wine possessed. Had I not visited Australia and California when I did, I doubt I'd have had the courage to try to pursue what was, frankly, a difficult path, because there'd have been no wines worthy of the social revolution going on all around me – enjoyable to drink, easy to understand, affordable to buy.

But I found in Australia a soulmate. And I sometimes feel as though purely by chance we've both been beating the same path to the same destination at the same time. Good wine; enjoyable, approachable wine available to all, affordable by all. Sometimes seeking to provide the greatest pleasure for the greatest number and achieving it. Sometimes saying, 'We're not frightened, we can equal those old-timers from Europe'. But more often saying, 'We're Australian, we don't copy anyone. Take us for what we are. And enjoy it.'

No vineyards in this picture? No barrels, no fermentation tanks? No people. Exactly. After a long, exhausting (honest! You try tasting a hundred red and white wines every morning, then having a big lunch, tours of the vineyard, barrel sampling and vat sampling of the new vintage, an ice cold beer to relax with, a glass of bubbly before dinner – and then dinner – every day! Hmm. Perhaps it doesn't sound that much like hard work after all) – I'll start again. After a long, exhausting trip, I need a couple of days' quiet and contemplation on the beach. This beach, at the mouth of the Margaret River in Western Australia, would suit me fine.

Green, golden-brown and blue – the colours of South Australia. Add a few gum trees breaking the skyline, and a dusty track winding away over the brow of the hill and this vineyard scene near Tanunda in the Barossa foothills could be repeated right across the state.

Australia setting the scene

AUSTRALIA DIDN'T HAVE MANY ADVANTAGES when it came to establishing a wine industry. There was no history of wine among the Aboriginal people because there weren't any native vines. None of Australia's trading partners in South-East Asia had ever had wine as part of their culture. And it didn't seem propitious that the nation which decided to colonize the vast continent was Britain. Now, if the French, or the Italians, or the Spanish…

We forget one thing. The British weren't much good at growing grapes at home, but they were the world's greatest connoisseurs when it came to appreciating the wine of other European countries, in particular the table wines of France and the fortified wines of Portugal and Spain. Since Australia was initially settled as a penal colony, the authorities were keen to establish a temperate wine-drinking culture, rather than one based on the more savage rum. And at the end of the eighteenth century, when New South Wales was gradually establishing itself, Europe was embroiled in war. The idea of a British Imperial vineyard not hostage to Europe must have seemed enticing. Well, it almost did work out like that. For considerable portions of the nineteenth and twentieth centuries, Australia provided a steady stream of unchallenging – and mostly fortified – wines that were lapped up by Britain. But by the last quarter of the twentieth century the country had embarked on a remarkable voyage of wine discovery that has placed her at the forefront of all that is best in the New Age of wine.

This position has been achieved without Australia enjoying many of the perceived benefits of Europe's classic regions, most of which are poised on the cusp between not being able to and being able to ripen their fruit. Unlike Europe, the general rule in Australia is more than enough sunshine and not nearly enough rain. Traditionalists say you can't make great wine under such conditions but Australia's winemakers have turned this to their advantage, using irrigation freely and highlighting the ripeness of the grapes in a succession of sun-filled, richly textured wines. These may initially have been inspired by the best of Europe, but they have created such a forceful identity of their own that Europe now often attempts to ape the style of these Down Under Wonders. In the meantime, a better understanding of how to bring grapes to optimum ripeness have led to an explosion of cool-climate wine regions on the fringes of this parched continent that challenge, but in no way imitate, the old classic regions of Europe.

Quick guide ◆ Classification system for Australian wine

Classifications Australia's system for classifying wines on the labels of bottles for export stems from an 1994 agreement with the EU. The Geograpical Indications Committee was set up in 1993 to begin to define areas of origin, dividing the wine-producing states into a number of zones, regions and sub-regions. The discussions, arguments and political wranglings that accompany such decisions will be in full voice for some years yet.

The system has to encompass certain peculiarities. The main one is the widespread use of regional blending in Australia: that is, trucking grapes from several different areas, possibly in different states, for blending together. Four major wine groups (Southcorp, Hardys, Orlando-Wyndham and Beringer Blass) make nearly 60 per cent of Australia's wine, and they rely a lot on blending varieties

and wines from different areas, especially for their big-selling brands, such as Koonunga Hill and Jacob's Creek, which are now important players in the wine scene. Whatever the origin of a wine, however, 85 per cent of its grapes must come from the area specified, whether it is a zone, region or sub-region, and it must be made of at least the same percentage of the named grape variety.

QUALITY CATEGORIES AND GEOGRAPHICAL INDICATIONS
● **The Label Integrity Program** This system (also called LIP) guarantees all claims made on the label, for example, the vintage, variety and region, by making annual checks and audits on specific regions, varieties and wineries.
● **Produce of Australia** This is the most general geographical designation. Any wine

sold solely under this category cannot have a grape variety or a vintage on its label.
● **South-Eastern Australia** This category covers most of the wine-producing areas of Australia and is widely seen, particularly on the big-selling brand name wines.
● **State of Origin** This is the next most specific category.
● **Zones** Many of Australia's traditional wine areas have been incorporated into zones. For example, Barossa is a zone within South Australia. Many zones are fairly meaningless, sometimes even covering areas that are desert but bureaucrats must have their fun.
● **Regions** These are the next level, for example, the Barossa zone is divided into the regions of Barossa Valley and Eden Valley.
● **Sub-regions** Some regions are divided into sub-regions, for example, Eden Valley consists of the High Eden and Springton sub-regions.

FOR MORE DETAILED MAPS SHOWING REGIONS AND SUB-REGIONS SEE

0 km 250 500
0 miles 250

N

ARAFURA SEA

DARWIN

TIMOR SEA

Roper

*CORAL
SEA*

Gulf of
Carpentaria

CAIRNS

*INDIAN
OCEAN*

Fitzroy

NORTHERN TERRITORY

Flinders

**GREAT SANDY
DESERT**

**TANAMI
DESERT**

Lake
Mackay

QUEENSLAND

GREAT DIVIDING RANGE

**HAMERSLEY
RANGE**

Lake
Disappointment

ALICE SPRINGS

Gascoyne

**MACDONNELL
RANGES**

1

GIBSON DESERT

Lake
Amadeus

BRISBANE

Lake
Carnegie

WESTERN AUSTRALIA

**SIMPSON
DESERT**

Barwon

GREAT VICTORIA DESERT

6

Lake
Eyre

Darling

19

Macquarie

20

21

Lake
Barlee

SOUTH AUSTRALIA

Lake
Torrens

Lake
Frome

FLINDERS RANGES

NEW SOUTH WALES

Hunter

22

Lake
Moore

Lake
Gairdner

Nullarbor Plain

23

NEWCASTLE

PERTH

2

Lachlan

24

26

SYDNEY

3

Murrumbidgee

25

CANBERRA

4

7

8

10

13

Murray

**AUSTRALIAN
CAPITAL
TERRITORY**

5

*SOUTHERN
OCEAN*

9

14

15

18

11

VICTORIA

16

17

MELBOURNE

12

*TASMAN
SEA*

Bass Strait

TASMANIA

HOBART

WINE ZONES

WESTERN AUSTRALIA

1. Eastern Plains, Inland and North of
   Western Australia
2. Greater Perth
3. Central Western Australia
4. West Australian South-East Coastal
5. South-West Australia

SOUTH AUSTRALIA

6. Far North
7. The Peninsulas
8. Mt Lofty Ranges
9. Barossa
10. Lower Murray
11. Fleurieu
12. Limestone Coast

VICTORIA

13. North-West Victoria
14. Central Victoria
15. North-East Victoria
16. Western Victoria
17. Port Phillip
18. Gippsland

NEW SOUTH WALES

19. Western Plains
20. Northern Slopes
21. Northern Rivers
22. Hunter Valley
23. Central Ranges
24. Big Rivers
25. Southern New South Wales
26. South Coast

QUEENSLAND

NORTHERN TERRITORY

AUSTRALIAN CAPITAL TERRITORY

TASMANIA

Grapes of Australia

Old Shiraz vines at Brand's of Coonawarra. Shiraz was the main grape in Coonawarra up until 1950 and played an important part in establishing its international reputation as Australia's leading red wine region. However, Brand's old Shiraz vines are some of the few left in Coonawarra.

THERE ARE THOUSANDS AND THOUSANDS of grape varieties in the world. So why does it often feel as if you are being given a choice of only Chardonnay or Cabernet Sauvignon or Shiraz when you buy a bottle of Australian wine? How come those thousands seem to have been narrowed down to only two or three? There are several answers. Most of the world's grape varieties are only used for dessert grapes or raisins, or are rarely grown, or are the wrong species for winemaking; in other words they might be capable of making wine, but it tastes foul. The indigenous vines of North America can produce wine – but just taste it! I thought the murky brew tasted like Euthymol toothpaste mixed with port last time I tried it. But that's America's problem not Australia's, because Australia has *no* indigenous vines. Even so, of the 1000 or so varieties that are at all significant for wine, only about 30 have international relevance.

Vine cuttings have been transported vast distances over the centuries and such movements of vines are not new, merely faster than they used to be. A few decades ago Chardonnay was seen as a Burgundian or Champagne variety. Now it's grown in almost every wine region of the world with aspirations, including every region of Australia. The crucial factor in the flavour of a wine is grape variety. Every grape has its own flavour, though most need specific climates to give their best. Thus Cabernet Sauvignon grown in too cold a climate like most of Tasmania produces thin, grassy wines; too hot, like in many of the inland irrigated vineyard regions in the Murray-Darling basin, and it risks being baked and raisiny. But when the worldwide movement of vines creates a chance combination of right vine, right climate and right soil, that's when classic wine styles can be established. A repeat of old classics or a creation of 'new' classics. A bit of both, but in Australia's case there's been a lot more creating of 'new' classics than aping of the old.

EARLY DAYS

There were grape vines in Australia from the time that Governor Arthur Phillip's First Fleet arrived in 1788 and, literally within days of landing they were being planted on the newly cleared land. We don't really know what varieties these first guys planted, because the first grapes rotted on the vine in the humid conditions. Vineyards gradually moved inland as settlers searched for decent conditions. By the 1830s, vineyards had been established in the Hunter Valley north of Sydney where vines flourish to this day. At last the new Australians could start worrying about what kind of vines might produce the best grapes. As I said above, there were no indigenous vines in Australia, and the First Fleet merely picked up whatever vine cuttings were available on the way out at places like Cape of Good Hope. But these boats were filled with sailors, soldiers and convicts. Not vineyard experts.

It wasn't until 1833 that expert selection of vines really got going. James Busby did an extensive tour of France and Spain, and returned to Australia with cuttings of more than 350 healthy grape varieties, including most of the classic varieties of France as well as Palomino, Muscat Gordo Blanco, Pedro Ximenez and Doradillo, which were to prove important in the production of the fortified and bulk wines. Busby's cuttings were particularly important in creating a good base for vineyards in the Hunter and South Australia. In the first half of the nineteenth century, cuttings were regularly collected from places at which sailing ships stopped en route for Australia: in particular, the island of Madeira and the Cape of Good Hope. Some immigrants, such as those from Silesia who settled in the Barossa, brought their own cuttings with them, notably Riesling and Shiraz. When Dr Christopher Penfold arrived in 1844, he had brought with him Grenache cuttings which he had collected in the Rhône Valley. For his McLaren Vale vineyard at Clarendon, Edward Peake imported a range of cuttings from Spain including Pedro Ximenez, Palomino and Doradillo, again classic fortified varieties, even if they made pretty dull table wine. Following the successful discovery of gold, vineyards became widespread in Victoria in the second half of the nineteenth century. Swiss and German growers used their contacts in Europe to source cuttings. Paul de Castella bought 20,000 Cabernet Sauvignon

These aren't my fingers (pink enough, but too pretty by half), but I have caressed, stroked and revered these wonderful old vines at Tahbilk. Many of the oldest vines in the world are in Australia, imported during the nineteenth century and still giving small amounts of fantastically flavoured grapes. They're ugly yet beautiful, seemingly half dead yet magnificently alive, so fragile you can rock them with your hand and fear they'll topple on your feet, yet they'll still be here next year, and the year after; maybe even when you and me are long gone their rickety boughs and tiny bunches of fruit will still be giving joy to a new generation of devotees.

vines from Bordeaux's Château Lafite in 1849 and Charles Louis Tetaz recalls Swiss and German growers from Geelong buying Pinot Noir from Dijon. Others brought in Marsanne and Roussanne so by the second half of the nineteenth century there was a pretty good mix of vines available – varieties from Spain and Madeira for fortifieds, warm climate red varieties from France for table wine and 'port' production and a few parcels of 'cool climate' varieties like Semillon, Riesling, Pinot Noir and Cabernet. Probably the biggest omission was Chardonnay.

However, which ones were to flourish would depend on what wine styles became most popular and by the beginning of the twentieth century, fortified wine, much of it destined for British throats, was dominating the market. Cool climate varieties went into retreat and many cool climate vineyard regions, especially in Victoria, fell into disuse. You might have thought the floods of immigrants after the Second World War from places like Italy, Greece and Yugoslavia might have brought an influx of those countries' grape varieties – but it didn't happen. They simply used whatever grapes they found to make their wines, and it wasn't until the 1970s that interest in good table wine began to revive and the new Australia began to emerge. In 1956 80 per cent of all wine production was fortified. Now it's a mere 5 per cent. The 1970s and '80s brought a great increase in the French 'classic' varieties (Cabernet, Merlot, Pinot Noir, Sauvignon and, obviously, Chardonnay) since these were the styles of wine the New World wanted to make. But the 1990s saw winemakers realize Australia already had a fantastic resource of old warm climate varieties like Shiraz, Grenache, Mourvedre and Verdelho as well as unfashionable but top quality whites like Semillon and Riesling. And as the new century blossoms, Australia's new confidence is expressed by increases in the classic Italian, Spanish and Portuguese varieties. Who knows, maybe the time is ripe for some old Yugoslav and Greek varieties as well.

Quick guide ◆ Top grapes

Australia's favourite wine grape varieties
(Total hectares planted)

Red grapes

Shiraz	37,016
Cabernet Sauvignon	28,871
Merlot	10,352
Pinot Noir	4270
Grenache	2322
Petit Verdot	1337
Sangiovese	657
Tempranillo	216

White grapes

Chardonnay	24,138
Semillon	6283
Riesling	3987
Sauvignon Blanc	2953
Muscat Gordo Blanco	2479
Colombard	2705
Verdelho	1612
Viognier	541
Muscat à Petits Grains	242

2003 figures ABS Vineyard Survey

Classic Red Grapes

Jim Barry's The Armagh Vineyard produces one of Clare Valley's top reds. The Armagh is about as big as Australian Shiraz can get – and that's pretty big. American oak is part of the secret, but old vines and the determination of the Barry family to trump their friends and colleagues in the valley are the true reasons behind the wine's brilliance.

EXPANSION FUELLED BY AN AMAZING GROWTH in exports (from 125 million litres in 1994 to 525 million litres in 2003) has meant unprecedented vineyard plantings around Australia. For red wines, this demand is being met by plantings of Shiraz, Cabernet Sauvignon and Merlot. Although planted in much smaller volume, Petit Verdot and Durif are proving successful in the warmer irrigated regions and so are also being used to meet export demand. Renewed respect for old-vine Grenache and Mourvedre has seen these former workhorse varieties (often blended with Shiraz) transformed into fashionable premium wines.

Interest in exotic Italian, Spanish and French varieties has seen a profusion (albeit on a relatively small scale) of plantings of grapes such as Sangiovese, Tempranillo, Nebbiolo, Barbera, Dolcetto, Lagrein, Saperavi and Marzemino. It's early days but there appears to be a market for well-crafted wines that display some point of difference from the sea of common varietals.

Shiraz is now Australia's most significant red wine grape. Fashionable as well as versatile, styles across the nation vary widely.

SHIRAZ

Heat is what this red vine, the Syrah of the northern Rhône in France, likes: in a hot, dry climate, planted in poor soil, it'll be happy as a sandboy and in Australia it responds magnificently.

Since it was first introduced to Australia in the 1830s and in the Barossa in the 1840s, Shiraz has been the great Australian grape. It could do anything: it could produce light, soft, jammy reds or blockbusters; it could make sparkling wines; and it could make fortified wines. It has remained the country's dominant red variety in spite of a fall from favour in the 1980s (accompanied by plummeting grape prices and the 1986 vine pull scheme which led to the loss of many, now-priceless, old Barossa vines first planted in the mid-19th century) and the challenge from Cabernet Sauvignon in the 1990s. More than 330,000 tonnes were harvested in 2004.

Shiraz has done best in the warmth of the Barossa and McLaren Vale where it produces rich, ripe, robust reds with irresistible velvety texture and heaps of flavour.

In the last 15 years or so, as well as growing in popularity as a delicious, approachable, fleshy quaffing wine, Shiraz has become prized as the variety which produces many of Australia's most distinguished wines. Low-yielding, unirrigated, century-old vines contribute to iconic wines such as Penfolds Grange, Henschke's Hill of Grace, Peter Lehmann's Stonewell, Grant Burge's Meshach and Wendouree's Shiraz.

While its home has been South Australia, Shiraz has always displayed its versatility and has been widely planted around the country – especially in recent times. Excellent expressions of the grape have been produced in regions such as the Hunter Valley, Grampians, Heathcote, Great Southern and Canberra; and all of them are thrillingly different, usually more scented than those of the Barossa and with a blacker, but fresher fruit.

CABERNET SAUVIGNON

Although Cabernet was recognized as a classic grape variety in Australia in the 19th century, it all but disappeared in the first half of the 20th century. This is probably due to the fact that it is low yielding and unsuited to the production of fortified wines. Plantings increased from the 1950s – indeed, an experimental 1953 Penfolds Grange was made from Cabernet Sauvignon – and by 1975, 15,000 tonnes were being harvested. This had doubled by 1990 (to 31,000 tonnes) and more than doubled again by 1996 (to 72,600 tonnes). The annual crush in

Plantings of Cabernet Sauvignon in Australia are still rising and modern winemakers are becoming ever more effective at helping it express the local growing conditions.

2004 was in excess of 250,000 tonnes, with South Australia still dominating production of the variety.

The best regions for Cabernet Sauvignon remain cool climate Coonawarra and Margaret River, with the Yarra Valley and the Great Southern making some impressive reds as do the warmer Clare Valley, Barossa, McLaren Vale and Langhorne Creek. Many of the larger companies producing quaffing Cabernet from the vast irrigated vineyards in the regions along the Murray River are now adding (up to 20%) fruit from these premium regions to improve the flavour profile and weight of their wines.

PINOT NOIR

Most of the Pinot Noir grown in Australia is picked early and used for sparkling wine base, when it is usually blended with Chardonnay. It grows best in cooler areas such as the Melbourne 'Dress Circle' (the Yarra Valley, Geelong, Macedon, Mornington Peninsula and Gippsland), Tasmania and the Adelaide Hills. Some promise is being shown in the Victorian Alps, Tumbarumba, Canberra and Orange.

Australia's most impressive Pinots so far come from Bass Phillip, TarraWarra, Diamond Valley, Coldstream Hills and Freycinet while Mount Mary, Yeringberg, Giaconda, Bindi and Rochford are also good producers. The quality of Tasmanian Pinot Noir has risen dramatically over the past five vintages: Freycinet, Domaine A, Providence and Apsley Gorge are among those wineries to shine.

While there is enormous variation between producers within any region, as a generalization it is possible to say that the

Pinot Noirs from the Adelaide Hills tend to be biggish, rich reds with sturdy structure and able to take some aging; from Tasmania the wines are lighter-bodied and more fragrant; from Macedon finer and tighter, though still with rich, concentrated savoury fruit and sometimes a scent of herbs; and from the Yarra Valley, opulent and velvety, with attractive, ripe flavours and fine, unintrusive tannins.

MERLOT

It is difficult to comprehend the speed with which Merlot has been taken up in Australia. Originally thought of as the fleshy grape that would fill out Cabernet Sauvignon and consequently planted in small amounts, there were less than 1200 tonnes harvested in 1988. This increased sixfold over the next eight years (to 7700 tonnes in 1996) and much more than that over the next six years (to 104,000 tonnes in 2002). The 644 vignerons growing Merlot in 2000 had increased to more than 1000 by 2004.

It is now the third most popular red variety (behind Shiraz and Cabernet) but few wines of real excitement have yet been made. I suspect that if Merlot weren't so popular in markets like the USA, we'd see a lot less planted here, because until recently it was thought of as a blender useful in softening the tougher Cabernet Sauvignon. However, in Australia most Cabernet Sauvignon isn't tough, and when it is, Shiraz has traditionally done an excellent blending job.

Another point worth noting is that Merlot has traditionally done best in fairly cool

conditions like those of France's Bordeaux. With the exception of winemakers like Brian Croser at Petaluma, who has always blended Merlot with Cabernet in his Petaluma red precisely because this was how the top red Bordeaux wines were made, most wine producers were hell bent on producing single-variety wines, and most of the cool climate effort until recently was focused on Pinot Noir, or white varieties like Chardonnay or Riesling. More effort is now being made with Merlot but I just don't expect to see a raft of fine Merlots suddenly appearing.

There have been a number of problems with growing Merlot successfully in Australia, from getting the right, virus-free clones to site selection and with making the wine: especially with the overuse of oak. At this stage, Coonawarra is the region that handles Merlot best, with good producers such as Brand's, Petaluma, Parker Estate, Hollick and Katnook. Other good examples from elsewhere in Australia have been made by Jim Irvine, Coldstream Hills, Elderton, Tatachilla and Evans & Tate.

It looks so unappetizing but this is the business end of winemaking – a squelchy mush of crushed red grapes and stains on your hands that will last for days. These grapes are Pinot Noir, which, by dint of bitter experience, I can tell you don't stain half as bad as Shiraz. Pinot Noir is one of the most challenging of all international varieties and continues to tantalize growers worldwide. Australia is no exception.

Classic White Grapes

Chardonnay vineyards at Leeuwin Estate in Margaret River, Western Australia. Leeuwin Estate makes thrilling Chardonnays that equal the top Burgundies of France with their nut and oatmeal richness and savoury depth. And they can age like Burgundy, too. Few people could have dreamt 30 years ago that Australia was capable of such quality.

A^S THE MAJOR WINE COMPANIES have become increasingly reluctant to purchase non-classic varieties from growers along the banks of the Murray River even for their most basic wine, those producers have been forced to replace unwanted varieties (such as Doradillo, Muscat Blanc, Palomino and Trebbiano) with classic varieties such as Chardonnay and Semillon. As with red varieties, much of the recent planting has been fuelled by export demand. However, plantings of reds outpaced whites so dramatically from 1999 to 2003 that a shortage of white wines occurred from the 2003 vintage (and is expected to last until about the 2006). So severe was the imbalance between reds and whites that Australia's largest plant nursery reported that 43 per cent of the cuttings they sold in 2003 were for Chardonnay.

Chardonnay is the most popular white grape in Australia by far, but this popularity is very recent – until the 1980s there was relatively little planted or sold. However the phenomenal success of wines like Lindemans Bin 65 and [yellowtail] means there is now an insatiable demand for the variety.

CHARDONNAY

Although there have been Chardonnay vines planted in Australia since 1920 (on the Penfold Vale vineyard in the Hunter bought by Tyrrell's in 1983), the first varietal Chardonnays weren't released until 1971 – by Tyrrell's and Craigmoor – and it wasn't until well into the 1980s that Chardonnay began to take hold in South Australia where it now produces vast amounts. Within 20 years, Chardonnay had become the dominant white wine variety in Australia and its current production in excess of 250,000 tonnes is significantly more than double its nearest rival, Semillon.

Huge volumes of quaffing wines are produced in the irrigated areas along the River Murray – especially in the Riverland, Murray-Darling and Riverina – under labels such as McWilliam's Hanwood, Jacob's Creek and Lindemans Bin 65. These are quintessential 'sunshine in a bottle' wines: fresh, clean, lively with ripe melon and peach flavours and a hint of oak. They are uncomplicated and refreshing – so long as they haven't been pointlessly sweetened up. The popularity of Chardonnay at the cellar door ensures that examples are produced in most areas of Australia.

At the top end of the market, there has been a move away from big, buttery Chardonnays with heaps of ripe peachy, toasty oak characters to more restrained, more tightly structured, finer wines with cool, minerally, savoury flavours and better potential for aging.

Australia's best Chardonnay regions are Margaret River, the Adelaide Hills, the Hunter Valley and the Melbourne 'Dress circle' (Yarra, Mornington and Geelong). Leeuwin's Art

Series, which has long been considered the country's top example of the variety, is under challenge from Giaconda in Beechworth. Vignerons are seeking extreme sites and cool regions, such as Tasmania and Macedon, to push the boundaries with this classic variety.

RIESLING

After Colin Gramp had introduced the German technology called cold pressure fermentation at Orlando in 1953, the quality of Riesling production in Australia was revolutionized by the enhanced control this gave over fermentation. For the next 30 years, Riesling was second only to Semillon as the most popular white variety in Australia. Then for a decade from 1982, the Riesling crush exceeded that of all other whites until the Chardonnay steamroller gained momentum.

Unlike all other classic varieties, the amount of Riesling grown in Australia has dropped substantially during the 1990s. However, most of this decline has occurred in areas which are unsuited to Riesling production. Australia's best Riesling region, the Clare Valley, increased the amount crushed in the 1990s and has enjoyed substantial growth since 1999.

Riesling was considered unfashionable in the 1990s but its current popularity has seen demand exceed supply in recent vintages. There have been significant improvements in quality in the Clare and Eden Valleys and this is seen in finer, more tautly structured, more citrus-scented Rieslings. These have intense lime juice and mineral flavours and bracing acidity in their youth but transform into deeper, more complex, toasty, honeyed, limey wines with age. Tim Adams, Grosset, Petaluma, Leo Buring 'Leonay', Mount Horrocks, Mitchell, Pike's and Orlando's Steingarten stand out. The renewed interest in cool climate Riesling has focused attention on cool to cold regions such as Great Southern, Tasmania, Canberra, the Grampians and Orange.

SEMILLON

Hunter Valley Semillon is different enough from any other expression of this variety elsewhere in the world to be considered unique: certainly, it is widely regarded as one of Australia's great wine styles.

Picked early, unwooded and bone dry, the best examples (when young) have minerally, lemon zest flavours and, despite a racy acidity that refreshes the palate, are not a lot of fun to drink unless they're from one of the infrequent sunny, dry years. More typically the alcohol is low and the ripeness hardly evident. But at about five to seven years of age, they begin to mellow and display wonderful toasty, honeyed, almost custardy flavours. These become more complex and

Late evening sunlight on Jeffrey Grosset's Riesling vines in the Polish Hill River region of Clare Valley. Rieslings from the Clare and Eden Valleys now rank as benchmark styles of the wine along with those of Germany and Alsace.

gentler with time without losing their zing. Top producers include Tyrrell's, McWilliam's (Mount Pleasant) and Brokenwood.

Most Semillons produced in the Barossa and Clare valleys are wooded and the best are vibrant, juicy whites with custardy oak and lemon citrus flavours. Top producers are Mount Horrocks, Tim Adams, Mitchell, Rockford, The Willows and Peter Lehmann (who have changed to an unoaked style with considerable success).

Margaret River Semillon has an uncharacteristic herbaceous, grassy character more reminiscent of Sauvignon Blanc. Moss Wood, Amberley and Evans & Tate make excellent varietal Semillon but the greatest successes have come with blends of the two varieties. Semillon/Sauvignon Blanc blends, especially from Margaret River, are incredibly popular as quaffing wines across the country.

Two-thirds of the Semillon crop, the dominant white variety in Australia until 1982, is grown in the Riverina where it makes the country's best sweet wines by allowing the grapes to develop the 'noble rot' fungus. Most of it, however, is used in cask wines or sold in bulk, but even at the lower end Riverina Semillon has a fair, citrus, waxy character. Varietal Semillon is distinctly unfashionable and so is often sold at bargain prices.

MUSCAT

The most famous Muscat produced in Australia is the Brown Muscat (a sub-variety of Muscat Blanc à Petit Grains) which makes the richly concentrated, syrupy, world-class fortifieds at Rutherglen in North-East Victoria. There are four levels of quality which approximate to richness, intensity, complexity and average age of the blended wine: Rutherglen Muscat, Classic, Grand and Rare. The solera system of the outstanding producers (Chambers, Morris, Campbells, Buller) for the Rare Muscat contains material dating back to the 1890s. The standard Rutherglen Muscat can be a delightfully fresh, clean, light-bodied, grapy fortified with a refreshing juicy finish. When aged in barrel, these Muscats become dense, heady, concentrated with deep raisiny, treacle and licorice characters, rose petal scent, lush texture and flavours that wash over the palate until long after the bottle's gone.

Muscat of Alexandria (called Muscat Gordo Blanco) is a high-yielding variety that is found in abundance in the irrigated vineyards along the Murray River. Its blunt but grapy aromatics improve the flavour profile of what would otherwise be bland, dull basic wines, but by itself it quickly cloys and you long for the enticing scent and irresistible fruit of the real Muscat grape.

Grenache vines near Lyndoch in the Barossa Valley. These ones were planted in 1936 and were lucky to escape the vine-pull scheme of the mid-1980s that ensured that many low-yielding vineyards of old Grenache and Shiraz were uprooted in favour of the more fashionable Cabernet and Chardonnay. Luckily the Australians came round in the nick of time to appreciate what they had in their own backyard and these old vines are now in demand as Australia rediscovers the virtues of Grenache.

Future Classics and other Grapes

AN INTEREST IN NEWER GRAPE VARIETIES in Australia is being fuelled by consumers eager to experiment with new tastes and by winemakers keen to find a point of difference from their competitors.

RED GRAPES

CABERNET FRANC

While there are about half a dozen examples of varietal Cabernet Franc made in Australia, almost all of its small production (5500 tonnes from 834ha of vineyards in 2003) is blended with Cabernet Sauvignon and Merlot with a view to making more complete, complex reds – and that's the best use for it.

GRENACHE NOIR

Largely because of its value in producing fortifieds, Grenache was the largest volume red varietal in Australia until the early 1970s, and second in importance to Shiraz until 1990. The value of dry-grown, old-vine Barossa and McLaren Vale Grenache has been rediscovered in the last decade or so. Some stunning varietals and blends (especially with Shiraz and Mourvedre) have been made. Recommended producers: Clarendon Hills, D'Arenberg, Henschke, Kilikanoon, Charles Melton, Peter Lehmann, Penfolds.

MALBEC

Like Cabernet Franc, Malbec is almost always used in Australia as a small part of Cabernet Sauvignon blends. Its production is tiny with 488ha planted in 2003. There are good varietal Malbecs made by Bleasdale and Ferngrove but most of the interesting wines are blends – powerful concentrated Shiraz/Malbec and Cabernet/Malbec from century-old vines at Wendouree, Cullen's unique Mangan blend (Malbec, Petit Verdot and Merlot) and Delatite's Dungeon Gully (Malbec, Merlot, Cabernet Sauvignon and Shiraz).

MOURVEDRE (MATARO)

Today, Mourvedre (also known as Mataro in Australia) is most often seen in blends with Shiraz and Grenache and like those two varieties has a long history because of its suitability to fortified winemaking. Unlike most other varieties, it produces about the same volume of grapes today as it did in 1980, although the majority of this is treasured, old-vine material from the Barossa, McLaren Vale and Clare. Charles Melton popularized the Shiraz/Grenache/Mourvedre blend and there are excellent examples by Henschke,

Penfolds, Mitchelton, Grant Burge and Langmeil. Very good varietal Mourvedres are made by D'Arenberg and Hewitson.

NEBBIOLO

It's unreasonable to expect Nebbiolo to shine in new, untried sites with growers who have limited experience of this recalcitrant, tannic variety, best known for producing Barolo in north-west Italy. With 100ha planted (2003) and Australia's interest in exotic grape varieties increasing all the time, there are several promising examples. Beringer Blass's Maglieri, Happs' Three Hills (from Karridale in the south of Margaret River), the King Valley's Pizzini and Scaffidi's One Tree Hill Gulf Breeze from the Adelaide Hills have all impressed me with their most recent vintages of Nebbiolo. Pioneers Brown Brothers and Dromana and the Murray-Darling's Trentham Estate also produce interesting examples.

PETIT VERDOT

Until recently in Australia, Petit Verdot (along with Cabernet Franc and Malbec) had been used as a minor contributor to Cabernet Sauvignon blends where its fragrance and high natural acidity were often greatly valued. As a late-ripening variety, its suitability for the warm irrigated areas along the River Murray and regions such as McLaren Vale (where Pirramimma has pioneered the variety) and Cowra has seen its emergence as a high quality, structured but immediately drinkable red with wild blackberry and blackcurrant perfumes and flavours, fleshy texture and firm but undaunting tannins. Kingston (Empiric), McGuigan, Zilzie and Trentham Estate make excellent examples.

SANGIOVESE

Tuscany's workhorse red grape is the most popular exotic variety planted in Australia with more than 600ha currently under vine from more than 150 growers. Pioneers include Coriole (which planted the variety 20 years ago), Brown Brothers, the King Valley growers, Pizzini and Dromana, who all produce good to very good examples. Other impressive Sangiovese wines so far include Maglieri, the Clare Valley's Cardingham Estate, Scaffidi (One Tree Hill Gulf Breeze) and Stonehaven.

TEMPRANILLO

Spain's classic red variety is Australia's fastest growing variety (in percentage terms) with just over 200ha (2003) from the tiniest of bases at the end of the 1990s. The vast majority of vines are yet to bear fruit. It's too early to make predictions but all the signs are positive for Tempranillo. Those doing well include Central Victorian High Country's Gapsted, Margaret River's Stella Bella, the Murray-Darling's Zilzie and Brown Brothers, which sources fruit from the King Valley.

ZINFANDEL

Given the cult status of Australia's best Zin, Cape Mentelle's benignly brooding alcoholic monster (fleshy, densely blackcurranty with licorice darkness and mighty tannins), it's surprising that Australia has so little. Nepenthe has gained attention for its fragrant, eucalyptus and wild blackberry Adelaide Hills version while the Eden Valley's Jim Irvine blends it with Merlot. The Clare's Wilson Vineyard makes a big, rich, alcoholic sweet Zinfandel.

WHITE GRAPES

CHENIN BLANC

Chenin Blanc does best in the warm climates of the Swan Valley and McLaren Vale. Here it is a light-bodied honeyed variety with ripe tropical fruit and golden plum flavours and is at its most attractive when it finishes crisp and dry. In the Swan Valley, it is the dominant white variety and is best known as a blending component of Houghton White Burgundy (HWB) or on its own at Moondah Brook. While vibrant, floral and fruity when young, these develop an impressive toasty complexity with age and have been mistaken for aged Hunter Semillon – most famously by Len Evans when he was judging at the Adelaide Show. He insisted that the trophy go to a wine that turned out to be the 1994 (if I remember correctly) HWB Show Reserve and was furious when it turned out not to be a Hunter Semillon. Well, that seems like justice done to me. He's always fooling me into swearing that his old Hunter Semillons are white Burgundies. *Touché*.

COLOMBARD

For Australia's third most planted white variety and on the increase, Colombard is surprisingly anonymous. That's because its ability to hang on to acidity in hot areas make it popular with the bulk growers, and it is mainly grown in the warmer areas along the River Murray where it is blended (mainly with Chardonnay and Semillon) for cask whites. Its clean, refreshing acidity and gentle perfume adds a dimension to these wines. Australia's most notable varietal example is La Biondina from Primo Estate.

MARSANNE

In Australia, the Tahbilk estate and Marsanne are almost synonymous: its 40-ha vineyard may well contain the world's oldest Marsanne vines (dating back to 1927) and the world's largest single planting of the variety. When young, this wine is fresh and fruity with delightful honeysuckle flavours: with age, it develops a mellow toastiness and a honeyed creamy finish. There are about a dozen producers of varietal Marsanne in Australia, including near neighbour, Mitchelton; some blend it with Roussanne (notably Yeringberg) and Viognier.

MUSCADELLE/TOKAY

There is only a small amount of Muscadelle in Australia. It is planted in the warmer regions such as the Swan Valley where it contributes a decreasing percentage of the blend for Houghton White Burgundy (HWB). It does best in Rutherglen where it is known as Tokay and is made into world-class fortified wines. Tokay shares Muscat's lush silky texture and its heady concentration of flavour and complexity but is less fleshy and has more savoury, tealeaf and fish oil (honest!) flavours counterpointed by malty, toffee and butterscotch sweetness.

PINOT GRIS/PINOT GRIGIO

This is currently the most trendy white wine produced in Australia. Although most plantings are only tiny, there are now more than 50 varietal wines labelled as Pinot Gris (in most instances) or Pinot Grigio, its Italian name. Most of these wines are from cold or cool regions such as Tasmania, Mornington Peninsula, Mount Benson, Macedon, the Grampians and Adelaide Hills. Most impressive so far are pioneers T'Gallant and Pipers Brook, Mount Langi Ghiran, Henschke, Pike & Joyce, Tim Adams and Primo Estate.

ROUSSANNE

Roussanne has become much more fashionable since Rick Kinzbrunner of Giaconda made his expensive but sublime Aeolia Roussanne and his Nantua Les Deux Roussanne/Chardonnay. Still grown in tiny quantities, it is made as a varietal wine by producers such as D'Arenberg and St Huberts and blended with Marsanne and sometimes Viognier by Mitchelton, Seppelt, Yering Station and Yeringberg.

VERDELHO

Traditionally used in Portugal for Madeira or white port, Verdelho used for table wines is unique to Australia: its popularity has soared

Yalumba produces Australia's best examples of Viognier – some of the fruit comes from their famous, stunningly beautiful Heggies Vineyard high up in the Eden Valley.

in recent years as drinkers have searched for a full-bodied, non-oaked alternative to Chardonnay and plantings have doubled since 1998. It has long been successful in Western Australia (especially in the Swan Valley) and McLaren Vale but has enjoyed new-found fame at the cellar doors in the Hunter (which alone has more than 50 examples made from the variety). Recommended producers: Chapel Hill, Lamont, Margan, Moondah Brook, Oakvale, Rothbury, Sandalford, Upper Reach.

VIOGNIER

Yalumba first planted Viognier in the Eden Valley in 1979 and is now reaping the rewards of its pioneering endeavours by producing Australia's best example of the variety, the Virgilius, and two other smart Eden Valley wines under the Yalumba and Heggies labels, as well as a fragrant and affordable Y label. There has been an explosion of interest in Viognier and plantings have increased at least tenfold in only a few years. There are now more than 50 wines including a few blends and various areas swearing that they will be the best (Heathcote and Canberra are the latest). In addition, many wineries are beginning to market Shiraz blended with a little Viognier (notably Clonakilla, De Bortoli/Yarra and Yering Station), a practice traditionally found in Côte-Rôtie in France's northern Rhône. As well as Yalumba, good Viognier comes from Elgee Park, Petaluma, Domain Day, Trentham Estate, Stonehaven, Belgravia and Mitchelton.

There's some water in the Creek – someone important must be expected and there are ways of making it run for a while. Yes. This is the Jacob's Creek – rather spoilt by an ugly modern road bridge. But, just to the left is where the first Jacob's Creek vines were planted in 1847. And – see that bottle on the facing page – that's a 1982 Jacob's Creek – the first one I ever tried. It was smashing.

Australian wine styles

NOT SO LONG AGO, IF I WERE TO OUTLINE the world's basic wine styles, the list would have been strongly biased towards the classics – Bordeaux, Burgundy, Sancerre, Mosel Riesling, Champagne. But the classics have, over time, become expensive and unreliable and this has given countries such as Australia the chance to invent styles of their own. Frequently these are from single grape varieties, and frequently these are from single regions – and that could be said of any forward-looking wine country. But there are certain styles that Australia, for better or worse, has pioneered.

IMPORTANCE OF BLENDS

The basis of inexpensive Australian wine (and quite a lot of the more expensive stuff, too) is the blend. Grapes can be grown anywhere and be blended with grapes from anywhere else. Every Australian winemaker is imbued with that philosophy, and it is reflected in wines that take some of their grapes from New South Wales, some from South Australia, some from Victoria; interstate blending, with wine being trucked great distances, is an everyday fact. The reason is that Australian winemakers only have time for the concept of terroir – that essentially European idea that a wine is shaped by the combination of soil, climate and exposure to the sun that it obtains in each individual vineyard – when it is applied to their top wines. Traditionally they have viewed climate as the major influence on wine style, and most Australian wines reflect, and are intended to reflect, the flavour of the grape, not the terroir. After all, even Grange is a blended wine

BRANDS

Brands such as Jacob's Creek, Lindemans Bin 65, [yellow tail], Banrock Station and Rosemount Diamond Label have been the driving force behind Australia's successful expansion into export markets. They enable large companies to take advantage of economies of scale and the technological know-how of the Australian industry to make and market good quality wines at cheap prices.

CULT WINES

There has recently been a proliferation of small volume cult reds – mainly Shiraz from the Barossa and McLaren Vale: Three Rivers, Torbreck's RunRig, Wild Duck Creek's Duck Muck, Turkey Flat and Dutschke's Oscar Semmler have been sourced from aged vines and, without any track record, most have achieved high prices, especially on the American market. The Langton's Classification (last revised in 2000) rates Australian wines on the

Quick guide ◆ Australia's Top Drop – the Jacob's Creek phenomenon

There really was a Jacob. There really was a Creek. The name of this phenomenally successful wine brand has now become such common currency, it's easy to forget whether or not it had any real provenance.

William Jacob was a surveyor who opened up the Barossa Valley in 1837. The creek is one he took a fancy to, so he called it after himself. And it's still there, even if it doesn't normally have any water in it. And there's a real vineyard at Jacob's Creek. It was planted by Johann Gramp in 1847. Gramp soon moved a kilometre up the road to found the Orlando Winery that to this day produces Jacob's Creek. So it's all very local and steeped in tradition. Well, up to a point.

First, they don't use grapes from that vineyard by the little creek any more. They're much too valuable. And it's not a big vineyard. Not big enough to provide grapes for the 78 million bottles sold last year. A lot, isn't it? But then Jacob's Creek is Australia's Top Drop, and, unusually for a wine brand, it has managed to keep a remarkable consistency, and sometimes can be truly excellent. I first drank it on a plane to Australia for my first ever serious wine trip. Hang on! What am I saying? I was flying to Australia for the Jacob's Creek export launch. I owe my first sight of Australian vineyards and my first experience of the daunting nature of the Aussie liquid lunch-cum-barbie to Jacob's Creek. You guys have a lot to answer for.

We drank a Shiraz/Cabernet red and it was a smasher – soft, ripe, plummy, spicy. Delicious. I thought all Australian red must be like this. But it seemed that this soft, easy-drinking style had only been developed very recently – at the Orlando Jacob's Creek winery. It seemed to me that if commercial, affordable red wine could be this good, the world must soon be beating a path to Australia's door. In fact, it took a few years but by the 1990s Australia was in export overdrive, her reds led by Jacob's Creek, her whites by Lindemans Bin 65 and Rosemount Chardonnays. And quality did stay good. I did a 20-year vertical tasting of Jacob's Creek reds with the impressive and likeable chief winemaker Phil Laffer – and the wines

basis of their performance at auction. To be included, a wine must have been produced for a minimum of 10 vintages and show a consistency of demand at auction.

BAG IN BOX WINES

Bag-in-box, or cask wine as it is called in Australia, tends to make up just over half of the table wine consumed in Australia. It has improved vastly in the past decade or so. Typically, it is now made from classic grape varieties grown along the Murray River cropped at much lower levels than previously. The four-litre cask is no longer the standard and there are plenty of two- and three-litre casks available. Generally, this means that the wine will be fresher and of better quality. Casks are now stamped with a Best Before date as wine companies acknowledge that they have a limited shelf life. The outmoded use of European names (such as Moselle, Lambrusco and Chablis) has all but disappeared and many casks acknowledge their varietal content. The lesser white casks tend to be very sweet and the inferior reds tend to show sugar, chippy oak and heavy, cloddish added tannins. The best (made by companies such as Yalumba and Hardys) are clean, fresh, uncomplicated wines which represent great value for drinking.

WINE SHOWS

Wine shows are held almost all over the world: in almost any wine shop you can find bottles and labels plastered with gold medals from obscure corners of the earth. Unlike many countries, Australia has a wine show system that really does reward quality, even if at the same time it tends to impose a uniform style. Award-winning wines sell better, so companies determined to win awards make wines in the precise style that they know the judges like. The result is an excellent basic level of quality, with varietal character, balance and structure all as they should be; but also a lack of quirkiness. Eccentric winemakers making quirky wines (and the world's finest and most interesting wines come into this bracket) tend not to get involved in the Australian show system because they know they'll get marked down for the very qualities that make their wines stand out from textbook examples.

Show judges continue to declare their preference for wines which have been given subtle oak treatment. Oaky wines, however, stand out in large classes at shows and continue to be rewarded. There is criticism of shows which give medals to unfinished wines and those bottled in several large batches – as the wine which wins a medal may not be the same one that the consumer purchases. With the expansion of the industry, marketing is becoming harder and so show medals are increasingly valued as an aid to selling wine. This has led to a substantial increase in the number of wines entered with consequent additional pressure on show judges. It has also led to a proliferation of wine shows. There have been calls for a rationalization of the system though any change looks likely to come slowly.

---

from the early 1980s were in excellent nick. (If you're wondering who could be so sad as to collect a vertical of Jacob's Creek, er, me actually.) But they hardly made a million bottles then, so quality control was easier. Correct. That's where Laffer comes in. He has to control, corral, cajole, coerce hundreds of growers from all over Australia to adhere to his standards. I don't know of any other major brand worldwide where such effort is made to hold the line on quality despite ever-increasing sales, and Laffer's award of the Qantas Winemaker of the Year prize in 2002 says a lot about how his peers regard him.

Grape variety, vineyard location or vintage variation are not the point of Jacob's Creek. It does make a lot of good wine, some very good wine (a Riesling, for instance), and classy Reserve and Limited Release varietals. But it's the image that has struck gold, backed up by decent grog. 'Australia's Top Drop'. Simple, effective. 'Australia's Other Great White', juxtaposed against a gleaming Sydney Opera House, a magnificent Great White Shark and the rest. For years you watched 'Friends' and up popped Jacob's Creek as the sponsor. You watch Wimbledon, or the British Open Golf – and there's Jacob's Creek. And you begin to understand there's a bit of class about this brand, and a minimum of cynicism in a very cynical section of the wine world. And when the managers tell you Jacob's Creek inspires

that Holy Grail for all brand owners – customer loyalty – you can sort of see why.

Jacob's Creek
Gosh. The sight of that label. The 1982 Jacob's Creek. I'm transported straight back to Qantas Economy Class somewhere between Singapore and Sydney on my first Australian wine trip. We didn't stop drinking this lovely, juicy 'sunshine in a bottle' till touchdown, and could have continued all day if we hadn't all fallen asleep as soon as we got to our hotel rooms – and missed our official welcoming reception. I'm told the champagne was delicious.

Quick guide ◆
The Grange story

Australia has many world famous wines today – but not so long ago it only had one – Grange. I have just a single bottle of it. The 1971, given to me by Max Schubert, its creator. And I treasure it as much as any wine in the world. Because it is as good as any wine in the world. Yet it was never supposed to exist. There's a fair bit of serendipity in wine. So, here's the Grange serendip.

Max Schubert was chief winemaker for Penfolds and a particular dab hand at making sherry. He'd gone to Europe in 1950 to learn about sherry, but had sneaked in a quick visit to Bordeaux on the way home, and was captivated by their red wines, capable of aging and improving for a generation and more. Fired up by their example he determined to produce something comparable in Australia, even though Bordeaux was cool and wet, South Australia was hot and dry; Bordeaux used grapes like Cabernet and Merlot which weren't on offer in South Australia, so Shiraz would have to do. And even though Bordeaux was usually aged in small oak barrels, many of them new. Max wasn't sure there was a single new oak barrel in all South Australia. And if there was, it would be big, not small.

The nose that started the red wine revolution in Australia. This is the late Max Schubert checking out a sample of his beloved Grange in the early 1990s.

Yet despite seeming to lack everything he needed, Max had the vision. A vision of flavour is something common to all great rather than merely good winemakers. Max had a vision of the great red Bordeauxs of the 1920s and the 1900s burnished and bronzed to something new and magnificent in the southern tip of the wine world. It would taste completely different because everything about its composition would be different. But its spirit would be the same, the spirit of the great red wines that had made Bordeaux the most fabled wine region in the world.

The first vintage was 1951 and until 1956 Max made deep dark reds from South Australian Shiraz, aged in a few reasonably small new oak barrels. Since he wanted the wines to age for a generation, it didn't worry him that after five years, not a bottle had been sold. But it worried the Penfolds Board who tasted the wine, thought it foul and banned further production. You don't deny a genius like Max. He went on making it in secret like a Colditz prisoner of war digging an escape tunnel. Until, in 1960, the directors tried the early Granges again. They'd been made to age. They needed to age. They had aged. Magnificently.

The wines were released and astonished the Australian wine world, and Max resumed 'official' Grange production as a hero rather than a pariah.

Nowadays Grange is thought of as the equal to any red wine in the world. It has inspired generations of Australians with the belief that they can equal the world's finest, and they often do. But were it not for a stubborn Barossa Deutschman called Schubert refusing to do as he was told, they would have had to wait goodness knows how long for a proud Aussie to challenge the old order – and win.

Penfolds Grange
An established world wine classic – supremely rich, concentrated but only really shows its magnificence after at least 10 years in bottle and will have decades of life ahead. My 1971 looks better every time I inspect it.

Best years Grange boasts an unbroken line of vintages beginning with the experimental 1951. The following are acknowledged as the best: 2001, '99, '98, '96, '94, '92, '91, '90, '88, '86, '84, '83, '80, '76, '71, '67, '66, '63, '62, '55, '53, '52. Vintages of the 1950s are extremely rare and valuable.

RED WINES

1 Big, spicy warm-hearted reds (Shiraz)
Almost every corner of the country has a stab at Shiraz, and the styles vary considerable. The most famous style is from the Barossa – tremendously rich, chocolaty, verging on the overripe but magnificent, sun-baked stuff. McLaren Vale's is rich and chocolaty, Clare Valley's is leaner but packed with dark, serious fruit. Padthaway and Wrattonbully makes wines full of damson fruit and chocolate richness, while Coonawarra's is dark and peppery. New South Wales' Hunter Valley was initially infamous for its 'Sweaty Saddle' flavour. It's still a bit meaty but full of ripe plum fruit. Victoria makes dark chocolaty Shiraz in the North-East, but wonderfully scented, damson-rich wines in the cooler regions like the Grampians and Heathcote. Western Australia produces cool but intense, dark plum flavours from Margaret River southwards. And even warm Queensland and cool Tasmania get in on the act.

2 Intense, blackcurranty reds
You may hear a lot about Cabernet Sauvignon tasting like blackcurrants. Well, if you really want a gobful of blackcurrant flavour in your Cab – Australia is the place to come. Coonawarra is the most famous Cabernet region and the most likely to fill your nostrils with blackcurrant scent. But you can also get blackcurrant in McLaren Vale and Barossa – warm and fat – or Clare Valley, drier, more austere. Victoria's styles are mostly rather leafy, but with fairly intense blackcurrant scent. That's the cool areas. There are parts of the Centre and North-East that use the heat to give big, rich styles. Hunter Valley's Cabernet rarely achieves real ripe rich fruit, though good vintages from Mudgee and Orange can produce lovely blackcurrant stuff. Some of Australia's most famous Cabs come from Margaret River in the West. Here the flavours are more likely to be black cherry, black plum, herbs and black olive.

Merlot generally makes rather soft wines in Australia, but Malbec can produce big, dark juicy flavours in Clare Valley and Langhorne Creek, while Petit Verdot makes intense damsony wine in the hot Murray-Darling and Riverina regions.

3 Soft, strawberryish charmers
To be honest, this isn't Australia's strongest style. The classics here are the gentle, mild-mannered, often charmingly scented Pinot Noir reds of Burgundy in France. Well, Burgundy is a pretty cool climate place, and Australia is mostly pretty hot. Early attempts to make Pinot Noir red in the warmer areas led to rather rich, overly jammy wines, although Murray Tyrrell in the sub-tropical

Hunter Valley had some notable successes. During the 1980s and 1990s, however, the achievement of true cool climate styles became an obsession for a lot of Australia's most talented winemakers, and there has been a gradual increase in the number of fine Pinot Noirs. But not all of them are soft and strawberryish; some of the Western Australian examples are strongly herb-scented; in cool years the cool areas like Mornington Peninsula and Tasmania can't keep a lean greenness out of their flavours. However, in warm years both of these regions do produce soft, strawberryish Pinot Noirs, and in Tasmania the East Coast and Coal Valley wineries produce positively exotic results.

Victoria's Yarra Valley has staked its reputation on Pinot Noir and there are wide variations between mild reds hinting at greeness in the cooler parts of the valley to relatively rich wine in the warmer zones. Victoria's cooler areas – the Alpine Valleys, Gippsland, Macedon Range and Geelong among them – also make delightful examples. Most of South Australia is a bit warm for this style, but Adelaide Hills produces some beauties.

4 Juicy, fruity reds
This is a style made famous by big brands like Rosemount's split label Shiraz-Cabernet and Jacob's Creek reds. Simple, bright, juicy red fruit flavours, uncomplicated pleasure, wine designed for the non-wine expert. Vaguely based on France's Beaujolais or Italy's Valpolicella styles, these have been a massive success, and are widely copied around the world for so-called 'red wine without tears'. Most of the commercial brands are not now as good as they used to be and have been diluted and sugared up to pander to a higher volume, low common denominator market. This is a great pity, and hopefully the fabulous 'more flavour for your money than any other country can offer' quality level will return. In the meantime, there are alternatives. Grenache is often used to make lovely juicy, easy-going reds – Peter Lehmann's Barossa Grenache is a classic example. Chambourcin is a little-known but tasty grape that works well in New South Wales and Queensland. And Brown Brothers have got what I think is a world exclusive on Tarrango – a grape 'invented' to give lighter, juicy Beaujolais flavours in hot areas – which is exactly what it does for Brown Brothers.

WHITE WINES
1 Full-fat, golden whites
The stratospheric growth in Australia's exports was led by soft, fleshy, golden Chardonnay whites. They provided ripe, easy to understand flavours, but also a blast of full-strength alcohol to a world for whom the only juicy, fruity whites on offer had been low strength, sugared-up Liebfraumilchs from Germany. Aussie Chardonnays tasted fat and ripe because they *were* ripe. The big mechanized vineyards that grew them were in hot places – 'sunshine in a bottle' they were dubbed. And that's exactly what they were.

In the early days it was names like Lindemans Bin 65, Rosemount, Wolf Blass Yellow Label and others that created waves. They're still going strong but the big brands are in danger of replacing the spice and butterscotch and the pineapple, peach and vanilla with blander, sweeter tastes. Nowadays the Hunter Valley and warmer parts of Victoria and South Australia are best at this fat, soft style. And as cool climate regions have developed, a less full-fat, less golden Chardonnay style has evolved. Warmer areas like Barossa Valley, McLaren Vale, Swan Valley and Riverina can offer the full-fat style by using vanilla-drenched American oak barrels to age grape varieties like Semillon, Marsanne and Viognier.

2 Tangy, citrus whites
New Zealand was the originator of this style with its famous zingy, nettley Sauvignon Blanc. Australia has always found it more difficult, especially using Sauvignon Blanc. There are some successes in cooler areas like Adelaide Hills, Melbourne's 'Dress Circle' regions, and southern parts of Western Australia. And Yalumba's Oxford Landing is a big brand that succeeds. However, the best tangy whites are not from Sauvignon. Semillon produces very lean results in Hunter Valley, and good leafy flavours in Western Australia. But Riesling is the best bet for really fresh bone dry styles – almost austerely citrus in Clare Valley, cool and perfumed in Eden Valley, and soft yet citrus and dry in Western Australia.

3 Warm-climate whites
For a country which has made such a noise about its warm climate red styles, it's taken Australia rather a long time to realize the potential for warm climate whites. But potential is there. Old plantings of Verdelho, Marsanne and Roussanne can give full, honeyed but dry wines, not usually aromatic but often with a satisfying waxy weight and quince richness when they're aged a bit. New plantings of Viognier have given scented wines with rich apricot fruit. Expect to see more of these.

4 Aromatic whites
The headiest of the aromatic styles is Viognier when it is grown in cooler sites. It can combine floral scent with delicate apricot fruit. Riesling in Australia is often citrus and very dry, but in some of the cooler areas like Tasmania, the Victorian Highlands and the southern parts of Western Australia it can be delicate and scented with lemon blossom. Gewurztraminer is generally heavy with rose petal scent and fat with lychee fruit. There are a few dry Muscats with attractive grapy perfume. Pinot Gris can be aromatic, but is usually made in a lighter, crisp, fresh style.

5 Mouthfuls of luscious gold
When De Bortoli released their astonishing luscious Noble One in 1982 they did so by touring the world and tasting it against Château d'Yquem – probably the most famous sweet wine in the world. And it often won! Noble One is a Semillon affected by 'noble rot' and there are now numerous examples of these rich peach and barley sugar, honeyed beauties in Australia, with Riverina being the leading area. Riesling also makes tremendous sweet wine, honeyed and intense with citrus acidity keeping it fresh.

FORTIFIED WINES
Australia's current fame may be for top table wines like Chardonnay, Cabernet and Shiraz, but there's one style in which she has equalled the world's best for well over a century – fortified wines – and, above all, the unbelievably rich Muscats and Tokays from North-East Victoria made mostly in wonderfully antiquated wineries by time-honoured methods. Australia also makes the other classic styles, in particular successful 'ports' and 'sherries'.

SPARKLING WINES
Tip-top fizz doesn't just come from Champagne in France. Australians make their best fizz in the same way as the French, they use the same grape varieties – Chardonnay and Pinot Noir – and some of the finest bottles are actually made by Champagne companies operating in Australia like Domaine Chandon – Moët and Chandon's antipodean operation. The style is usually a little riper than in France but the sparklers have the same soft creamy, yeasty depth of good Champagne. Tasmania is proving to be one of the world's best sites for sparkling base. Other good areas are Macedon Ranges, Tumbarumba, and the cooler parts of Yarra Valley.

Australia also makes sparkling reds – usually from Shiraz, sometimes from Merlot, Cabernet or Grenache. These are magnificent wild beasts packed with pepper and blackberry fruit, and with enough deep colour to stain your tongue.

In the Vineyard

Peter Leske of Nepenthe in the Adelaide Hills is a happy lad – the sun's shining and these Cabernet Sauvignon grapes are healthy, ripe – and harvested safely.

A USTRALIA HAS LED THE WORLD so effectively in winery techniques and innovations that it's easy to regard her vineyards merely as fodder-providers for the wizards of the winery to turn into wine. Just make sure the figures are correct – the winemakers say – the right sugar ripeness level in the grapes, the right acidity, the right pH (that's a way of measuring the balance between acid and alkaline in a grape. It took me years to figure it out, but a low figure is acid and a high one is alkaline; you always want a reasonably low figure because acidity is crucial in making a wine taste appetising). Where were we? Oh yes, you'll need to check the physiological ripeness of the pips and the skins, because if the pips are still green and the skins haven't fully matured they will leach out a raw bitterness into the wine that you'll never be able to get rid of, however much of a wine wizard you are. But hang on. I'm talking about flavour here, the character the grapes might impart to the wine. Dear, oh dear, I'll be talking about one vineyard giving different flavours to those of another in a minute. The Aussie winemaker wants the figures to be right – just deliver me the figures – and all the transformation of grape juice into a wine of infinite taste possibilities will be performed by the magicians of the winery.

That was then. Now is different. The relationship between winemakers and grape-grower or vineyard is now remarkably close in all the best wineries – but you do still find winemakers who just want 'the figures' – and not so long ago that's all that most of them wanted. In the 1980s reaching well into the 1990s, the cult of the winemaker reigned. The winemaker, usually this self-confident testosterone-fuelled male, reckoned that he could 'create' the right flavours by scientific trickery regardless of where the grapes came from. Indeed, while Australia was building its reputation as the master of consistent, tasty, affordable wine brands, this attitude probably didn't do much harm, and may actually have been the correct one. But not any more. As we head into the second half of the noughties, with significantly more grapes being grown in Australia than there are homes for, and with large companies simply tearing up the contracts of broad acres farmers who thought grapes

One of the great pests Australia's grape-growers have to contend with is the kangaroo. They are virtually impossible to keep out of the vineyards and can cause havoc once they're in. But I dunno, as a gooey-eyed visiting Pom, I think the little darlings are an absolute delight.

Growing grapes in hot climates: Romavilla Winery outside Roma, Queensland. I'm not sure anyone would establish vines here nowadays, because, except for a few rows at Alice Springs, this is the hottest vineyard area in Australia and these vines bake under the searing sun. Not surprisingly fortified wines are the most successful style. But spare a thought for the pioneers. This is where Queensland's wine industry began in 1863.

Growing grapes in cool climates: Hoddles Creek Vineyard, Upper Yarra Valley, Victoria. This looks more like a Christmas card than a vineyard scene, but then Hoddles Creek was chosen for a vineyard site precisely because it is so cold, way up in the forest on the edge of the Yarra Valley. Hardys were after really cool climate, barely ripe fruit to make into sparkling wine and Hoddles Creek fits the bill perfectly.

Quick guide ◆ The vineyard year

Work in the vineyard This follows a basic pattern the world over, but the timing of each operation is dependent on both the prevailing climate and the weather conditions that year. The approximate dates for budburst, flowering and harvesting will vary from region to region, cool climate regions such as Tasmania following approximately a month behind warm climate regions such as Riverland in South Australia.

Winter (July-August): the leaves fall, the sap descends and the vine becomes dormant. Pruning can be done at any time during the winter.

Spring (September-November): the sap starts to rise, and the first signs of growth appear, from mid-September to mid-October: the young vine must be protected against frost from now until early summer. The buds are also vulnerable to pests and diseases: sprays help to control these enemies, though organic and biodynamic growers use other methods. Ploughing and hoeing aerates the soil and clears weeds; fertilizer may be applied. As the ground warms up, new vines can be planted. Once the vines begin to shoot, the new growth needs to be tied to the wires, otherwise the foliage would shade the fruit and prevent it from ripening; the final trellising takes shape.

Summer (November-December): eight weeks after budbreak, the vine flowers for about 10 days and then the fruit sets; cold or wet weather can cause poor fruit set and reduce the size of the harvest. Summer pruning, or leaf plucking, may be necessary to allow more sunlight to reach the fruit. At véraison (when the fruit changes colour) a green harvest may be done to reduce the size of the crop, and superfluous clusters removed. Netting or bird scarers may be used to protect against bird damage.

Autumn (January-April): picking often begins as early as mid-January in Queensland and takes place in mid-April in Tasmania.

Putting on anti-bird netting – in many areas of Australia birds are a menace. This isn't surprising. When you clear forests or plant old grazing land with vines the word is going to get round the bird population pretty fast that that there's a lovely juicy source of fruit coming on stream. So, many vineyards have to net their vines as soon as sugar levels start to build in the grapes. Otherwise, with little critters like silvereyes and destructive scavengers like parrots you can lose half your crop in just a couple of days.

were like any other agricultural crop – grow the biggest crop you can at the lowest possible cost and you'll be rich, cobber – it's becoming glaringly evident that the site of your vineyard, the varieties of grapes you grow there, and the methods you use to mature the vines and harvest the grapes, are of paramount importance.

I'll be talking about vineyards again throughout this book, but let's look at a few of the characteristics of the modern Australian vineyard. First, soil matters – but not to an overwhelming degree as it does in the cool, damp classic areas of Europe like Bordeaux, Burgundy, Champagne and Germany's Mosel Valley. That's because most Australian vineyard regions are not cool and damp. 'Sunshine in a bottle' is what made Australia famous, and if your vineyards are warm and dry virtually any kind of soil can produce good grapes. Indeed, in a hot place you sometimes want a heavy, fertile soil to hold moisture better so you don't waste your irrigation water. But in cool, damp regions you need soils that drain well and preserve some warmth. Clay doesn't drain well and, since it holds water, is a cold soil. In cool areas this means grapes will rarely ripen fully. So the soil type is vital. Coonawarra in South Australia is the most obvious example of this; its red top soil over limestone produces far superior wines to those grown on clay soil right next door. The infertile granite soil of Macedon near Melbourne and Queensland's Granite Belt allow grapes to ripen in challenging conditions. Pemberton, Frankland River and other parts of cool southern Western Australia rely crucially on warm, free-draining gravels to ripen their crops.

Climate matters too. Most of Australia's vineyards are in regions which would be thought of as pretty warm and dry in European terms. Which means that so long as you have a water supply to keep your vines alive, you'll ripen your crop. But the modern passion in Australia is to prove that she can grow great cool climate wines as well as warm. So soil matters for that, and so does local climate. The east coast and parts of the south of Tasmania are protected from the cold, wet westerly and southerly winds that lash much of the island – and produce beautiful, generous-flavoured wines. The Yarra Valley near Melbourne has so many different local climates that it produces everything from frosty cool sparkling wines, to rich, scented Shiraz. Sometimes this is to do with protection from wind and rain. Sometimes this is due to altitude. One of the ways Australia has created cool climate wines is to climb up the mountain slopes or develop the high country plateaux. As you go higher, the temperature drops, so your grapes will ripen more slowly and with better acidity. That's why the Granite Belt way up in sub-tropical Queensland can still make crisp, fresh wines – the vineyards rise up to over 1000 metres. Victoria's King Valley, Alpine Valleys and Beechworth again can offer you full-blooded Shiraz, sturdy Nebbiolo, fragrant Riesling or lean, taut sparkling wine depending on altitudes that can rise to over 1000 metres at Beechworth's Stanley. And if you stand in the broiling Barossa Valley and look up into the hills to the east – that's the Eden Valley up there, just a few kilometres away. But you're at around 250 metres in the Barossa, and the High Eden and Eden Valley zones rise to 550 metres. That's the difference between rich Barossa Shiraz and delicate, scented Eden Valley Riesling.

Australia has also had to make major compromises – or innovations: it depends how you look at it – in the way she cultivates the grapes. European vineyards have usually been developed over the centuries by local communities. In many of the best vineyard sites in Australia, there are *no* local communities to provide labour. Many parts of South Australia's Limestone Coast are miles from human habitation. The large developments in much of Western Australia don't have a knowledgeable local workforce to call on. So Australia became a leading proponent of mechanized vineyard management – things like pruning and picking all being done by machine. The jury is still out on the effect on quality, especially with machine-pruning, but mechanical harvesting is now a fact of life in all modern vineyard countries, and many superb wines result.

And there's one more point. Water. Australia is the driest continent on earth. Most of its vineyards can't survive without irrigation. Sometimes this water can be collected from winter rains. More often bores are sunk into aquifers or water is sucked from the small number of large rivers. Both these methods are now at their limit or past it. Salination and pollution of water sources and creeping decay of the soils that depend on them is a real factor that Australia must face up to, or all the great advances she has made will count for nothing.

Left: Australia's greatest river, the Murray, right in the heart of the vineyard area at Renmark, South Australia. The Murray mops up all the water from the west side of the Great Dividing Range and then begins its extremely languid and serpentine route of 2600km until it reaches the sea, south of Adelaide. By that time it hasn't got much water left, because it's been extracted for irrigation. Well over half the vineyards in Australia rely upon the Murray and its tributaries, the Lachlan and the Murrumbidgee, for their water. Without the rivers, there would be no modern Australian wine industry.

Below: Flooding at Langhorne Creek, South Australia. This is the old way of doing things. The Bremer River rises just south-east of Adelaide and flows down to the sea at Lake Alexandrina. Since time immemorial it has flooded in the spring and created a rich, alluvial flood plain with deep, fertile soils at Langhorne Creek. Bleasdale use the floodwaters to irrigate their vineyards – and they don't need to irrigate any more all year.

Oak barrels have played a large part in Australian wine. The spicy vanilla flavour of new oak barrels adds enormously to the flavour and character of table wines like Chardonnay, Cabernet and Shiraz. But old barrels like these are also very important in the maturation and development of the great fortified wines that Australia excels in.

In the Winery

THE AUSTRALIAN WINE INDUSTRY HAS ENJOYED spectacular success in managing domestic growth and making a strong push into export markets, and its winemakers can be found – often using their technical knowledge to push the boundaries – working in many parts of the Americas and Europe.

The foundation on which this success has been based is Australia's outstanding research and teaching institutions. Roseworthy Agricultural College (now part of the University of Adelaide), established in 1883, has had an intense focus on viticulture and oenology and a Diploma in Oenology since 1936. A second institution, Charles Sturt University at Wagga Wagga, started offering tertiary studies in viticulture from 1975. The first formal research into wine took place in 1934. Lobbying by the wine industry led to the formation of the Australia Wine Research Institute (AWRI) in 1955 which has been a major force for change since then. AWRI has conducted research into all facets of winemaking and viticulture.

TECHNICAL WIZARDRY

The introduction of stainless steel pressure tanks and refrigeration – initiated by Orlando's Colin Gramp in 1953 – led to dramatic improvements in the freshness and fruit purity of white table wines. Riesling, in particular, became extremely popular as a result and led the boom in white wine sales which lasted until into the 1990s. Production techniques for whites continued to change during the 1980s and '90s, especially with the increase in popularity of Chardonnay as winemakers experimented with barrel fermentation, use of oak and the choice of enzymes and yeast cultures.

In the 1960s, the technology used in white winemaking was adapted to large volume production of reds. The giant Potter red fermenters enabled temperature-controlled red winemaking in closed tanks before the stable finished wine was transferred to barrels for oak maturation. While the method of large volume red winemaking hasn't changed a great deal since then, there have been refinements which have added to the choices available to producers, such as the use of roto-fermenters (for gentler but more complete extraction of colour and flavour from the grapes) or micro-oxygenation (bubbling low levels of oxygen into wine to soften tannins and make young wines more approachable).

The work of Max Schubert on the barrel fermentation of reds has been vastly influential although, because it is labour-intensive, its use has tended to be reserved for the upper quality levels of reds. The prohibitive cost of using oak barrels for commercial reds led to cost-cutting shortcuts such as the use of oak chips, oak staves and added tannins – but don't take this as a criticism. These rather 'industrial' methods of adding the vanilla richness and the spicy scent of oak were perfected in Australia by people like Wolf Blass and transformed the flavours of cheap reds without incurring the heavy costs of aging the wine in new barrels. Oak chips are used by hanging a great big 'tea bag' of toasted oak chips in the vat during fermentation, and, just like when you make a cup of tea, the liquid leaches out the flavour from the 'tea bag'. A slightly more sophisticated method is fixing oak staves or 'planks' in the stainless steel vats during fermentation and maturation, and these also give off their oak flavours far more cheaply than a barrel would. Wolf Blass realized that oaky reds would be commercially popular and made this his trade mark.

In recent years, many winemakers have looked at ways to make more food-friendly wines by reducing their oakiness. For top-level wines from top-quality grapes, this isn't a problem, but when you're making cheap wines out of high-yield, diluted grapes – you've got to get the flavour from somewhere. Oak chips used to supply it, now sugar does. I think I preferred the oak chips. Ironically, the worst abuse of oak now takes place at the top end – especially the enormous but virtually undrinkable cult 'icon' wines – highly alcoholic, strikingly oaked wines that are finding a ready market – especially in the USA.

BLENDING

One of the freedoms which Australian winemakers enjoy is being able to blend grapes from different regions if they believe that this will make a better wine. Two of Australia's greatest winemakers of the first half of the twentieth century, Maurice O'Shea and Colin Preece made full use of this in spite of the inadequacy of transport at the time. The country's greatest wine, Penfolds Grange, is almost always a multi-regional blend honed to the style developed by Max Schubert. The brands behind Australia's export push in recent times – Jacob's Creek, Lindemans Bin 65, and the like – would not be possible unless the companies that make them were able to source the fruit for these wines from several regions. In fact, one of the most encouraging recent developments with these quaffing wines has come from companies such as McWilliam's and Angove's which are blending wines from premium areas such as Coonawarra to improve the flavour profile of fruit from the vineyards along the Murray River – without increasing prices.

So Australia became a hotbed of innovation – first in winemaking science, but latterly in viticulture as well. Wine schools like Roseworthy and Charles Sturt are respected worldwide. Dr Richard Smart is probably the world's most famous vineyard doctor and has radically changed the way we think about suitable vineyard sites and how to maximize yield without risking quality – worldwide. I sometimes think, listening to Dr Smart, that there isn't a field, a slope or a hillock in the world that he couldn't turn into a vineyard if you let him. And between them all they've created glorious and individualistic wines. But there's another point, just as important. They've facilitated mass production of consistent quality brands at a level the world has never seen before. And they've devised methods of labelling and marketing them that now see other nations adopting Aussie-style names and flavours as a crucial first step in trying to export their wines to the world.

That's a big tanker truck there. I mean, look at how small the blokes are, then look at the tanker truck, then look at the tanks. These are the wine tanks at Orlando, probably full of a small part of the 78 million bottles of Jacob's Creek that are produced each year. It may look industrial, but the high tech stainless steel wineries of Australia produce some of the most consistent and reliable big volume wines in the world. And with towering storm clouds like this, let's hope it's not vintage time.

Latest high-tech stainless steel presses and fermentation and storage tanks, such as these giant ones at Angove's vast processing facility in the Riverland, enabled Australia to mass produce brands that have performed at a level of quality and consistency no other country in the wine world has ever matched.

Wizards of Oz

AUSTRALIA'S REPUTATION AS A WINE COUNTRY was built by personalities. Other countries built their reputations on the places where the grapes grow. You don't think of France and start spouting people's names, because most of them don't ever appear on the label. You talk of Bordeaux, of the different villages in Bordeaux, maybe even separate properties or châteaux in those villages that have performed particularly well. But actual people? No. In Burgundy it's the village, the different patches of land on the various slopes that are better or worse. The people are regarded as custodians rather than creators. Or countries build reputations on styles. The style of France's Champagne. The style of Spain's Rioja or Sherry. The style of Portugal's Port or Madeira. The style of Chianti. Even the style – or lack of it – of Liebfraumilch. Personalities don't enter into it.

And then you come to Australia. Well, the one thing Australia didn't have was any centuries-old tradition of vineyard site or wine style that they could build on. Europeans brought a wine culture of sorts with them in the 60 years after the First Fleet landed in 1788. During the nineteenth century some good vineyard areas were discovered, but just as many vines were planted for no better reason than that they were close to a state capital or close to the gold mines. Some of these chance plantings were lucky and flourished. Just as many faded away, and through the first half of the twentieth century, whatever wine tradition Australia might have been starting to develop, withered away too. But as the second half of the twentieth century hurried in to the last few decades, it became clear that what Australia did have was personalities determined to impose their wills and ways upon wine. People who were gritty, determined, focused, passionate, imaginative and opinionated. Shy, retiring and conciliating? No. Never. What would that have achieved in God's Own Country, where sometimes the only motto worth knowing is 'You gotta have a go'. And have a go they did.

I mean, just let me tell you about my first day on my first wine visit to Australia. We drove up to the Hunter Valley, north of Sydney in an old minibus and tumbled out to be met by four kings of modern Australian wine. Not protected by PR people, shielded by marketeers and flunkies – but just there standing in the dust waiting to cast a beady eye over these pale-faced Poms. Good God. What a crew. Murray Tyrrell – the 'mouth of the Hunter', a magnificent curmudgeon who brought Australian Chardonnay to the world's attention and fiercely defended old tradition while nurturing the new. Len Evans. Even other people say he invented modern Australian wine. Len would probably say he did a whole lot more than that. But here he was, Mr Wine, shouting a cheery g'day – and was that 'Pommy bastard' I heard under his breath? And next to him, with jowls as crumpled as a British Bulldog's cheeks, Max Lake, the man who would probably say he began the whole boutique wine revolution that now sees the independent estates of Australia – virtually all created since Max Lake's seminal Lake's Folly first saw the light of day in 1966 – producing some of the greatest wines in the world. 'And I re-introduced Cabernet to the Hunter'. Yes Max. 'And Petit Verdot... and new oak barrels...' OK. OK. And the big bushy-browed guy, bursting with so much energy you think the top of his head's going to fly off – James Halliday, who is now the most influential wine writer and judge in Australia as well as a mean wine producer himself. Every one, an enormous personality. Every one fired up with self-belief. Every one never known to be wrong.

And this is the spirit that has created the modern Australia. The sheer lack of tradition allied to the typical Australian's determination to prove himself is of enormous importance in how the modern Australia developed. Australia looked out at the world and decided which wine styles and grape-growing and winemaking techniques it liked the look of and set about adapting them. But Australia isn't like Europe. Even the most temperate of places like Victoria's Yarra Valley or Western Australia's Margaret River aren't really like Bordeaux or Burgundy. And, to be honest, their wines don't taste like Bordeaux or Burgundy. They taste like themselves. Those Aussies. Those Hallidays, those Schuberts, those Crosers, those Evanses. 'Top of the World, Ma' in a Strine accent.

Len Evans: *Ah, Len, where would we be, where would the modern world of Australian wine be without you? In no other country has one man had such an influence on the creation, promotion – and consumption – of a wine industry.*

Mick Morris: *The keeper of the flame. A century ago Australia was famous for its luscious fortified wines. Underneath the eaves at the Morris winery a few centenarians still lurk, so rich and powerful that just a dab will transform a barrel of a young 'un.*

Bailey Carrodus: *A mischievous maverick who delights in going his own way in winemaking and wine styles, in 1969 Carrodus determined to revive the glories of Yarra's 19th-century wines and he has done so with panache and brilliance.*

James Halliday: *A bristling bundle of energy, talent and opinion who has managed to be both poacher and gamekeeper, becoming Australia's top wine critic as well as one of its leading wine producers.*

Jeffrey Grosset: *The man who put the steel back into Riesling. At a time when Riesling was unfashionable and undervalued, Grosset created a style of austere mineral purity and stark citrous scent in the Clare Valley that proved irresistible to critics and drinkers alike.*

Brian Croser: *Croser has been a great leader, a great teacher and a great innovator in Australian wine. But above all, he's been a visionary, for ever refusing to let Australia believe there isn't more that can be achieved.*

Murray Tyrrell: *Tyrrell, while managing to preserve Hunter Valley traditions, also created Australia's first commercial Chardonnay, Tyrrell's Vat 47, and the first Aussie Chardonnay I ever tasted.*

Philip Shaw: *Rosemount is a modern winery, dedicated to modern, crowd-pleasing wines. Shaw was the man entrusted with creating these styles and, until he left in 2003, did so brilliantly.*

Peter Lehmann: *Without Lehmann's passionate defence of Barossa as the world's greatest resource of 19th-century vines and of its traditions, the Valley's greatness would just be a fading memory.*

Wine Tourism

THIS MAY NOT SOUND RELEVANT to a book on Australia – but it is, it really is. I can remember everything about my first trip to France to visit the vineyards. The first vines I saw near Blois on the Loire. The drive down towards Tours on the tiny road that hugged the chalk cliffs looming over us in the evening sun. The Cave at Amboise, and me striding in to meet my first vigneron. The Loire? White wine, surely. So I confidently ask for it and M. Dutertre says – actually, we're rather better known for our red – or something like that, in his wonderful thick French accent that impressed my girlfriend rather more than my failure to know which colour of wine to ask for.

We drove on. Down to Bordeaux, out of the city on the D2 road and the factories and suburbs fall away, the forest closes in – but not for long. The trees part and a slope of vines sweeps up to my right. Château La Lagune. A famous Classed Growth. I've read about it, I've tasted it. And here it is. Château Cantemerle is next and the famous names of châteaux and villages – Cantenac, Margaux, St-Julien, Pauillac appear in glorious profusion of road signs and hoardings by the side of the road as it rolls bucolically, joyously through the gorgeous vines. I remember every château we visited. And even now, these are the first ones I look for on a list of Bordeaux wines.

There was more on that trip – much more – Provence, the Rhône, Burgundy, Alsace and Champagne, and in each area one village or another, one vineyard or another, one smiling winegrower, one welcoming merchant would find a place in my heart that they hold still. And if I sometimes find myself making irrational decisions in my choice of favourites – blame the road signs and the cafés, the cellars and the slopes, the winemakers and wine sellers I first got to know on my first ever wine trip. My first ever wine tourism trip.

Because that's what it was. It wasn't called wine tourism because hardly anyone did it and most winegrowers were amazed to get a visitor – and a foreign one at that. But it was, and it remains, the most potent, the most emotionally effective way of maximizing your pleasure. If you've seen the vines, talked with the person who hoes the earth, crushes the grapes and ferments the juice, you add so much to the pleasure of a wine's flavour. No wine ever tastes as good as one you drink at the vineyard or take away with you after a visit.

So how's Australia doing in the wine tourism stakes? Well, better and better, and in places like New South Wales' Hunter Valley, Victoria's Yarra Valley and South Australia's Barossa Valley and McLaren Vale, you'll find high quality wine and tourism going arm in arm like nowhere else in the world.

In 1996, there were fewer than 900 Australian wine producers. Just eight years later, that figure had more than doubled to around 1800 and the majority of these will be longing for you to visit. After all, a lot of them are going to find it very difficult to get retail listings, and having you pop by in your hire car is the best possible way for them to make a sale – and maybe create a loyal customer. It makes sense for them – indeed for many it's a necessity – but it also makes sense for us. Wineries and vineyards aren't situated in the middle of busy fretful cities. Apart from the strictly industrial contract vineyards of some of the inland areas, wineries and vineyards are usually situated along the banks of rivers, up the slopes of mountains, in the twists and turns, the nooks and crannies of land that couldn't be used for grain and cattle. In other words, in some of the loveliest, most tranquil yet uplifting countryside that inhabited Australia has to offer.

All the state capitals have some vineyard areas close by. These are often the original plantations and they generally have a well-developed sense of what the wine tourist might want. Some of the originals are in the middle of nowhere – like the fascinating string of vineyards in the upper reaches of Victoria. More often than not, these were developed to help sate the thirst of the goldminers – so you get double pleasure – the history of gold, the inheritance of the towns and sometimes the gold mines themselves – and long-established vineyards and wine styles. And increasingly, there are new and exciting developments miles from civilization, with determined enthusiasts planting vines simply because the conditions are so good for top quality wine. These could be anywhere. The tablelands of Queensland

There's not much that will get me out of bed at dawn on a wine trip, but a balloon trip will. In the purest, most serene part of the day you'll see the vineyards and their world waking up below you as the golden fingers of early sunlight hurry the shadows of nighttime away.

and New South Wales, the Gippsland Coast in Victoria, the Limestone Coast in South Australia, or the spread of excellent but remote vineyards across the southern coast of Western Australia.

So how to set about it? Well, first you will normally need a car. Distances are rarely small and can be considerable. So. Here it is in capitals. DON'T DRINK AND DRIVE. Spit the stuff out. If you can't see a spitoon, spit it out in the yard. You'll get all the flavour of the wine, but keep a clear head. Next – contact regional tourist associations and local wine promotional groups (see page 164). Even the small places will have someone on the case to help you. They'll give you information to show you where the wineries are, where you can stay, where you can eat and so on. It's all part of the experience.

After that, you can just drive about and see what happens – I do that sometimes and invariably turn up some new exciting discovery. But it's probably best to plan, deciding whether you want to visit the big places, or the small, or both. Australia has everything, from superb tourist-orientated setups like Sirromet near Brisbane, to architectural delights like Yering Station in the Yarra to wonderful 'mom 'n pop' operations like Helm near Canberra where Ken Helm will hold court in his tiny, jumbled delight of a tasting room for as long as you'll let him.

You'll meet the winemakers, see the vines, and try the wine. And for ever more the bottles from places you visited will be just that bit more special. And do I remember my first Australian wine tourism trip? How could I forget? I was playing General Peron in *Evita* in London and managed to wangle five days off to go to Australia and back! I drove up to the Hunter Valley in a van with a bunch of bad boys. I ate 48 rock oysters, drank a dozen stubbies of Coopers Stout, met legends like Murray Tyrrell, Max Lake, Len Evans and James Halliday. Recovered. Flew to the Barossa. Met legends like Bob McLean of St Hallett, Wolf Blass, Peter Lehmann, Max Schubert. Nearly didn't recover. Flew home as they closed Adelaide airport for bush fires. And I've loved every one of them since.

WINE REGIONS

AUSTRALIA IS a vast continent with an array of different climates and vineyard conditions which are being increasingly recognised by its many talented and imaginative winemakers.

South Australia page 36
Australia's biggest grape-growing state produces almost half the country's total production. It covers many climates and most wine styles, from bulk wines to the very best.

New South Wales page 76
New South Wales's strongest suit is its big ripe wines, the original Australian classics, from the smaller premium-quality regions. Better viticultural and winemaking practices have brought significant quality improvements in the large, irrigated vineyards along the Murrumbidgee, Lachlan and Murray rivers.

Victoria page 98
Despite its relatively small area, Victoria has probably more land suited to quality grape-growing than any other state and currently leads Australia's boutique winery boom.

Western Australia page 122
Only the south-west corner of this vast state is suited to viticulture. Despite producing only a tiny percentage of Australia's wines, there is plenty of exciting quality and a myriad individual styles.

Tasmania page 142
The generally cool climate has attracted high quality winemaking, resulting in delicate Pinot Noir, elegant Chardonnay and Riesling and the real star, fabulous premium fizz.

Queensland and Northern Territory page 150
Queensland isn't a major player in the Aussie wine stakes but the wine business is expanding fast and increasingly good wines are being made. And there is even a vineyard out at Alice Springs in the middle of the desert.

Bliss. Me, and what looks like – ooh – a good year's supply of grog in the barrel cellar at St Hallett's in the Barossa Valley.

SOUTH AUSTRALIA

SOUTH AUSTRALIA IS not only the engineroom but also the standard-bearer for Australian wine. Thanks to the massive irrigated Riverland plantings along the banks of the Murray River, the state generally provides over half of Australia's wine. But thanks to many of Australia's most famous wine companies in the traditional quality regions of Clare, Barossa, McLaren Vale and Coonawarra, for many people South Australian wine *is* Australian wine.

All the biggest Australian wine companies are either based in South Australia, or have substantial operations there. The focal point of this activity is the Barossa Valley, an easy hour's drive north of Adelaide. The Barossa remains, in particular, a producer of ultra-typical, full-bodied Australian reds, with voluptuously sweet, rich fruit reaching its zenith in Penfolds Grange, Australia's greatest red. Going south from Barossa to the Adelaide Hills, the climate becomes cooler. Sauvignon Blanc, Chardonnay and Pinot Noir thrive as the numerous small vineyards vie for space with Adelaide's inhabitants intent on a home in the Hills. North of the Barossa is the Clare Valley, a regular producer of limey Riesling and intense Shiraz and Cabernet Sauvignon.

South of Adelaide, the McLaren Vale produces a surprising range of reds and whites, united by the generosity of their flavour. Finally, there are the vast open expanses of the Limestone Coast Zone. Coonawarra and Padthaway are already famous, but the emerging regions of Wrattonbully, Robe, Mount Benson and Bordertown point the way for the future where limestone-laced soils, plentiful underground water and a moderately cool climate all contribute to the making of elegant, premium wines from the classic core of grape varieties, led by the blackcurrant and mulberry Cabernet Sauvignon of Coonawarra.

Sheep graze as they have done for generations and in the background vineyards reach up from the Barossa Valley floor on to the arid slopes above Tanunda.

SPOTLIGHT ON
South Australia

You cannot really understand why Henschke is so important in the world of Australian wine until you have climbed up into the hills above the Barossa Valley, tipped your cap to the tiny Gnadenberg Church and then turned and walked thoughtfully into the vineyard over the little country road. You are strolling between the vines of the Hill of Grace vineyard, one of Australia's most famous Shiraz vineyards. Some of the vines are 150 years old, ungrafted and planted by Stephen Henschke's great-great-grandfather sometime in the 1860s. Taste the superb Hill of Grace Shiraz wine, and you are tasting a bloodline of fruit and experience and emotion that goes right the way back to the original settlers taming this land a century and a half ago.

SOUTH AUSTRALIA MAY BE THE COUNTRY'S major producer of wine but it isn't wine that is the subject on everybody's lips – it's water. South Australia manages to produce an average of 530 million litres of wine a year, and yet it is the driest state in Australia. And if it weren't for the Murray River, I'm not sure many people would even live there, let alone have the slightest chance of producing such vast amounts of wine. The Murray is a zillion-gallon resource rising in the mountains of New South Wales near Canberra and then following a sluggish serpentine route of nearly 2600 kilometres before trickling out into the ocean at Lake Alexandrina, south-east of Adelaide. And I mean trickling, because most of the water in this mighty river has been taken out and used for irrigation or drinking by the time its remnants reach the ocean.

The exploitation of the Murray for irrigating hundreds of thousands of hectares of otherwise uncultivable barren land was one of the great agro-industrial feats of the twentieth century, and, along with the exploitation of its tributary rivers, primarily the Lachlan, the Murrumbidgee and the Darling, these waters have created massive prosperity for the inland regions of Queensland, New South Wales, Victoria and, above all, South Australia. But they're running out. And South Australia is at the end of the line. Her politicians are facing the unenviable task of trying to persuade states like Queensland and New South Wales to reduce water usage so that South Australia fruit- and grape-growers can survive. The reaction of many bush communities in those states has been very much of the two finger variety, and it isn't helped when areas like Clare and Barossa or Langhorne Creek, which have existed without supplementary irrigation for the vines for well over a century, decide that they too want a pipeline to pump millions of litres of water from the river so that investor companies and the large brand owners of Australian wine can plant ever more vineyards, often in places where the vine has never grown before. I mean, does the world need a significant increase in the amount of South Australian wine produced just now? No, it doesn't.

Does this all sound a bit pessimistic? I'd prefer to call it realistic. There are areas where water isn't a problem. Coonawarra, for instance. Not only does it rain a fair bit, but the bottom south-east corner of South Australia is lucky to sit on top of a giant aquifer of pure water running slowly to the coast. The trouble here is the name Coonawarra is so famous there's been a completely unjustifiable expansion of the region onto unsuitable soggy land nearby. Coonawarra's fame is due to beautifully cool, elegant reds grown only on bright red terra rossa limestone. There are thousands upon thousands of hectares of

Quick guide ◆ South Australia

Location Despite being the source of almost half Australia's wine, most of South Australia has no vineyards at all. They are tucked into the bottom right-hand corner south, north and east of Adelaide. The high-quality wines come from Barossa Valley, Eden Valley, Clare Valley, Adelaide Hills, Coonawarra and Padthaway. Riverland is the bulk-wine region. Limestone Coast is the exciting new zone down on the coast.

Grapes Anything and everything. Classics are Shiraz, Cabernet Sauvignon and Riesling. Shiraz from Barossa is one of Australia's

great success stories: the best comes from old vines, has great depth of leathery, rich fruit and will age for years. It's equally good, too, in McLaren Vale and sometimes softer and juicier. Cabernet Sauvignon makes wines of good complexity and concentration in Coonawarra, and plump, blackcurranty ones in McLaren Vale. Higher-altitude vineyards in the Clare or Eden Valley give leaner, ageworthy wines. Pinot Noir, especially in the cooler sites such as the Adelaide Hills, can be perfumed and good. Riesling reaches great heights of quality in the Eden and Clare Valleys and the hills to

the east of Barossa; these lime-and-toast-flavoured wines age superbly. Softer wines come from Padthaway and Coonawarra. Chardonnay is at its best in the cool vineyards of the Adelaide Hills and the Eden and Clare Valleys, or in warmer Padthaway. Coonawarra also makes some richer versions. Sauvignon Blanc is most pungent in cool regions like the Adelaide Hills but Padthaway also makes some tasty wines. Viognier is doing well in the Eden Valley.

Local jargon Don't confuse South Australia on a label with the more general South

such soils near Coonawarra – the whole area is called The Limestone Coast. But they're not called Coonawarra. So you can't get so much money for your wine. Ah, well, time will tell. There are lots of Limestone Coast vineyards being developed, from Padthaway and Wrattonbully to the north, out west to Mount Benson and south to Mount Gambier. Maybe some of them will prove they're better than Coonawarra, I don't see why not. And by then, perhaps the whole of Australia will have a national water policy to ensure that everyone benefits from this precious resource, but no-one abuses it.

ADELAIDE'S FIRST VINEYARDS

It was probably evident that water was going to be a bit of a problem right from the start in South Australia, but, as with the other states, settlers immediately planted vines when they first arrived in 1836. These have largely disappeared under the tarmac and brick of modern Adelaide, though a patch of Penfolds' Magill vineyard still survives, hemmed in by suburbia. The first substantial vineyards were to the south of Adelaide – Morphett Vale, Reynella, McLaren Vale and across the hills to Langhorne Creek. Of these McLaren Vale and Langhorne Creek survive and flourish. The move north came in the 1840s when German settlers arrived in the Barossa

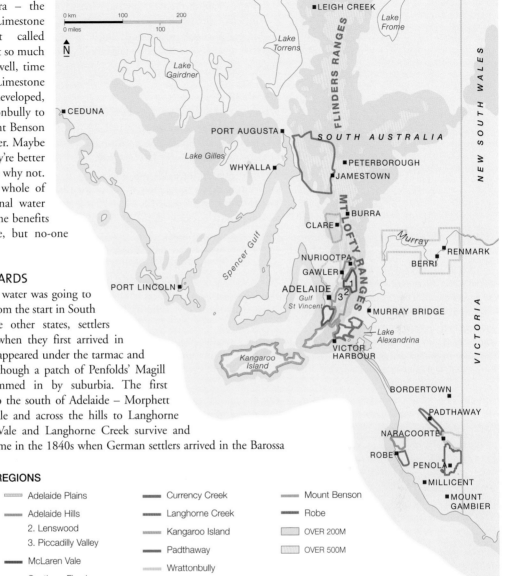

WINE REGIONS AND SUB-REGIONS

- Southern Flinders Ranges
- Clare Valley
- Riverland
- Barossa Valley
- Eden Valley
  1. High Eden
- Adelaide Plains
- Adelaide Hills
  2. Lenswood
  3. Piccadilly Valley
- McLaren Vale
- Southern Fleurieu
- Currency Creek
- Langhorne Creek
- Kangaroo Island
- Padthaway
- Wrattonbully
- Coonawarra
- Mount Benson
- Robe
- OVER 200M
- OVER 500M

Eastern Australia appellation that includes the whole of Victoria, New South Wales and Tasmania and parts of Queensland and South Australia.

Climate This ranges from 'cool climate' regions like the Adelaide Hills and Coonawarra, to hot, dry ones like Barossa. Many regions are restricted in their growth by the lack of available water.

Soil The soil is a mix of sandy loam, red loam, various clays and fertile volcanic earth. Coonawarra has terra rossa over limestone.

Aspect Varies widely, from flat Coonawarra to vines on quite steep slopes in the Adelaide Hills, the Barossa Ranges and parts of the Clare Valley.

Do regions matter? They do, but it's a horribly complex picture. Wines from the Adelaide Hills are generally cool climate; Barossa Valley wines, from further inland, are bigger and beefier; and Coonawarra, Clare and Eden go for intensity without the brawn. Other regions, including bulk-producer Riverland, deliver big, ultra-ripe flavours.

Do vintages matter? In Adelaide Hills and perhaps in Coonawarra too, otherwise only stylistically – the quality remains good.

Organization South Australia is home to many of Australia's largest wine companies, but many of the small boutique wineries are increasingly high profile and export widely.

A few facts 66,633ha of vineyards, 42 per cent of Australia's total plantings; 49 per cent of total production; 432 wineries.

Valley and established a vineyard and winery community that has played a dominant part in Australian wine ever since, and left it with some of the world's most ancient vines, because the phylloxera vine aphid, which has ravaged vineyards worldwide and throughout much of Australia too, has never taken hold in the state, allowing original plantings of such vines as Shiraz, Grenache and Mataro (Mourvedre) to survive to this day.

RIVERLAND

Hardly any of South Australia's famous wines come from the Riverland. Is that fair? Well, I admit, the labels don't actually spell out that they come from the Riverland – but when you see the words South Eastern Australia on the label of a famous brand like Penfolds or Lindemans, Wolf Blass or Jacob's Creek, you can be pretty sure that there's a great slug of Riverland fruit in there, because the Riverland is the sweep of South Australia that borders the Murray River, from Morgan in the west to past Renmark in the east almost on the Victorian border. As the great Murray lazily twists and turns, its sluggish flow sometimes so slow you'd swear it didn't even want to reach the sea, vast vineyards have been established on the banks using irrigation water to produce prodigious amounts of cheap grapes. How good they are depends on how hard the growers try to restrict the generous yields and use ripening methods that maximize quality rather than quantity. But while the Big Brands try to hold down costs, and the world's supermarkets demand budget-priced own label Australian reds and whites, it is from here that the majority of fruit will come.

Both Renmark and Mildura have been through tricky times but, by and large, they and the other Murray Valley regions of South Australia and Victoria flourished, and so did the Riverina region which lies on the Murrumbidgee River in New South Wales. Today, the grapes for all the low-priced, but attractively fruity, red and white Australian wines the world laps up will have come from these vast, mechanized, irrigated vineyards.

Vast, isn't it? This is Angove's 500-ha Nanya Vineyard near Renmark in Riverland. I can't say I've walked around it as it's 5 kilometres from end to end but I have driven it in a dusty old ute and even that took some time. However, it is economies of scale like this that enable Australia to be such an efficient and effective producer of high-quality, high-volume, low price wine.

This large-scale irrigation has helped Australia to transform the quality of budget wine worldwide, but it is a relatively recent phenomenon. When it comes to quality, the heart and soul of the South Australian wine industry is still in the water-starved, sun-soaked fields and vales to the north and south of Adelaide.

ADELAIDE HILLS

The area north of Adelaide is dominated by the Barossa Valley (see page 46) and the Clare Valley (see page 54), but there are also significant amounts of grapes grown on the baking Adelaide Plains just north of the city and one star producer – Primo Estate. However, the spotlight today is on the search for cooler conditions near to Adelaide, and for those we need to head east, into the hills that are already steeply rising out of the city long before you reach the edge of the suburbs. There's an impressive and rather beautiful motorway that assaults the hills head on yet still reveals much of their beauty. But there are smaller roads up from the city – to Summertown, to Norton Summit, Basket Range, Lenswood or Cudlee Creek. If you've got the time, and want to experience the sheer intensity of the beautiful, cramped tortuous hill valleys, smell the perfume of the gum trees that crowd in on all sides, and feel a fabulous sense of release from the pressures of the city, take one of these small roads, and take your time.

But it is this magic and tranquillity of the Adelaide Hills that seriously limits its potential as a vineyard region. No-one doubts that it produces marvellous fruit, which can be cool climate and restrained in areas like Piccadilly that nestle high up under the slopes of Mount Lofty, South Australia's not very high highest mountain, yet there's also remarkable Shiraz and even Zinfandel in the warmer pockets and glades that wine people have sought out amid the forest. Ah, but if it's ideal for growing grapes it's equally ideal for homes, hideaways, weekend retreats – and these have often won the battle for land in the past. And there's another battle. About water – what else, in South Australia? Adelaide desperately needs the water that the Hills and the forests draw down as rain. The Government does allow some of it to be siphoned off for irrigation, but there are a lot more votes in decent tapwater, lawn sprinklers and urban industrial needs down in the city than there are in vineyards in the Hills.

So, we're never going to see an enormous amount of grapes grown up here, but the quality of the wines they create does mean that Adelaide Hills yields considerable influence in the South Australia wine world, not least because some of the wine industry's highest achievers have vineyards here – Brian Croser of Petaluma, Tim Knappstein of Knappstein/Lenswood and Henschke of Hill of Grace fame, among others. But Croser is the real catalyst here. He'd begun his career in the 1970s, an era when cool climate wine-making had scarcely been conceived of in Australia. But Croser was passionately determined to establish a cool climate culture in South Australia, and founded his Petaluma winery in 1976 with this in mind. His eyes were already on these misty, wooded valleys high in the hills above Adelaide, and in 1978 he began planting vines on the steep slopes of the Piccadilly Valley, some of which are so cool they can only ripen fruit enough to act as the acidic but excellent base wine for his Croser fizz.

Piccadilly is about as cool as you can get, up at 570 metres height, and that's exactly why Croser chose it, but Tim Knappstein and Stephen Henschke run it close at Lenswood with vineyards between 530 and 570 metres. But they're not quite so cool because they're slightly north and slightly east of Piccadilly. This is how it works. There are a number of north-south ridges in the Hills. As you head east, the ridges get lower, rainfall is lower, and temperature creeps higher while you descend to the plains of the Murray River basin. As for north-south – Mount Lofty, south-east of Adelaide city, is the highest, wettest and coolest point. As you head north, the height drops, the valleys broaden and the heat increases. Around Gumeracha and Chain of Ponds, it becomes pretty open country, with the Barossa Valley dipping away to the north, and High Eden to the north-east. The wine styles become accordingly fuller and riper. However, you can also get warmer by going south from Mount Lofty, as the Hills become much lower, and Kuitpo, down south, has produced some exciting Shiraz, as has Mount Barker, to the

Quick guide ◆
The great Murray River

Australia has to thank the foresight and determination of two American brothers, the Chaffeys, for transforming the annual flooding of the Murray River into the most important resource in Australian viticulture. They arrived in Australia at the end of the 1880s, having successfully established irrigation schemes in the California desert. The headwaters of the Murray River are numerous streams fed by the melting snowfields of the Great Dividing Range. Every year the river used to bulge and burst with the thaw. The waters flooded vast expanses of empty, arid land that gratefully lapped up the moisture – but to no avail, since no-one knew how to exploit this annual bounty.

First at Renmark in South Australia, and then at Mildura further upstream in north-west Victoria, the Chaffeys built pumping stations, dams, locks and irrigation channels to harness the Murray River. As a result, verdant market gardens and vineyards were planted where nothing but saltbush desert had existed before. Now not only do most of Australia's wines come from these vast, inland irrigated carpets of vines, but also most of her fruits and vegetables too.

The beautiful wetland centre at Hardys' Banrock Station winery in the Riverland. Over-exploitation of the Murray has caused considerable damage to the river and Banrock Station is a highly successful effort to restore some of the Murray's original eco-system. It is supported by a donation from every bottle of Banrock Station wine you buy.

McLaren Vale is one of the original vineyard areas in South Australia, situated just south of Adelaide. Intense sunshine produces high ripeness, but regular cooling winds from Gulf St Vincent create rich but balanced wines.

south-east of Mount Lofty. And higher altitude will always give you cooler conditions. This may all sound a bit gimmicky, but the Adelaide Hills are marginal for vineyards. Tiny differences of height, aspect to the sun and soil do make a difference – just 100 metres higher or a kilometre to the west can make one patch of land perfect for world-class Chardonnay and Pinot Noir, and the next patch much better suited to peppery, brawny Shiraz – or even Zinfandel!

SOUTH OF ADELAIDE

Head south of Adelaide, and you're in Fleurieu. Which all sounds a bit French. Well, it is. It's easy to forget that when Australia was being explored, the French were pretty keen on a slice of the action. Lieutenant Flinders of England and Captain Baudin of France were both busily charting South Australia's coast when they met in Encounter Bay near the mouth of the Murray River. The whole of the area up to Adelaide lay before them including the magnificent peninsula pushing out seaward to the south-west. Flinders named it Cape Jervis. No, not very catchy is it? Baudin christened it the Fleurieu Peninsula. Isn't that a much grander title? Those French always did have style.

But apart from the name, the French didn't have a lot more to do with the region, which was quickly developed by a very English bunch of settlers. In wine terms this is relevant. North of Adelaide it was the German settlers, especially those of the Barossa Valley, who were most important. South of Adelaide, the settlers were overwhelmingly English, and in McLaren Vale, the chief vineyard area, supplying the English was what they did almost to the exclusion of all else for the best part of a century.

In fact the first grapes were probably planted as early as 1838 at Reynella, on the north side of McLaren Vale. In time Reynella became famous as the headquarters of the Hardy Wine Company (they're still going, now as part of the world's biggest wine company, Constellation), and Thomas Hardy and Sons were the driving force in creating the British market for 'sherries' and 'ports' and great, beefy 'ferruginous reds' and 'tonic Burgundies' such as Tintara and Emu which kept generations of damp old Englishmen and women tolerably contented up until tastes changed and the market for these wines collapsed in the 1960s.

But the conditions that had created such wines didn't change, and though McLaren Vale went through a tough decade or two like its northern cousin, the Barossa, by the 1990s rich, ripe, alcoholic reds were back in vogue – and that's what McLaren Vale does best – just like the Barossa. And like the Barossa, McLaren Vale isn't just one homogeneous chunk of land. It's a very beautiful, calm, pastoral place, shaped a bit like a shoe horn bounded to the north-west by the deep gorge of the Onkaparinga River and to the south-west by the great golden hummocky ridges of the Willunga escarpment. And over to the west, the Gulf St Vincent. The gulf is very important, because it creates sea breezes every day that considerably cool down the vineyards, especially those near the sea. These coastal vines are largely new and only made possible by a new irrigation scheme using waste water from Adelaide, purified and pumped south. They're very imaginative in Australia when it comes to water. But the truly great McLaren Vale vineyards are further inland, where the grapes are more able to bake on the vine, and fabulous Shiraz, Grenache and Mourvedre are the result. But there is a wide variety of soils and conditions in what is a relatively contained area. Up towards the Mount Lofty Ranges to the north-east, there's a powerful aquifer that brings the water table up to within 2 metres of the surface during winter. Areas like Blewitt Springs are sandy and produce looser-textured wines, while areas like Seaview and the vineyards that run up onto tough ground towards Chapel Hill and the Onkaparinga Gorge produce dark, intense reds, as brooding and magnificent as any in Australia.

There are several other vineyard regions in Fleurieu. Windswept Kangaroo Island, off the coast, produces some decent stuff – and even Jacques Lurton, the go-getting French flying winemaker, has bought land here. The Southern Fleurieu peninsula has quite a few vineyards, and I've had some lovely wines from Currency Creek, which stretches along the banks of Lake Alexandrina to the mouth of the Murray.

But the most important of these other areas is Langhorne Creek centred on the floodplains of the Bremer and Angas rivers. That sounds impressive, doesn't it, but the Bremer is a small river and the Angas is a *very* small river. The first time I visited, I drove down from Mount Barker and somehow thought I would happen upon some vast fen courageously defended against imminent inundation by doughty old-timers manning the bilge pumps night and day. No need to. The rivers do flood, most springtimes, and the floodwaters are allowed to flow across the fields that spread for a few hundred metres from the river banks. But it's only for a few hundred metres. Then the ground rises and the waters can't get any further. Even so, it's an efficient if old-fashioned irrigation method and the super-fertile soil soaks up the water. But once a year is enough – usually in early spring, and then the vines get on with life without any need for further irrigation. However, these old-established flood plain vines are in the minority. But it's still very flat and very fertile on the slightly raised land, and the Langhorne Creek red wine has a famously soft and mellow quality to it. Langhorne Creek grapes formed the basis of the hugely successful Wolf Blass wines; Jacob's Creek's quality was similarly based on Langhorne Creek fruit, as was Saltram's famous Metala, and now, with irrigation pumped by pipeline from Lake Alexandrina, there are about 6000 hectares of vineyards, mostly providing the Big Brand owners with fruit, though some independent producers like Bleasdale, Bremerton and Step Road are growing increasingly tasty reds from Cabernet Sauvignon, Shiraz and Malbec in particular.

LIMESTONE COAST

This large area is exactly what it says. It's the whole bottom chunk of South Australia, bordered by Victoria to the east, the ocean to the south and west and stretching up north about as far as Bordertown on the main Adelaide-Melbourne road. And it really is a limestone paradise – probably the largest single limestone resource in the world. Its wine reputation is centred on the limestone of Coonawarra (see page 50), for decades one of Australia's most famous red wine regions, but there are numerous other Limestone ridges and outcrops, many of which are now being developed.

The best known of these is Padthaway, about 90 kilometres north of Coonawarra, with similar limestone though a slightly warmer climate. Originally set up to provide large quantities of basic white wine, it quickly proved much better than that, growing a succession of award-winning Chardonnays, and, nowadays, some superb reds, notably from Shiraz. Most of the 3720 hectares are on the flat, but there are 300 on really challenging terrain in the Padthaway Ranges which produce reds of startling intensity. The crop is largely processed elsewhere by the Big Companies, but Hardys operates the very good Stonehaven Winery here, and if you can find a bottle of Henry's Drive, you're in for a rare treat.

Heartland wines are a rare treat too, this time from Wirrega, in the north, near Bordertown (they display a furious black power to their fruit) and Wrattonbully, just to the north of Coonawarra, is proving to have outstanding potential for deep, scented reds that almost have an Italian bitter chocolate twist to them. But again as elsewhere in the Limestone Coast, most of the fruit is processed elsewhere.

Otherwise, the main limestone action is out towards the coast. From the Comaum Range just east of Coonawarra, there are 12 limestone ridges stretching north-south, all old coastlines, and all suitable for vines. Just about every centimetre of Coonawarra is now planted with vines, but St Mary's just west of Coonawarra is already producing lovely reds, and there's a serious amount of vines planted out on the coast at Robe and Mount Benson. Conditions are cool and windy, but I've tasted some outstanding Sauvignon from vineyards on windward slopes and intense Shiraz from vines on the protected leeward side. And even south of Penola, and way down by Mount Gambier there are vines. In fact, out at Kongorong, west of the town, I've seen vineyards where there seems to be no soil at all, just quartz-like limestone, piled up between the vines that stores the heat so well that even in the windy, wet south, the grapes are ripening not far behind those of Coonawarra.

The Wrattonbully region, just north of Coonawarra, is proving to have outstanding potential for deep, scented reds, but again as elsewhere in the Limestone Coast, most of the fruit is processed elsewhere. These are new plantings belonging to Yalumba. We won't really know how good Wrattonbully can be until we see labels appearing dedicated to Wrattonbully fruit alone. But look at that dark red soil. It's the famous terra rossa again.

This is such a South Australian panorama. Bright green splashes of vines, angry red earth, the parched golden colour of pasture land in the heat – and in the distance, stands of elegant river gums and the promise of brief respite from the heat in the high hills. This is the Heritage Vineyard in the Barossa Valley, with the Barossa Ranges rising in the background.

BAROSSA

I SUPPOSE YOU COULD CALL IT a kind of maturity being reached. The moment when the world's most influential wine critic decides to give one of your wines a perfect score. 100 out of 100. Legitimacy. Now we can hold our head high versus the view of mankind. Was this what the Barossa producers were thinking when Trevor Jones was awarded a sweet full house in February 2000?

Well, no, I don't think so. Legitimacy? These guys have been tilling the land and making stupendous wine for 150 years. Hold their head high? Australians have accepted Barossa as a supreme producer of mighty red wines since the nineteenth century, without any need to go around awarding marks. The Australian way of rewarding merit is through its national system of competitive wine shows in each state's capital city. The Barossa is awash with trophies and gold medals awarded down the years and still being awarded today. Hell, when you've got more 100-year-old vines than anywhere else in the world, when your vines span three centuries of vintages, some of them still battling away after being planted in the 1840s and 1850s... Legitimacy? Maturity? Barossa has it like no other wine region in Australia, and few regions in the world can top it.

It all started with the Germans. Well, the Silesians. In the 1840s Silesia was part of Prussia and three shiploads of Lutheran religious refugees turned up in South Australia desperate for good weather, religious freedom and somewhere to settle and rebuild their

These old vines at Seppeltsfield are coming up for their centenary soon and will go on providing rich black fruit for fortified 'ports' for as long as anyone will let them.

BAROSSA AND EDEN VALLEYS

TOTAL DISTANCE NORTH TO SOUTH 31KM

▦ VINEYARDS

N

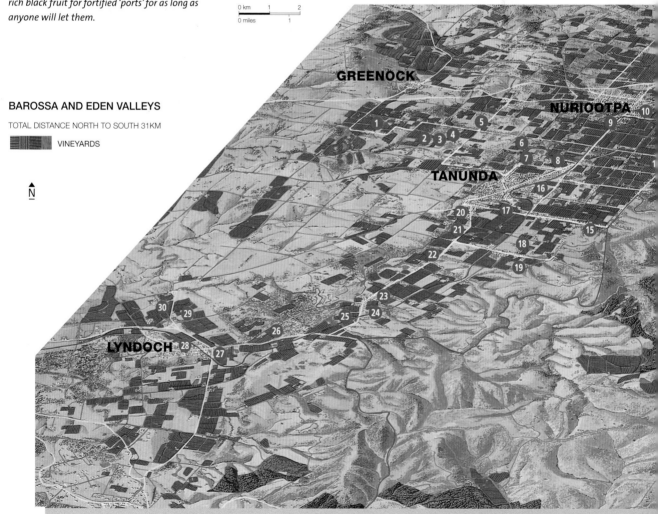

WHERE THE VINEYARDS ARE

This map is a marvellous panorama of the whole Barossa region. One of the things that always strikes me in South Australia is how seemingly insignificant the mountains are. The Mount Lofty Ranges stretch up the right of the map, yet these ancient hills have been worn away over the millennia into hummocks of storm-smoothed rock. They are still a vital few hundred metres above the valley floor, creating cooler, windier conditions for viticulture, and since they are some of the first obstacles the westerly winds have encountered since coming in from the Indian Ocean way over in Western Australia, whatever moisture there is will drop mainly in these hills.

As you can see, most of the vineyards have lakes next to them, to catch winter rains for irrigation in the dry summers, when each vine may need 5 litres of water a day. The valley floor gets far less winter rain and almost none in summer. Not only that, subterranean water to the west of the North Para River is too salty to be of much use for irrigation. Consequently, most vineyards lie east of the river. But the dry land to the north and around Nuriootpa and Greenock can produce stunning reds from old vines: Penfolds Grange is based on fruit from the Kalimna Vineyard north of Nuriootpa. Further south, wineries such as St Hallett, Rockford and Charles Melton have built enviable reputations.

In the Eden Valley hills, water is less of a problem – so long as you build large catchment dams to hold the winter rains. It is cooler here, due to the height of the hills: most vineyards are at 400–500m high, and produce some of South Australia's top white wines.

SELECTED WINERIES

BAROSSA VALLEY
1 Greenock Creek
2 Barossa Valley Estate
3 Two Hands
4 Heritage Wines
5 Torbreck Wines
6 Veritas
7 Peter Lehmann
8 Richmond Grove

9 Penfolds
10 Elderton
11 Willows Vineyard
12 Wolf Blass
13 Saltram
14 Haan Wines
15 Bethany
16 Basedow
17 Turkey Flat

18 Rockford
19 Charles Melton
20 Glaetzer
21 St Hallett
22 Grant Burge
23 Orlando
24 Miranda
25 Jenke Vineyards
26 Kellermeister/Trevor Jones

27 Schild Estate
28 Burge Family Winemakers
29 Charles Cimicky
30 Yaldara

EDEN VALLEY
31 Yalumba
32 Thorn-Clarke
33 Henschke
34 Mountadam
35 Irvine

EDEN VALLEY = WINE REGION

▬▬▬ REGIONAL BOUNDARY

0 km   1   2
0 miles   1

This is Orlando's famous Steingarten Riesling vineyard in the Eden Valley. It is with more than a touch of irony that the name Steingarten or 'Garden of Stones' was chosen for its name when this rocky ground was first planted in 1962.

Red grapes Shiraz is the star red, dominating current plantings as well as new ones. Cabernet Sauvignon is also important, but the next most precious resource is hundreds of hectares of old Grenache and a little ancient Mataro.

White grapes Riesling is still the leading grape, mostly planted in the Eden Valley, but there is almost as much Semillon and Chardonnay, and a small amount of Sauvignon Blanc and Chenin.

Climate The Barossa enjoys arid summers. The Eden Valley and the Barossa Ranges are cooler with more rain, but it's winter rain when the vines are dormant, so irrigation is often needed.

Soil Topsoils range from heavy loam with clay, to light sand; some soils need the addition of lime to counteract acidity. Subsoils are limestone, quartz-sand and clay, and red-brown loams.

Aspect Traditional valley floor estates are best at producing big reds; estates in the higher Eden Valley are excellent for cooler climate styles.

communities. Their descendants still dominate the Valley, as grape-growers, as winemakers. Just listen to these names – Johann Gramp, Leo Buring, Stephen Henschke, Wolfgang Blass, Peter Lehmann, John, Colin and Ben Glaetzer – the names of Barossa winemakers, ancient and modern. Add to these a delightful assembly of old Lutheran bluestone churches, bakeries offering Streuselkuchen, rather than buns and cakes, delicatessens displaying Mettwurst and Lachsschinken, and the strains of lusty-lunged choirs and brass bands at practice cutting through the still, warm air of a summer's evening – and you know the Barossa is different. Indeed, the fabric of the Barossa as a delightful place to live and raise your family is in a bit of a time warp. Many of the aged vineyards are in a time warp and had they not been owned by fiercely independent and fiercely proud German families, they would probably have been uprooted and replanted with Chardonnay and Merlot long ago. Because, although the descendants of those early settlers did establish first vineyards, and then wineries, the wineries paradoxically became too successful.

Most of the famous old names are now just part of vast conglomerates. Wolf Blass is part of the American-Australian giant Beringer-Blass. It sounds wonderfully German. It isn't; not any more. Leo Buring, Kaiser Stuhl, Seppelt – these have all been swallowed up by the rapacious Southcorp. Johann Gramp's Orlando winery is now owned by the French behemoth Pernod-Ricard, and many of Australia's largest-scale and most efficient wineries now cluster round the old settler towns of Nuriootpa, Tanunda and Angaston. Indeed, today more than half of all Australia's wine is made by these big Barossa-based companies. But not many of the grapes for these wines are grown in the Barossa by the descendants of the Silesian settlers who used to provide the fruit, since the accountants in charge quickly realized that far cheaper fruit was available from the sprawling irrigated vineyards in the Murray Riverland than would ever be offered by the Barossa. This produced a massive crisis in the 1980s, but never underestimate the resilience of these old Barossa Deutsch families. Led by the formidable Peter Lehmann, and followed by such visionaries as Rob Hill-Smith of Yalumba, Stephen Henschke, Charles Melton and Robert O'Callaghan of Rockford, the Barossa discarded its over-reliance on outside companies and set to work reviving its own reputation based on the great old vineyards.

By the beginning of the new millennium, the pendulum had swung the growers' way. Enthusiasts worldwide realized that some of the world's oldest pre-phylloxera vines still survive in Barossa. The incomparable flavours these centenarians offer has meant that 'boutique' or small-scale, high quality wine production now flourishes in the Barossa. The big companies are still there, and put these precious grapes to far better use than before but now, when they try to browbeat a grower, the grower has somewhere better to turn.

It wasn't only the Germans who established the Barossa. George Angas, a Scot who owned a vast holding of 11,330 hectares (or 28,000 acres, for which he paid £1 an acre) spread across the Barossa and the surrounding hill country, was the person who paid for the three shiploads of Silesian refugees who arrived and settled in 1842. The Hill-Smiths who founded Yalumba turned up at Angaston from Dorset in England in 1849. Vineyards weren't their only interest, but the fact that we can still walk out in the fields at Turkey Flat and gently stroke the bark of Shiraz vines planted in 1847 – we can pick off a grape if we want, and suck its sweet flesh from the skin – shows how successful vineyards were. And it wasn't always just deep red table wines. 'Port' and 'Sherry' were made to a fantastically high quality level. Seppelt's examples are justly famous, and Kellermeister's Old Barossa Tawny and Barossa Liqueur Shiraz Tawny also got straight 100's from the mighty Robert Parker. And during the 1950s, Australian *white* wine was revolutionized in the Barossa Valley, and Barossa Pearl, an easy-glugging fizzy white, became one of the top selling wines in Australia. Excellent Semillon whites are still made in the Valley, but most of the white wine action has moved up into the hills of High Eden and the Eden Valley just to the east.

BAROSSA VALLEY VINEYARDS

Vineyards were established in two main areas: the gently undulating valley floor, along the North Para River from Nuriootpa down to Lyndoch, and on the hills to the east. The valley floor is hot and dry; soils veer from infertile yellow clays to deep red loam, suited to the production of dark, intense red wines. There's little rainfall, and there's little subterranean water suitable for irrigation.

But there are significant differences in the styles of red wine each particular area produces. Blending has always been an important part of Barossa winemaking, and most of the best wines are blends of more than one vineyard. As one master blender told me as we surveyed the components of a great Shiraz he was creating – we've got some low yield grunts, and we've got some florals. We need them both. And he was right. Although some producers, perhaps seduced by the American market's fascination with intensely lush, high alcohol 'grunts', do simply go for a positively over-ripe, piledriver style, the most complete wines are blends. Stonewell to the west has ironstone in the soil and makes powerful sturdy wines. Greenoch, just north, is finer, while Ebenezer and Light Pass to the north-east are sandier and produce immediate intensity without the staying power of Stonewell, or the perfume of the higher cooler vineyards of Lyndoch and Williamstown at the southern end of the Valley.

And if you're still not content, you've got the hills to the east. These are the Barossa Ranges, that used to be thought of simply as Barossa. But Eden Valley and High Eden are very different from the Valley floor. They're windswept, often quite steeply sloped, cool, and always short of water. Some venerable vines like those in Henschke's Hill of Grace vineyard are too well-established to worry about drought, but younger vines need all the help they can get from drip irrigation just to stay alive in the dry years. The results are superb. Henschke's Shirazes are world famous. Adam Wynn has also made outstanding Shiraz as well as top Pinot Noir at Mountadam, in the High Eden sub-region. But Eden Valley is known best for its whites, and above all for its Rieslings which are definitely as fine as those of the Clare Valley, and because of their haunting scent of a lemon grove in summer, are sometimes even better.

COONAWARRA

Poor, tiny, neglected Coonawarra station – a shed, a dunny, an overgrown platform, and years since the train last stopped. And beyond? A sea of vines on black clay soil traditionally regarded as swampland fit only for grazing. Ah, how times change.

Red grapes Success with Cabernet Sauvignon makes this by far the predominant variety in Coonawarra today, though there is a good deal of Shiraz and Merlot, and a little Pinot Noir and Cabernet Franc.

White grapes Chardonnay is the most widely planted variety, but there's also Riesling and some good Sauvignon Blanc.

Climate These are the southernmost and, therefore, coolest of South Australia's vineyards. Frost is a significant problem during the early part of the growing season. The easily accessible water table gives high yields of good quality. Vintage can take place from early March to as late as May.

Soil An area of terra rossa (literally 'red soil'), or crumbly red loam, covers the low ridges, with both black cracking clay and sandy soils over a clay base on lower ground.

Aspect It is flat here – uniformly so, and with its long growing season, high light intensity and unique soil structure, it is ideal for vines.

Coonawarra is not the place it was when I first visited. Then, it was dead easy to understand. You drove for ages through bleak, empty countryside south from Murray Bridge. You rumbled over the railway tracks to the little town of Naracoorte, and then you were back out in the open, some lovely tall gums now and then by the road, but as you looked west – nothing – just flat, flat land. Somewhere out there was the sea. The first visit I made was in the summertime. There were cattle. The second visit was in winter. West of the road was a marsh.

But you drove on, and just as you'd got used to Glen Roy National Park providing something pretty to look at on the left-hand side of the car, the road took a little jig right, straightened out again – and there you were. The Coonawarra vineyards. From that corner, pretty much straight as a die for 15 kilometres, the road ran south to Penola, the local town. All along the right, and in parts along the left, there were famous vines, of companies like Wynns, Lindemans, Rouge Homme, Redman, Mildara and Brand's – all deservedly famous for producing what many critics had hailed as Australia's best red wines.

The secret lay in this thin, cigar-shaped land, 15 kilometres long and varying between 2 kilometres and only 200 metres wide. The Terra Rossa. The red soil. In the days when Bordeaux wines were regarded as the ultimate expression of red grape quality, this cool, well-drained, isolated little patch of land gave the most Bordeaux-like results in Australia for the Cabernet Sauvignon grape – although sometimes a little peppery Shiraz was mixed in as well. They didn't really taste like Bordeaux, but they were pretty light and refreshing in traditional Australian terms – and they did have a remarkable blackcurrant intensity of pine, as well as a leafy greenness from the cool conditions that wasn't all that far away from Bordeaux in style. The wines were easy to identify and understand. The conditions in which the grapes grew were precise, compact and absolutely obvious even to an amateur. If your grapes grew on the slightly raised limestone ridge with the red soil, they could give you the classic Coonawarra flavours. If you dropped off this red soil ridge to damp black clays towards the sea, or strayed inland onto the sandy loams and pallid chalky clays towards the east – your grapes wouldn't ripen. Simple as that. So they weren't Coonawarra grapes.

WHERE THE VINEYARDS ARE

Well, here it is, one of Australia's most famous vineyard areas in all its glory. It is a spectacular place to grow vines, but it just so happens to be dumped in the middle of what is virtually a swamp. When the rain starts, you keep to the roads or take a pair of water-wings. Penola – the little town at the bottom of the map – means 'big swamp' in the local Aboriginal language.

But if you take the main road north out of Penola, for about 15 kilometres you travel along the low limestone ridge of Coonawarra. This slight increase in altitude raises the road and a thin strip of land either side a crucial metre or so above the surrounding waterlogged clay soils, and provides brilliant conditions for growing an abundance of healthy vines.

The best land has a thin covering of red-brown topsoil which lies directly over a layer of calcrete and then limestone. This terra rossa topsoil is extremely fertile, so the best quality comes from thin coverings of as little as a couple of centimetres on top of barely perceptible rises in the land.

However, those vines you can see to the west of the railway are on black clay soils, and many of the vines stretching east are on white clay, some of which (both black and white) is little more than partially reclaimed swamp. Neither is capable of properly ripening Cabernet or Shiraz grapes.

The underground water that nourishes the Coonawarra vines is remarkably pure, but as more and more water is drawn out of the Great Artesian Basin by Coonawarra and other nearby emergent wine areas, damaging salts are likely to be leached from further inland. A water-sharing agreement between South Australia and Victoria, just to the east of the map on Coonawarra's eastern border, aims to limit any water extraction in the future.

N

COONAWARRA

TOTAL DISTANCE NORTH TO SOUTH 24KM

VINEYARDS

SELECTED WINERIES

1 Rymill
2 Penley Estate
3 Brand's
4 Wynns Coonawarra
5 Di Giorgio
6 Zema Estate
7 Jamiesons Run
8 Majella
9 Lawrence Victor Estate
10 Katnook Estate
11 Highbank
12 Leconfield
13 Yalumba (The Menzies)
14 Bowen Estate
15 Balnaves
16 The Blok Estate
17 Hollick
18 Punters Corner
19 Parker Coonawarra Estate
20 Lindemans

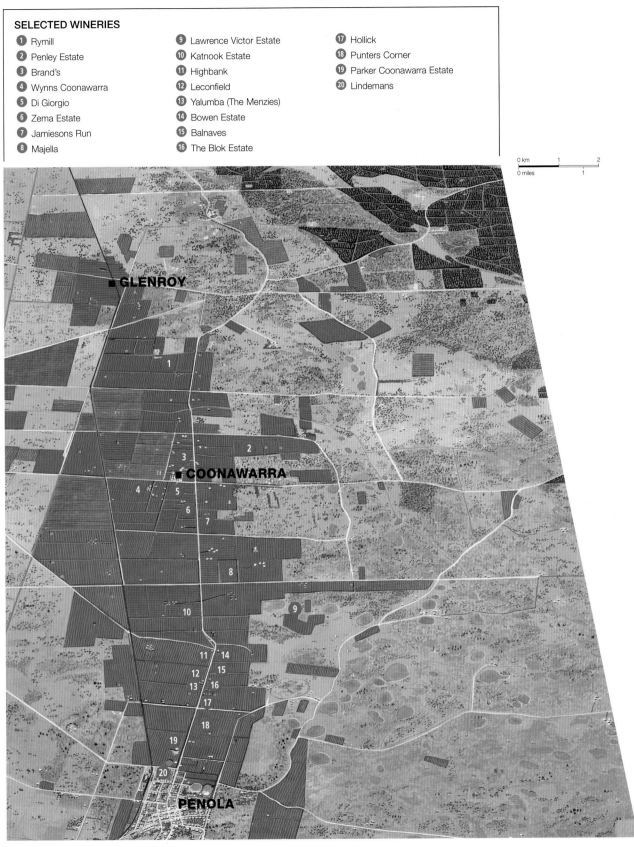

Oh, the sad price of success. They are Coonawarra grapes now. In a series of court cases the previously sacred Coonawarra boundary has been shamelessly stretched and gerrymandered. The worst excesses are to the west, over the railway line, on to the flat black clays. Here there are now hundreds of hectares of vines where previously there were none and the absurdly generous limit of the Geographical Indication (GI) has two quite illogical loops outwards in its western boundary. Since there can be no vinous reason for these deviations, I can only assume someone paid the right lawyer the right amount of money to get themselves included. There are also extensions south and way north – to patches of land that have no historical claim to the name Coonawarra, but at least they are on outcrops of this precious Terra Rossa land. Is this land so rare? Well, actually, it isn't. There's absolutely heaps of it down in this region, the entirety of which is now called the Limestone Coast. But it isn't Coonawarra. Or wasn't until the lawyers got involved.

ABOVE AND BELOW GROUND

This whole Coonawarra phenomenon deserves a closer look. First, let's look at what goes on beneath the ground. Most of the great vineyards of the world owe their presence to a river which has carved its path to the sea, creating a mixture of valley slopes and river plains that provide the unique conditions needed for grapes to ripen. Coonawarra's uniqueness is the fact that there aren't any rivers: there are mountains to the east; there's sea to the west; but there are no rivers to connect one to the other.

There is a lot of water, though, falling in the mountains every winter. And it seeps, bit by bit, just below the surface across the bleak swathe of bogland that makes up the southern tip of South Australia. They call this the rump end of the Great Artesian Basin

The vivid red terra rossa soil in the heart of Coonawarra covers a bed of soft, porous limestone with a constant water table below, providing perfect drainage and an ideal environment for root nourishment.

at least, that's how I interpret their vernacular. Depending on who you talk to, the water has seeped from neighbouring Victoria or all the way from Queensland. And depending on how far the water has come, it could be thousands of years old or hundreds. Anyway, it's so pure you almost need to add salts to it to make it suitable for vines. And there's lots of it, just below the surface.

That's all very well. But what about what happens above ground? What about the climate; and, for that matter, what about the soil itself? What's it all to do with wine? Let's go back a bit. About 600,000 years.

The area was under water then, with the shoreline marked by the Comaum Range east of Coonawarra. But two things happened. First, there was a reversal in the earth's magnetic field – we're due another one now – followed by a slow but continual upheaval in the land that has by now raised Coonawarra 60 metres above sea level. Second, about every 50,000 years, there has been an ice age and the seas have retreated. With each subsequent warm period, the seas have crept back to find the land sufficiently raised that a new beach is established, and a new ridge is built up of limestone over sandstone. There have been 12 ice ages in the last 600,000 years. There are 12 ridges between the Comaum Range and the sea – one for each ice age – running north to south, parallel to the shore. Between each ridge the land is a sullen mix of sandy soil over a clay subsoil, or black cracking clay. On the barely perceptible ridges, a thin sprinkling of fertile reddish soil sits above a tough limestone cap. Break through that cap and the limestone becomes so damp and crumbly you can poke your finger into it and waggle it about. And a yard or two further down, the pure mountain waters from the east seep slowly towards the sea. The underground water provides one of the best natural resources for irrigation that any wine area in the world possesses – that is, if the vines need it: many of the older vines' roots tap directly into the water. Given that Australia is a hot country, this should be a recipe for the efficient production of vast amounts of reliable, low cost wine.

CHILLY VINEYARDS

But there's one other thing. It's not hot in the south of South Australia. Coonawarra, 400 kilometres south of Adelaide, is surrounded by the chilly Southern Ocean. Most of the rain dumps uselessly on the area during the cold, damp winters, often waterlogging all but the scattered limestone ridges. Springtime is squally, and often frosty too. Summer starts out mild but dry, yet in February and March there are often hot spells that can scorch and exhaust the vines: then the bore holes pump day and night, providing life-saving irrigation. And as the grapes slowly ripen into April, the weather can break into sour, joyless early winter before the harvest is in and stay unfriendly and raw until the following spring.

RED WINES

Some of Australia's greatest reds have been made on this thin strip of land, where the climate makes vines struggle all year but the famous red soil and subsoil, and bountiful water cosset and spoil them. Since the first vines were planted in 1891, French-style reds, primarily from Shiraz and Cabernet, have dominated. But it wasn't until the 1960s that the world began to appreciate the relatively light yet intensely flavoured qualities of these reds. And of course during the 1980s, as Australia's New Wave searched hungrily for cool climate conditions – here was one that had already proved itself over the generations – the 'Bordeaux' of Australia, ready and waiting. The trouble was everyone wanted a piece – big companies, small companies without cool climate vineyards, rich men from big cities, poor men from the region who smelt gold and, having endured a lifetime of Coonawarra's tough conditions, didn't want to give it all away to city slickers and bully boys. And so it stands now. There are some splendid Coonawarra reds being made at the top end where yields are kept down and the Cabernet really does ripen. And those extension soils have shown that they can ripen whites pretty well – and the pale sandy clays can even give reds a chance if yields are low. But Coonawarra used to be rare and precious. It is in danger of becoming too everyday, too commonplace. In which case we consumers won't pay a silly price. And the silly price is why everyone wanted a slice of the action in the first place.

CLARE VALLEY

The Church has always played a strong role in Clare Valley wine – Sevenhill monastery, established in 1851, is still a leading producer. But this is St Mark's Church at Penwortham and the vines are Riesling belonging to Jeffrey Grosset, whose wines are already so good that he doesn't need any extra help from the Almighty.

Red grapes The main plantings in Clare are Shiraz and Cabernet Sauvignon, with some Malbec, Merlot and Grenache.

White grapes Riesling is the principal variety, with significant amounts of Chardonnay and Semillon plus some Sauvignon.

Climate The heat should lower grape acidity and send sugars soaring, but instead it produces light wines, especially Rieslings, with an unexpected natural acidity and delicacy.

Soil The main subsoil is of calcareous clay. In the north, there's a sandy loam topsoil, in the centre, red loam, and in the south, red clay.

Aspect Vineyards are planted at 400–500 metres above sea level, in the narrow valleys running from north to south, and in the foothills to the west. Aspects vary, with twisting contours.

It really doesn't matter from which direction you approach Clare Valley. The place is always going to seem like an oasis. It's almost as though it's been put there to remind you that South Australia is Australia's driest state, and every mile you go north from Adelaide is a mile closer to the red hot desert heart of Australia. So the shocking verdant green of the Clare Valley seems as one last warning – do you really want to go any further north than this? This could be the last splash of green you see until you reach the other side of Australia at Darwin.

I know that sounds a bit dramatic, but the Clare really is an unexpected oasis on the harsh dry road north. I've approached it over the escarpment to the west. I've driven up from the Barossa Valley through a countryside of pale, wan, exhausted beauty, so flat, so hot, where every hillock or stand of gums is an event, and every derelict, corrugated iron shack reminds you of one more ancient settler who decided to 'have a go' before discovering that this is hard land, too hard for most to bear.

But more often, to reach Clare I've driven out on the flat northern highway from Adelaide, past the old airfield, through the suburbs of Elizabeth, Gawler and Tarlee, leaving the Barossa Valley's charms over to the east as I make my way through arid, dun-coloured cereal fields that made me think – doesn't grain need *any* rain to survive? – and the only signs of life are the occasional silo, or a cloud of dust on some unsealed road that spears away to the horizon and which may only see a truck or two a day, but is the lifeline of this spare rural world.

It's getting hotter and drier – is that possible? – and I'm looking for the Clare Valley, a famous cool climate vineyard area? And suddenly, in a dip in the land just north of Auburn, there's a field of deepest green. Vines – the first vines of the Clare Valley – healthy, vigorous, their leaves waving gently in the breeze.

The breeze? What breeze? There wasn't a whisper of cooling wind on the way up here when I stopped off at Tarlee for an ice cold beer. There is unmistakably one now, taking the harshness out of the hot afternoon sun. And the air feels fresh, hillside fresh. Without once realizing that I was climbing at all, I've reached over 400 metres above sea level. At last some of the reasons for Clare's reputation as one of Australia's great cool climate vineyard regions are falling into place.

Don't worry. They'll fall out of place again. The Clare Valley may have a reputation for elegant, balanced Riesling, but it also produces some of the most startlingly concentrated, brawny Shiraz in South Australia. Its 'ports' and Liqueur Tokays are pretty exceptional, too. In one vineyard Riesling struggles to ripen by late April. A couple of kilometres north-east, another vineyard harvests the warm climate port variety, Touriga Nacional, in February. I'll try to explain.

People have been experiencing the relief of reaching Clare's gentle Valley ever since they began pushing north from Adelaide, and the town itself was established in 1846. I've seen Clare described as a frontier town and as the 'hub of the north' in its early days.

WHERE THE VINEYARDS ARE

Clare Valley is only 25 kilometres long, but a surprising number of different growing conditions exist for its near 2000 hectares of vines. To call it a valley isn't actually accurate, as the watershed at Penwortham forms a plateau from which three river systems run, two north – including the Clare – and one south. The area, however, with its remarkably crisp, fragrant whites and elegant reds, is baffling. It seems too hot and dry. Certainly altitude is very important. None of the vineyards seen here are at less than 400m. But Clare has one of the lowest summer rainfalls of any Australian quality wine region and could do with more. And it relies on sea breezes from the west and south-west to cool the vines and would certainly prefer to have an uninterrupted flow.

CLARE VALLEY

TOTAL DISTANCE
NORTH TO SOUTH
33.5KM

VINEYARDS

N

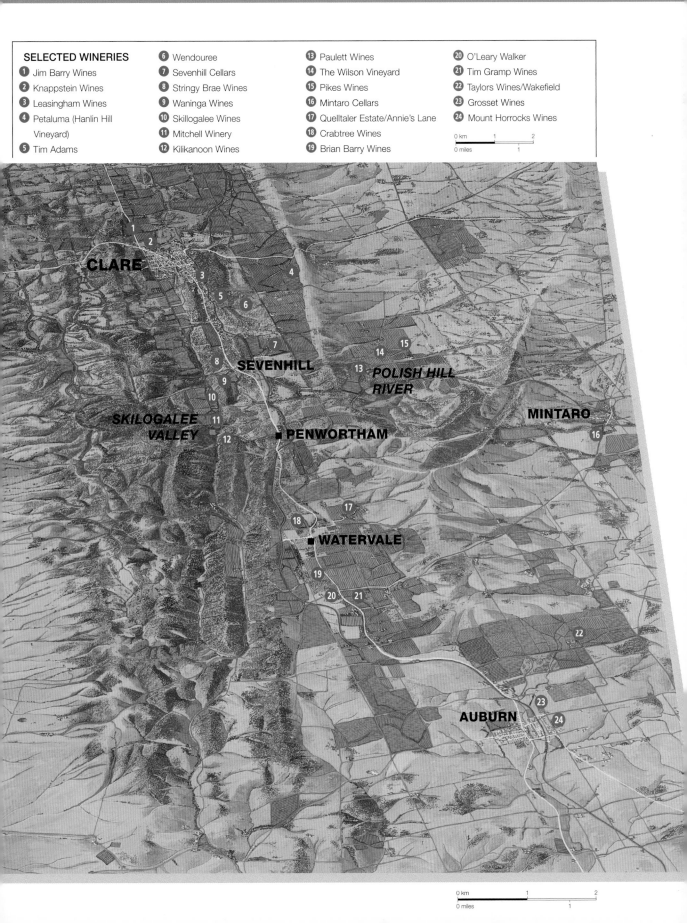

SELECTED WINERIES

1. Jim Barry Wines
2. Knappstein Wines
3. Leasingham Wines
4. Petaluma (Hanlin Hill Vineyard)
5. Tim Adams
6. Wendouree
7. Sevenhill Cellars
8. Stringy Brae Wines
9. Waninga Wines
10. Skillogalee Wines
11. Mitchell Winery
12. Kilikanoon Wines
13. Paulett Wines
14. The Wilson Vineyard
15. Pikes Wines
16. Mintaro Cellars
17. Quelltaler Estate/Annie's Lane
18. Crabtree Wines
19. Brian Barry Wines
20. O'Leary Walker
21. Tim Gramp Wines
22. Taylors Wines/Wakefield
23. Grosset Wines
24. Mount Horrocks Wines

0 km 1 2
0 miles 1

CLARE

SEVENHILL

POLISH HILL RIVER

SKILOGALEE VALLEY

PENWORTHAM

MINTARO

WATERVALE

AUBURN

0 km 1 2
0 miles 1

I'll buy that. There's still a touch of that feeling, even today, because Clare is 130 kilometres from Adelaide, and beyond Clare, endless parched plains stretch away to the north, towards Jamestown and Port Pirie. Ever since its foundation, Clare has been a focal point both for trading and for the refreshment of tired limbs and parched throats for the whole area. It's been a boom town several times. Copper was discovered nearby in 1845. Clare serviced that boom. There were massive wheat plantations established during the 1870s. Clare serviced these too. World-class slate reserves were discovered at neighbouring Mintaro, and there was a silver rush leading to the formation of the Broken Hill Propriety Co – Australia's largest company – in 1855. Once again, this small town reaped its share of the benefits.

What is left now is a traditional market town – still quietly prosperous long after those early frenzied years – and vines. Vineyards throughout much of Australia were established to slake the thirsts of wealth-crazed pioneers in the nineteenth century. Those of the Clare Valley were no exception, though one distinct novelty, for Australia, was the establishment of Sevenhill Jesuit monastery in 1851. Naturally the brothers planted vines. Just as naturally they are still making wine.

Clare was luckier than many areas in that there was a genuine effort made to plant only the better grape varieties – and particularly Cabernet Sauvignon, Malbec and Shiraz. But then, as elsewhere in Australia, these were largely supplanted in the early twentieth century by varieties planted for the production of cheap fortified wine and brandy which the market demanded in vast quantities. However, the re-establishment of Clare Valley as a quality region during the 1950s and 1960s saw the better red varieties dominate new vineyard plantings once more, along with the white grapes Riesling and (more recently) Chardonnay and Semillon.

VINEYARD AREAS
The trick was to have planted the vines in the right place. The term 'valley' isn't really an accurate description of this region. There are in fact three valley systems in Clare Valley, stretching both south and north with a watershed plateau in the middle at Penwortham. Incorporated into this are five sub-regions with differing soils at different heights above sea level – and differing mesoclimates too. Confusing, especially since Clare seems to get about as much heat as, and even less rain in the growing season than the impossibly hot fortified wine centre of Rutherglen in Victoria. Well, it does and it doesn't. Except in the valley bottom, it would be impossible to establish vineyards without irrigation. Storage dams for winter rain are the most effective source of water, although the rather over-ambitious expansion of vineyards by investor groups of Big City businessmen has made the recent extension of an irrigation pipeline from the Murray an expensive, inevitable necessity. And the tumbling landscape allows a wide variety of aspects to the sun, while nights are generally chilly and breezes arise to cool the vines during the day.

There is some disagreement about these cooling breezes because they have a fair way to travel inland from the sea which is 50 kilometres away to the west and south-west. It seems that, by and large, these breezes only get up in the late afternoon, cooling the vines in the evening and at night, but not affecting the most intense heat which occurs in the early afternoon. So ripening is not hindered, but acid levels in the fruit remain high. Some locals say it is the daily fade-out, around 4pm, of the hot, northerly winds that is the crucial factor in cooling the vineyards, especially in the north-facing valleys above Penwortham.

Altitude certainly seems to help. The excellent Enterprise and Petaluma vineyards, both giving outstanding Riesling wine, are over 500 metres high, facing west over the town of Clare. The Skillogalee Valley, south-west of Sevenhill, is not far short of 500 metres and protected from the north. Ripening is delayed here and the fruit flavours are particularly fine and focused. With Polish Hill River, directly east of Sevenhill behind a ridge of hills, it's not just altitude. The locals say the hills lop off at least 20 minutes of sun at the end of every day. Certainly the grapes do ripen two or three weeks later than those at similar altitude in the main valley. Again – delayed ripening, intense flavours.

Soil also plays a major role. Deep, dark loams below Watervale produce ripe, fat reds and whites, yet the ridge of limestone north of Watervale provides white wines with a lean, citrus tang that such a warm climate should deny. In the Polish Hill River area the shaly soil was relentlessly overworked by early Polish settlers and is now a poor acidic mix that again seems to retard ripening and limit yield. Sometimes the reds do seem a bit too lean, but that same minerally austerity makes for haughty, imperious Rieslings. And if you turn into Taylors' vineyards just north of Auburn – the soil's red. Taylors have 523 hectares here and reckon they're the biggest family owned vineyard/winery in Australia. They also reckon there's more famous terra rossa around Clare than in Coonawarra. And Honeysuckle Creek runs through their property. Honeysuckle? Isn't the local Aboriginal word for honeysuckle – Coonawarra?

And all the while the Sevenhill Vintage Port sits patiently in its barrel, and the 100-year-old Grenache and Shiraz vines at Wendouree and in Tim Adams' Aberfeldy and Sheoaks vineyards creep to ripeness as the sea breeze wipes the fire from the sun and the hot northern winds retreat into the arid northern plains. A paradoxical place, the Clare Valley? It certainly is.

Springtime in the vineyards in the Polish Hill River region of Clare Valley. The storage dam has collected whatever winter rain has fallen – and it will all be needed because Clare rarely gets much rain from spring to autumn, the vine's growing season.

Tim Adams
Wines with exceptional depth of flavour are the hallmark here. The peppery Aberfeldy Shiraz is a remarkable wine from 100-year-old vines growing near Wendouree in the Clare Valley.

TIM ADAMS

Clare Valley
✴ *Shiraz, Cabernet Sauvignon, Grenache and others*
✴ *Riesling, Semillon, Chardonnay*

Every wine area needs someone like Tim Adams: a top-class winemaker, committed grape-grower and, above all, passionate devotee of the region itself. Clare Valley is an idyllic sylvan interlude of elegant gum trees, rustling in the breeze, and swathes of bright green vines in an otherwise arid part of South Australia. Nice place to live? The best in the world, says Adams, as he welcomes you with a rugged smile and a daunting handshake, and then proceeds to show you a string of superb wines matching modern know-how with old-fashioned sensitivity to the Clare Valley style.

The darkly fruity and sweetly oaked Aberfeldy Shiraz, almost medicinally spicy Fergus Grenache and straight Shiraz are outstanding. His Riesling is an Australian classic – very austere, tingling with the icy flavours of minerals and citrus peel, but as scented as a lemon grove. His Semillon is also austere, haughty, but with a richness of custard and limes drizzled with honey that can take 5–15 years to fully reveal its beauty. He also makes a sweet botrytis Semillon which is very difficult to get hold of.
Best years: (Aberfeldy Shiraz) 2002, '01, '99, '98, '97, '96, '95, '94, '93, '92.

ANGOVE'S

Riverland
✴ *Cabernet Sauvignon, Shiraz, Grenache and others*
✴ *Chardonnay, Chenin Blanc, Colombard and others*

Angove's, the first winery established in the Riverland back in 1886, was producing 300 tonnes of grapes by the turn of the 20th century. The fourth generation of the Angove family are in control today and have made a great deal of progress in the past decade. The company has been sourcing grapes from Padthaway, Coonawarra, McLaren Vale and Clare and either releasing them as regional wines under the Sarnia Farm and Vineyard Select labels or using the fruit to add depth to their other wines.

Angove's has also been redeveloping the vast 500-ha Nanya vineyard with new root-stocks and grape varieties (there are now 18 different ones planted here), improved trellising and computer-controlled drip irrigation and fertigation. If you've got the energy you can walk the rows – all 5km of them – and experience what life was like before the advent of mechanical harvesting. Production now exceeds 1.3 million cases a year, virtually all of which is at budget prices. Best wines are the Sarnia Farm varietals, Bear Crossing Chardonnay, the Vineyard Select Clare Riesling and Angove's stunning range of Australia's best brandies, often under the St Agnes label.

Angove's
Angove's Bear Crossing wines are sold in aid of the Australian Koala Foundation. The Chardonnay is pretty decent stuff for a big volume brand.

ASHTON HILLS

Adelaide Hills
✴ *Pinot Noir, Merlot, Cabernet Franc*
✴ *Riesling, Chardonnay, Pinot Gris, Gewurztraminer*

This tiny (3.5-ha) vineyard lies in one of the coolest parts of the Adelaide Hills at 600m on a ridge-top overlooking the Piccadilly Valley. Stephen George, and his partner Peta van Rood, choose to do almost all the work themselves and so it hasn't been expanded

Ashton Hills
This vineyard is one of Adelaide Hills' coolest sites and provides delicious table wines as well as restrained, delicate sparkling wines.

since it was planted in 1982. Says George, 'It's probably the only vineyard in Australia that hasn't expanded in the last 20 years.' There has been rigorous experimentation with different varieties (Cabernet Sauvignon has been replaced by Pinot Gris and Gewurztraminer), clones (15 of Pinot Noir), trellis design and management systems and so George believes that they have now 'got it right'. Their wines are among the best from the region: fine, delicate, steely Riesling; subtle, restrained, austere Chardonnay; and fine, complex, savoury and silky-textured Pinot Noir.
Best years: (Pinot Noir) 2003, '02, '00, '99, '98, '97.

Balnaves
Balnaves has been growing high-quality Cabernet Sauvignon for many years but only started to make their own wines in 1996.

BALNAVES

Coonawarra
✴ *Cabernet Sauvignon, Merlot, Shiraz, Cabernet Franc, Petit Verdot*
✴ *Chardonnay*

No other region does Cabernet quite like Coonawarra and so it is not surprising that 70% of the 50-ha Balnaves vineyard is planted to that variety. The Balnaves family has been in Coonawarra since 1854. They must have had something to do with sheep because this was about all that would survive the conditions in the early days. Nowadays, however, their name is synonymous with wine – as growers, consultants and producers. They first bought land in 1949, watched others grow grapes until they planted theirs in 1975, then watched others make the wine till they started their own label in 1990. The winery was built in 1995, which was when top winemaker Pete Bissell came on board. The Cabernet Sauvignon is outstanding with ripe, brambly, blackcurrant flavours, velvety texture and seamlessly integrated oak. It is among Coonawarra's best and is moderately priced. The Cabernet/Merlot and The Blend (Cabernet Sauvignon, Cab Franc and Merlot) represent great value while the flagship Reserve Cabernet – 'The Tally' – is an enjoyable blockbuster.

Best years: (Cabernet Sauvignon) 2002, '01, '00, '98, '96.

BAROSSA VALLEY ESTATE

Barossa Valley
❋ *Shiraz, Cabernet Sauvignon, Merlot, Grenache*
❊ *Chardonnay, Semillon, Riesling*

Initially established by local grape-growers as a quality co-operative and now half owned by industry giant HARDY. Its name is somewhat misleading, however. It implies that it is a vineyard-owning operation, whereas in fact it owns no vineyards whatsoever. But all through the Barossa Valley you'll see 'Barossa Valley Estate' signboards up outside vineyards with someone's name below. These are all contracted growers, many of them in some of the best sites in the Valley. If you want to know what they look like – well, that's me and my Akubra hat on the title page, standing in one just along from the famous Jacob's Creek.

Barossa Valley Estate
From low-yielding, unirrigated vines, E & E Black Pepper Shiraz is the flagship wine here, and black pepper is a good description of its powerful style.

Its flagship reds are huge, gutsy Barossa beauties E & E Black Pepper Shiraz, Ebenezer Shiraz and E & E Sparkling Shiraz, all bursting with ripe plum fruit, spice and vanilla oak. There's also good quality in the other Ebenezer wines (such as the full-flavoured sparkling Pinot Noir) and some of the Barossa's best value in the Moculta and Spires ranges.

Best years: (Shiraz) 2002, '01, '98, '96.

JIM BARRY

Clare Valley
❋ *Shiraz, Cabernet Sauvignon and others*
❊ *Riesling, Chardonnay and others*

My mum always said what a charming boy Pete Barry was. Well, he is. He's got enough Irish charm oozing out of his jovial Irish eyes to kid even such a wily old Irish girl as my mother. And every time I get near the Clare Valley I know I'll fall for it too and suddenly, there I'll be, at four in the morning and having a right old time when I should have been tucked up hours ago. There's a bunch of wild boys in the Clare, a charming, irresistible Irish kind of bunch, and Peter's the leader. But they all have two sides to them. They play. Do they play! But they also make excellent wine, have successful serious wineries and are passionately involved in the whole society and community of the Clare Valley. To be honest, all the Barrys – and there are several generations of them in Clare – have got a roguish charm about them. It's just that I usually fall into Peter's clutches first.

But while I'm fearing for my liver, he's showing me lovely tangy Rieslings, deep, strong Cabernet and a rich chocolaty McCrea Wood Shiraz. And then he'll show me The Armagh, a heady palate-busting Shiraz designed to overwhelm anyone of a

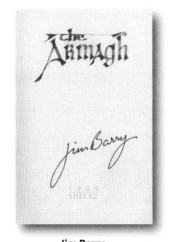

Jim Barry
The Armagh is about as big as Australian Shiraz can get – and that's pretty big. Ancient vines and family passion are part of the secret.

sensitive disposition. But it works and now sells for huge sums. Serious wine. Serious winery. Seriously successful.

Best years: (The Armagh Shiraz) 2002, '01, '99, '98, '96, '95, '93, '92.

Wolf Blass
This is Blass's white masterpiece: a spicy bouquet along with a very intense, full-flavoured citrous character and excellent acidity.

WOLF BLASS

Barossa Valley
❋ *Cabernet Sauvignon, Shiraz*
❊ *Riesling, Chardonnay*

It's easy nowadays to lose sight of the massive importance the name Wolf Blass once held in Australian wine. Wolf Blass is a man, a diminutive, passionate bundle of energy from the Barossa, who is the greatest wine popularizer in the history of Australia – itself the greatest popularizer in the world of wine.

Back in the 1960s and '70s most Australians didn't drink table wine at all, so Wolf Blass set out to use the superb, ripe-tasting South Australian fruit – especially Cabernet Sauvignon and Riesling – to create crowd-pleasing wines that never welched on quality. I remember in the late 1980s still being bowled over by the irresistible mint and blackcurrant juiciness of his Cabernet and the amazing mix of sunny ripeness and lime juice aggression that marked his Riesling.

Nowadays Wolf Blass is a crucial component of the multinational company, Beringer Blass. Some of the wines are still good, but they are neither as affordable nor as unashamedly enjoyable as once they were. Riesling has probably kept its character better than most of the other styles. Regional varietals under the Blass label reflect the winemaking style rather than regional taste and merely go to show that regionality is much better interpreted by small producers than by large multinationals. Ultra-expensive Black Label and Platinum reds are impressive.

Best years: (Black Label) 2002, '01, '99, '98, '97, '96, '95, '90, '88, '86.

Bleasdale
Bleasdale's flagship wine is named after its founder, Frank Potts who set it up in 1850, making it one of Australia's oldest wineries.

BLEASDALE

Langhorne Creek
❈ *Shiraz, Cabernet Sauvignon, Malbec, Merlot, Petit Verdot, Cabernet Franc*
❧ *Verdelho, Chardonnay, Riesling*
What you must do at Bleasdale is ask to see the pictures of the floods. Either the occasional summer floods where absolutely everything gets drenched, or the regular winter/spring floods where the overflowing waters of the Bremer River are directed into all the vineyards stretched along the river banks and provide the simplest but most spectacular example of irrigation in Australia. It works and it's been done like this since 1850.

A lot of the winery hasn't changed much either, but although Bleasdale has time-worn charm about its winery and vineyards, it's a serious operation, quite capable of making good quality modern wines and certainly in the last few years the reds in particular have improved.

Apart from YALUMBA, this is Australia's oldest family-owned winery. It was established by Frank Potts in 1850 and named after one of Australia's most admired viticulturists of the time, the Rev John Bleasdale. It has been revitalized in the past few years under the direction of fifth generation winemaker, Michael Potts, and CEO, David Foreman, with substantial investment enabling Bleasdale to expand its fermentation capacity and increase tank, barrel and warehouse storage.

Bleasdale whites often get forgotten but their Verdelho is pretty fair stuff. Even so, their nicely laid-back approach is better suited to red wines. They have several good reds based on Shiraz and the traditional Bordeaux grapes – and Malbec is in favour here. My favourites are Frank Potts – a rich serious blackcurranty blend of the Cabernets, Malbec, Merlot and Petit Verdot

– and Generations Shiraz – a powerful black chocolate, ripe, long distance runner.
Best years: (Frank Potts) 2003, '02, '01, '00, '98.

Bowen Estate
Doug Bowen's Shiraz is a benchmark wine with exquisite fruit definition and fleshy, hot peppery, blackberry flavours.

BOWEN ESTATE

Coonawarra
❈ *Cabernet Sauvignon, Shiraz, Merlot*
❧ *Chardonnay*
Doug Bowen is one of the most highly regarded red winemakers among the small Coonawarra wineries. As part of his winemaking studies he prepared a report on Coonawarra's potential way back in the early 1970s, before the area was fashionable, and immediately put his money where his mouth was by setting up a vineyard and winery in 1972. His 35-ha estate is largely given over to a wonderfully peppery, spicy Shiraz and an elegant, discreetly herbaceous Cabernet Sauvignon. There is also a Bordeaux-style blend.
Best years: (Shiraz) 2000, '98, '97, '96, '94, '93, '92, '91.

BRAND'S

Coonawarra
❈ *Cabernet Sauvignon, Shiraz, Merlot*
❧ *Chardonnay, Riesling*
Brand's was a famous Coonawarra name that had fallen upon hard times until it was taken over by industry giant MCWILLIAM's. For once the Goliath has greatly improved the David's performance, and chief winemaker Jim Brayne's influence has lifted standards dramatically. The accent is still on red wines, aided by excellent vineyards which include a precious patch of old Shiraz planted in 1896, which provides the top Stentiford Shiraz and shows how good Coonawarra Shiraz can be. All the reds are full-flavoured

Brand's of Coonawarra
The fruit for this wine comes from the Brand's Laira Vineyard where the Shiraz vines, now more than 100 years old, are some of the oldest in the Coonawarra region.

but I think they're still a work in progress – massively improved from their uninspired fruitlessness before, but not yet front rank Coonawarras. Cabernet, for instance, is fairly leafy – which is fine – but leafiness requires a bit more fruit back up than this normally has. The leafiness sits more easily on the Merlots.
Best years: (reds) 2001, '00, '99, '98, '97, '96, '94, '90.

BREMERTON

Langhorne Creek
❈ *Cabernet Sauvignon, Shiraz, Merlot, Malbec, Petit Verdot*
❧ *Sauvignon Blanc, Chardonnay, Verdelho*
The purchase of Bremerton Lodge in 1985 was the first step. Almost a decade later, Craig Willson left a career in regional newspapers to manage an expanding grape-growing and winemaking business.

Another 10 years on, Bremerton is a family business (with daughter Rebecca as winemaker), has 115ha under vine, a new

Bremerton
Verdelho was originally planted in Langhorne Creek in 1850 and today it has very much come back into fashion for drinkers who want full-bodied but unoaked whites.

winery at nearby Matilda Plains, and annual production under their own labels of about 25,000 cases.

The flagship, Old Adam Shiraz, is opulent and fleshy with ripe blackberry, dark plum and sweet smoky, vanilla oak flavours while Walter's Cabernet, Selkirk Shiraz and the quaffing Tamblyn red blend are quintessentially Langhorne Creek – each is ripe and rich, has a smooth, velvety texture, and is shot through with good ripe black fruit.
Best years: (Old Adam Shiraz) 2003, '02, '01, '00.

Burge Family Winemakers
Old-vine Grenache/Garnacha from the Barossa Valley is in high demand today as Australia rediscovers the virtue of this wonderful fruitbomb grape variety.

BURGE FAMILY

Barossa Valley
🍇 *Shiraz, Grenache, Cabernet Sauvignon, Merlot, Touriga, Mourvedre, Zinfandel, Nebbiolo, Souzao*
🍇 *Semillon, Muscat Blanc à Petit Grains*
Established in 1928 by Percival Burge, the winery survived through the difficulties of the Great Depression as a producer of dessert-style fortifieds. Things changed for the better when the current winemaker, Rick Burge, returned to the Barossa in 1986 and bought his cousin Grant's share in the family business.

Since then, the voluble and aimiably opinionated Burge has focused on making estate reds from the family's 10-ha vineyard: most notably the Draycott Shiraz, Olive Hill Shiraz Blend and Garnacha – from 80-year-old Grenache vines. The vineyard, where he reckons to spend 40% of his time, is at the heart of Rick Burge's winemaking philosophy. While its small, 3000-case production means that it may not enjoy the profile of some of his neighbours, there is a devoted band of wine lovers who can't get enough of these opulent, lushly textured reds.
Best years: (Draycott Shiraz) 2002, '01, '99, '98.

GRANT BURGE

Barossa Valley
🍇 *Shiraz, Merlot, Cabernet Sauvignon, Grenache, Mourvedre, Petit Verdot*
🍇 *Riesling, Sauvignon Blanc, Chardonnay, Semillon, Muscat (White Frontignac)*
Time flies; from one of the brightest of Barossa's bright young boys of the early 1970s, Grant Burge is now a highly mature senior citizen, with an extremely successful business based on the most extensive vineyard holdings in Barossa under single-family ownership. Generously flavoured wines are the order of the day, and there was a time at the end of the millennium when there was so much rich cloying oak flavour sloshing around in the glass that you really wondered why bother with the grapes? Which would be a crying shame given how much good vineyard land Burge owned in all corners of the Barossa Valley. But in recent years, there's been an easing off on the oak. The wines are still well-oaked, and consequently rich, but you can see serious quality fruit there as well and start making informed judgements about the wines rather than about the bank balance of the cooper.

Top label is Meshach Shiraz and other wines include chocolaty Filsell Shiraz and Cameron Vale Cabernet, snappily fresh Thorn Riesling and oaky but balanced Zerk Semillon. Shadrach Cabernet, a Rhône-style blend, Holy Trinity, and the excellent value Barossa Vines range are recent additions.
Best years: (Meshach) 2002, '01, '99, '98, '96, '95, '94, '91, '90.

Grant Burge
Named in honour of Meshach William Burge, Grant Burge's great-grandfather, this oaky, highly concentrated wine is Grant's flagship – plummy, meaty game aromas, along with ripe tannins, high alcohol and long aging potential.

LEO BURING

Barossa Valley
🍇 *Shiraz, Cabernet Sauvignon*
🍇 *Riesling, Semillon, Chardonnay*
Owned by Southcorp, Leo Buring was once unchallenged as Australia's finest producer

Leo Buring
The top of the range Eden Valley Riesling from Leo Buring are labelled Leonay. If you see an older vintage from the 1970s snap it up.

of Riesling, notably from the Eden and Clare Valleys, though many newer wineries are now snapping at its heels. These wines mature magnificently, peaking at 10–20 years. Those from the Eden Valley retain a lime juice character and flavour all their life, while those from Clare have an added touch of toast. If you see the word 'Leonay' on the label you know it is a special bottling and I am continually amazed when some guy in the Clare or Barossa Valley creeps reverentially up and offers me a blind tasting of a deep green-gold liquid, virtually touching his forelock and genuflecting as he proffers the bevy. Well, I should know by now. It'll be 'Leonay' and I should add on at least 10 years and maybe 15 to my guesses to how old it is. I mean – look at our 'Best years' list. How many others in this book or any other go back to 1972? And this is for white wines!

If I was being brutally honest I'd have to suggest – reverentially, on bended knee, all that – that they should smarten their act up again. But, despite the great John Vickery who made all those superb Leonays being alive and kicking, Leo Buring is now part of Southcorp, the vast conglomerate that seems to have lost track of the fact that it owns more of Australia's wine heritage than anyone else. Until recently, they have shamefully failed to respect it. I sense a change for the better, but if they'll allow me to use their kind of language – well, here goes. Southcorp. Exploit your assets! No, you heard me right. I didn't say abuse your assets, I said exploit. Exploit their history, their wine styles, their great vineyards. Exploit them by making them better than they've ever been and thereby build a conglomerate so full of commitment and belief that no corporate raider will ever again be able to trample casually over your crown jewels. And Leo Buring is a crown jewel just longing to be polished back to gleaming excellence.
Best years: 1999, '98, '97, '94, '93, '91, '90, '87, '86, '84, '79, '73, '72.

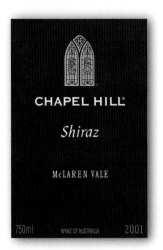

Chapel Hill

The McLaren Vale region is famous for Shiraz. Chapel Hill's vines are low-yielding and up to 30 years old. With aging in both American and French new oak, the result is powerful and bold Shiraz with lots of spicy, vanilla and ripe berry flavours.

CHAPEL HILL

McLaren Vale

✻ *Cabernet Sauvignon, Shiraz and others*

✽ *Chardonnay, Verdelho*

Outstanding winery south of Adelaide that always manages to marry superb quality with value for money and also makes very astute use not only of local McLaren Vale grapes but also fruit from Padthaway and Coonawarra. This allows winemaker Pam Dunsford to craft red wines of great richness from differing percentages of Shiraz and Cabernet. Pam's top red is a stupendous Shiraz/Cabernet blend called The Vicar. It's so good that I sent a case last year to an old friend who'd just become a high court judge. Inexplicably, my friend forwarded it to his brother, who was surprised, but drank it with great pleasure. It was some time before I discovered his brother had just been made a bishop, and my friend thought I'd got the wrong 'bro'.

Pam also makes excellent unwooded and Reserve Chardonnay from a variety of sources, sometimes including Western Australia, and lean but fragrant McLaren Vale Verdelho. Now owned by the Swiss Schmidheiny group who also own Cuvaison in California's Napa Valley.
Best years: (Shiraz) 2002, '01, '00, '98, '97, '96, '95, '94, '93, '91.

CLARENDON HILLS

McLaren Vale

✻ *Shiraz, Grenache, Cabernet Sauvignon, Merlot*

These aren't wines that you can approach in a technocratic frame of mind. They're such rip-roaring bruisers – rather like the iconoclastic owner Roman Bratasiuk – that you have to take them for what they are – intense, brooding, massive interpretations of superb old vines, especially Grenache and Shiraz (Astralis Shiraz is his larger than life flagship wine).

Well, I hope he'll appreciate that I've never had the chance to taste them in a 'technocratic' way. They never turn up in flights of McLaren Vale wines that I'm judging. So I've tasted most of them in Adelaide's Chinatown. With fabulously original, unexpected and brilliantly conceived dishes served on plain white china and received rapturously by the hedonistic crowd I hang out with.

Clarendon Hills wines take their chance, just like everyone else's – but I hope that Roman will be pleased to hear that his inspired, idiosyncratic gobfulls of wine fantasy are just perfect with the inspired, idiosyncratic gobfulls of China's best that wash down our gullets together in hilarious harmony. I'm not sure what I'd do if I met one of his wines in a serious wine-tasting line up. Oh, by the way, he also makes Pinot Noir and Merlot, but these wines rather get lost in the rush.
Best years: (Astralis) 1999, '98, '96, '95, '94.

Clarendon Hills

This controversial winery in McLaren Vale has rapidly become famous for highly extracted reds. The Grenache wines come from 75-year-old vines in the Blewitt Springs Vineyard and are marked by saturated black cherry fruit and high alcohol. And that's not the half of it.

D'ARENBERG

McLaren Vale

✻ *Shiraz, Grenache, Cabernet Sauvignon*

✽ *Chardonnay, Viognier, Marsanne, Riesling, Sauvignon Blanc*

This winery first sprang to prominence in the second half of the 1960s, with a 1967 'Burgundy' (largely Grenache) which won seven trophies and 25 gold medals from major Australian wine shows, an astonishing record by the standards of the time, followed up by a 1968 Cabernet Sauvignon which won the coveted Jimmy Watson Trophy in 1969.

d'Arenberg

Characterful, old-vine reds based on Shiraz and Grenache are d'Arenberg's strength. Made with traditional winemaking equipment and techniques and rigorous selection, the flagship reds are rich, heady and extravagantly flavoured. Some of the old vines for The Dead Arm date back to the 1890s.

Things then settled down until the 1990s when Chester Osborn took over from father d'Arry, and with the help of savvy marketing (e.g. wine names like The Dead Arm Shiraz, The Coppermine Road Cabernet, The Dry Dam Riesling and The Last Ditch Viognier) and impressive winemaking that combines keen technical skill with great sensitivity for the traditional equipment that still is much in evidence at d'Arenberg, Chester has proceeded to make exceptionally lush cherry, currant, berry, spice and plum-filled reds and weighty whites, with an appropriate lick of new oak. These are big, brash, character-filled wines that are continually being joined by new ideas from Chester's super-active imagination.

And don't count d'Arry out of the equation just yet. The pair of them are Australia's greatest vinous double act, and through all the humour and the fun shines a passionate belief in what they do.
Best years: (Dead Arm Shiraz) 2002, '01, '00, '99, '98, '97, '96, '95, '94.

FOX CREEK

McLaren Vale

✻ *Shiraz, Cabernet Sauvignon, Cabernet Franc, Merlot, Grenache*

✽ *Verdelho, Sauvignon Blanc, Semillon, Chardonnay*

Impressive, opulent, superripe McLaren Vale red wines are the key to this recent success story – the winery produced its first wines as recently as 1994 and since then Reserve Shiraz and Reserve Cabernet Sauvignon have wowed the critics; JSM (Shiraz/Cabernet) is rich and succulent; the Merlot is a little lighter but still concentrated and powerful. Vixen sparkling Shiraz is also lip-smacking stuff, but I have to say, the wine I

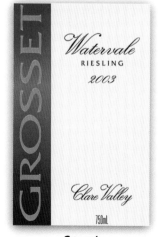

Fox Creek

The JSM blend, mainly Shiraz with some Cabernet Franc and Sauvignon, is a hedonistic mouthful of wine with good concentration, ripeness and succulent berry flavours.

most warm to is Shadow's Run – a red blend named after and enthusiastically promoted by the winery's black and white sheep dog, Shadow. The whites are comparatively ordinary, albeit fair value for money.

GLAETZER

Barossa Valley

❋ *Shiraz, Cabernet Sauvignon, Grenache, Malbec*

❋ *Semillon*

One of Australia's most dynamic young companies specializes in producing traditional Barossa Shiraz of almost breathtaking quality. This was the grape variety with which Colin Glaetzer forged a reputation for himself and BAROSSA VALLEY ESTATE while he was winemaker there for a decade from 1985. The Glaetzer family company was formed in 1995 and is based at the contract winemaking facility, Barossa Vintners, in which Glaetzer is a shareholder and which Colin and his son Ben manage. The top wines are the flagship Glaetzer (from 80-year-old vines) and The Bishop (30- to 60-year-old vines) Shiraz, sourced from the

Glaetzer

Glaetzer specializes in producing Shiraz from some of the oldest and unirrigated vines in the Barossa. The wines have great concentration and complexity with none of the overripeness that can characterize some Australian Shiraz.

Ebenezer area. There is little to separate these vibrant, opulently flavoured reds in which the integration of powerful oak and intensely concentrated fruit is a feature.

Ben Glaetzer is irrepressible and is the driving force behind the family export label, Amon-Ra, the cult wines of McLaren Vale's Mitolo Winery and the budget-priced Heartland label that is making superb use of Pinot Gris and Viognier from Langhorne Creek as well as reds from Wirrega in the Limestone Coast. The Wirrega Vineyards are near Bordertown, in the north of the region, and the wines' phenomenal intensity, almost medicinal richness and denseness of texture and heady gunpowder scent are re-defining what is possible in the Limestone Coast with Shiraz, Cabernet Sauvignon and Petit Verdot.

Best years: (The Bishop Shiraz) 2002, '01, '99, '98, '96.

GROSSET

Clare Valley

❋ *Pinot Noir, Cabernet Sauvignon, Merlot*

❋ *Riesling, Semillon, Sauvignon Blanc, Chardonnay*

If democratic elections were held for the position of King of Riesling in Australia, Jeffrey Grosset would be a shoo-in. The crystal clarity of the Polish Hill Riesling, with fragrant whispers of herb and spice, and the fractionally richer Watervale Riesling, with a vibrant twist of lime, evolve with shimmering beauty over a 10-year period. The fact that he's now started using screwcaps will only enhance the austere beauty of these wines. But Jeffrey doesn't just do Riesling. Gaia, a Cabernet-dominant Bordeaux blend, redolent with blackberry and sweet cassis

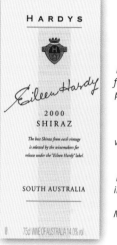

Grosset

Much of Australia's finest Riesling comes from the Clare Valley and Jeff Grosset's two versions, the Watervale and the Polish Hill, are benchmark stuff with the ability to age for 10 years or more.

fruit, somehow introduces finesse into a region more famous for blockbusters. His brilliant Adelaide Hills trio of Semillon/ Sauvignon Blanc, Piccadilly Chardonnay and Reserve Pinot Noir are the kind of wines you have to camp outside the winery door overnight for on the eve of release if you're going to get a bottle or two. It would be worth the lack of sleep, the cold, and the foggy dew forming on the end of your nose, because these are classic renditions, as scarce as hen's teeth, but fine wines if you can lay your hands on them.

Best years: (Riesling) 2003, '02, '01, '00, '99, '98, '97, '96, '94, '93, '92, '90.

Hardys

The Eileen Hardy label is a tribute to the matriarch of Australia's best-known winemaking family, and the finest parcels of Shiraz and Chardonnay from each vintage are selected for these wines. The Shiraz is a complex, spicy-peppery wine with lots of fruit and oak influence, now made mainly from McLaren Vale grapes.

THE HARDY WINE COMPANY

McLaren Vale

❋ *Cabernet Sauvignon, Shiraz, Merlot, Pinot Noir*

❋ *Chardonnay, Semillon, Sauvignon Blanc, Riesling, Gewurztraminer*

BRL Hardy (formed when twin Riverland co-operatives Berri Estates and Renmano took over the then family-owned company of Thomas Hardy) is now Australia's second-largest wine company, newly renamed as the Hardy Wine Company, and through its merger with Constellation of the USA it is part of the official Largest Wine Company in the World. The group now includes Banrock Station, BAY OF FIRES, BROOKLAND VALLEY, Kamberra, Berri, Renmano, Hardys, HOUGHTON, Hunter Ridge, Moondah Brook, REYNELL, YARRA BURN, STONEHAVEN and LEASINGHAM brands.

The greatest of the Hardy wines are the Eileen Hardy Shiraz (made from basket-pressed McLaren Vale and Padthaway grapes), Eileen Hardy Chardonnay (the ultimate grape-fruit-with-melon Padthaway style), some superb 'Beerenauslese' sweet Rieslings, and the 'vintage port' – probably Australia's best port-style wine. I shared a bottle of the 1954 once with Peter Dawson, the delightful and talented head winemaker. The quality was memorable for two things. The fabulous still youthful flavours – and the lack of hangover. I doubt if a bottle of 50-year-old Portuguese Port would have left me feeling anything like so fresh in the cold light of dawn.

The National Trust-classified and beautiful buildings of Chateau Reynella just outside Adelaide house Hardy's corporate headquarters. There are various keenly priced labels – Tintara, Nottage Hill, Stamps of Australia and, especially, the tasty VR (Varietal Range) and VR Reserve.

Best years: (Eileen Hardy Shiraz) 2002, '01, '00, '98, '97, '96, '95, '93, '88, '87, '81, '79, '70.

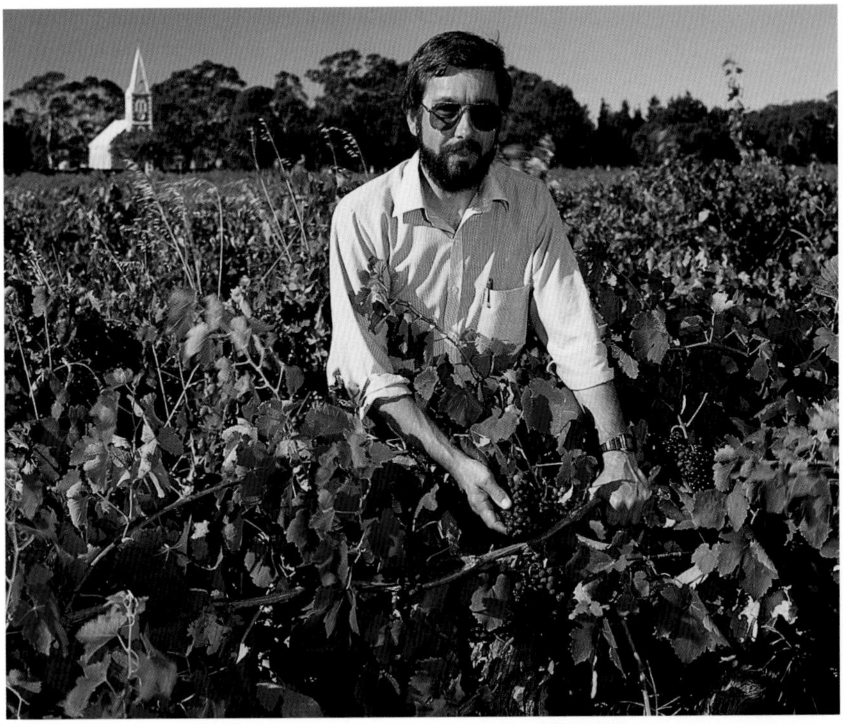

Stephen Henschke proudly shows off the first of 'the Grandfathers' in the Hill of Grace vineyard. They'll ripen slowly to give a Shiraz of such sweetness, power and scent that it is now one of the most sought-after and rightly expensive wines in Australia.

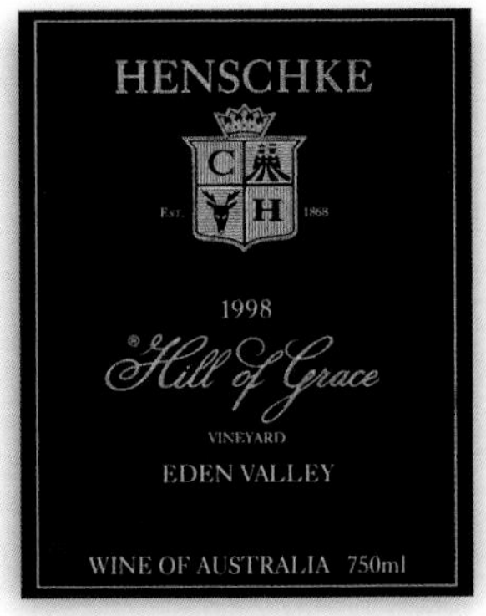

Henschke

Hill of Grace, a stunning wine with dark, exotic flavours, comes from a single plot of low-yielding Shiraz, first planted in the 1860s. It is now one of Australia's most expensive wines.

HENSCHKE

Eden Valley

Shiraz, Cabernet Sauvignon, Merlot, Pinot Noir, Grenache

Riesling, Semillon, Chardonnay, Pinot Gris, Sauvignon Blanc, Gewurztraminer

You cannot really understand why Henschke is so important in the world of Australian wine until you have climbed up into the hills above the Barossa Valley, tipped your cap to the tiny Gnadenberg Church and then turned and walked thoughtfully into the vineyard over the little country road. You are strolling between the vines of the Hill of Grace, some of them 150 years old, Shiraz vines, ungrafted, planted by Stephen Henschke's great-great-grandfather some time in the 1860s.

Nowadays every ancient vine in the Barossa is eagerly sought out and lovingly cossetted, but less than a generation ago few Barossa folk cared for these low-yielding wizened old vines. Stephen and Prue Henschke did. Hill of Grace Shiraz, along with Penfolds Grange, is now Australia's most avidly collected red wine – and deservedly so – for its fabulous exotic richness does seem to express a purity, the very essence of a vineyard, like few other wines worldwide.

Henschke is not just Hill of Grace – they have another awe-inspiring Shiraz vineyard a couple of kilometres away called Mount Edelstone. These vines are mere striplings – at 80 years or so old – and in any other company would be regarded as superstars. A further memorable, licorice-rich, herb-scented red is Cyril Henschke Cabernet, a chewy yet sweet-fruited Bordeaux blend. Other notable reds are Johann's Garden Grenache, Henry's Seven Shiraz blend and Keyneton Estate.

Their Eden Valley Semillon and Rieslings are both exceptional, and both reds and whites from their cooler Lenswood vineyard in the Adelaide Hills are subtle, delicious – and modern. Yes, modern even to the employment of the screwcap on an increasing number of the early-drinking wines. And over all these new endeavours, the ancient 'grandfather' vines stand looking on in silent approval.

Best years: (Mount Edelstone) 2002, '01, '00, '98, '97, '96, '94, '92, '91, '90, '88, '86, '84, '82, '80, '78.

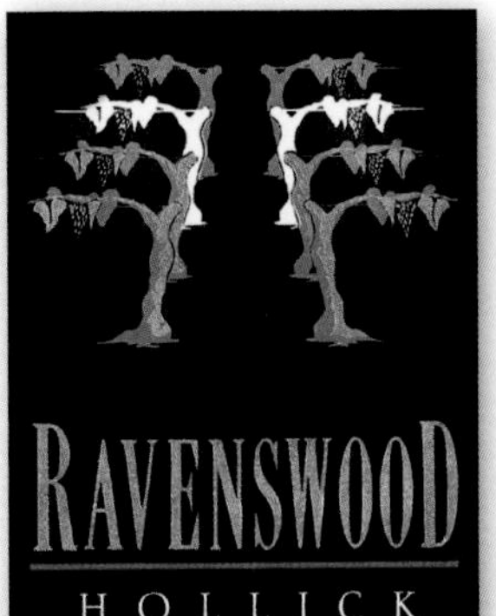

Hollick

Ravenswood Cabernet is the top wine here – the vines are planted on one of the original Riddoch plantings in Coonawarra.

HOLLICK

Coonawarra

Cabernet Sauvignon, Merlot, Shiraz, Pinot Noir

Riesling, Chardonnay, Semillon, Sauvignon Blanc

I can't resist riling Ian Hollick. Just as he's trying to impress me with his serious Cabernets and Shirazes, I cry 'Show me your sparkling Merlot!' And he does. But you can sense this isn't the wine that a serious Coonawarra pioneer wants to be known for. Anyway, it's a delicious red fizz. Thank you, Ian. On to the serious stuff.

Hollick set up their Coonawarra vineyard in 1975. They now have 52ha there as well as 20ha in Wrattonbully. They've always made serious, dry reds – proper reflective Coonawarra styles, mostly based on Merlot, Cabernet and Shiraz, with a top-of-the-line range led by Ravenswood Cabernet. These never quite have the sheer blackcurrant ripeness that some Coonawarra Cabs achieve, but I'm not sure that's what Ian wants anyway. But they have also always championed Riesling – they don't make much white, but their Riesling, Chardonnay, Semillon and Sauvignon are good.
Best years: (Ravenswood) 2002, '01, '00, '99, '98, '96, '94, '93, '91, '90, '88.

Katnook
The Odyssey Cabernet Sauvignon, one of Katnook's flagship reds, is made in tiny quantities. Spending 30 months in new French oak followed by three years' bottle age, the wine will easily age for a decade or more.

KATNOOK ESTATE
Coonawarra
✶ *Cabernet Sauvignon, Shiraz, Merlot*
✶ *Sauvignon Blanc, Chardonnay, Riesling*
Katnook is one part of the Wingara Wine Group, which owns large vineyards in Coonawarra (as well as being the largest contract grape-grower) and Deakin Estate in the Murray Darling and it also processes a great many tonnes of grapes into juice or newly fermented wine. But Katnook is proudly Coonawarra, and winemaker Wayne Stehbens is *fiercely*, proudly Coonawarra. He once met me on the Coonawarra boundary after I'd been critical of the region, with a noose and a spade. He'd probably worked out which bough to hang me from as well.

Strangely, it's Katnook's whites that have thrilled me most – in what is really a red wine area. I can hear Wayne dusting off that noose again. The Katnook Riesling is the

most powerful and concentrated of its kind in the area. The Sauvignon Blanc is that Australian rarity – a really tangy, green-tasting mouthful; the Chardonnay is long-lived and herbal with melon flavours; the Cabernet Sauvignon certainly did go through a period when the fruit was too meagre. It still gives a dry style but has more fruit at its core. Odyssey Cabernet and Prodigy Shiraz are the flagship reds. A new venture has been to create a 'celebrity' wine range with golf star Nick Faldo. And I thought the Sauvignon Blanc was the best. No, you dig, Wayne; I'll just swing in the breeze.
Best years: (Odyssey) 2002, '01, '00, '99, '98, '97, '96, '94, '92, '91.

Kilikanoon
This is a fuller style of Clare Valley Riesling and comes from Mort's Block, a renowned vineyard in the Watervale area of the valley.

KILIKANOON
Clare Valley
✶ *Shiraz, Grenache, Cabernet Sauvignon, Mourvedre*
✶ *Riesling, Semillon*
Winning six out of the seven trophies awarded at the 2002 Clare Valley Show provided the trumpet fanfare for Kilikanoon's entrance to the world of wine.

Winemaker and part-owner, Kevin Mitchell, was raised in the Clare where his father, Mort, has been a grape-grower since the 1960s. The starting point was Mitchell's purchase of the Kilikanoon property in 1997 and blood being thicker than water, access to his father's and other old vine vineyards. Since taking on partners in 2002 his access to fruit has increased and production has soared from 2000 cases (1997) to 35,000 (2003). The Oracle and Covenant Shiraz and Prodigal Grenache are complex, opulent and fleshily textured with wonderful depth of flavour. The whole range, however, is consistent, excellent and modestly priced. Future plans include a collaboration with the Barossa Valley's Rolf Binder (see Veritas page 73).
Best years: (Oracle Shiraz) 2002, '01, '99, '98, '97.

Knappstein
Knappstein's Clare Valley Riesling has an intense fruity citrus-scented style and will benefit from three years of aging or more.

KNAPPSTEIN
Clare Valley
✶ *Pinot Noir, Cabernet Sauvignon, Merlot, Malbec, Shiraz*
✶ *Sauvignon Blanc, Chardonnay, Semillon, Gewurztraminer*
Knappstein, originally set up by Tim Knappstein in 1976 (see KNAPPSTEIN/LENSWOOD below) has now been well and truly subsumed into the large Lion Nathan group who bought the company in 2001; to emphasize the change 'Tim' has been dropped from the label, and PETALUMA stalwart Andrew Hardy, having taken charge of winemaking in 1996, now produces a range of full-flavoured reds and whites as well as plotting to build a brewery in the valley and joining up with Peter Barry (see Jim BARRY) to ambush visiting wine writers and deprive them of sleep and sobriety.

The best wine is the Riesling, often high-toned when young, but developing serenely over many years. An elegant, mildly herbal Cabernet/Merlot blend, faintly foresty Shiraz and premium Enterprise Cabernet Sauvignon and Shiraz are among many releases, some of which incorporate a percentage of Adelaide Hills fruit, sourced via Petaluma's numerous vineyards and contracts in that area.
Best years: (Enterprise) 2002, '01, '00, '99, '98, '97.

KNAPPSTEIN/LENSWOOD VINEYARDS
Adelaide Hills
✶ *Pinot Noir, Cabernet Sauvignon, Merlot, Malbec*
✶ *Chardonnay, Sauvignon Blanc, Semillon*
In 1981 Tim and Annie Knappstein, who had established the KNAPPSTEIN winery in Clare Valley in 1976, also bought land at Lenswood in the Adelaide Hills. After they sold Knappstein to PETALUMA in 1992 they concentrated all their efforts on their Lenswood operation, and further purchases have

Knappstein/Lenswood Vineyards
Tim and Annie Knappstein make delicious, intense, tangy Sauvignon Blanc in the Adelaide Hills.

brought their distinctly cool climate holdings here to 54ha. With Lenswood they have since exceeded their old reputation with a string of fine, tangy Sauvignon, elegant Chardonnay and perfumed Pinot Noir and since 2001 a Gewurztraminer. In warmer years they also release a Semillon and a rich, sturdy Bordeaux blend called The Palatine.

In 2004 Tim Knappstein began winemaking at a new 2000-tonne capacity winery, Woodside Wines, processing his own fruit and those of local growers.

Best years: (Pinot Noir) 2002, '00, '99, '98, '97, '96, '95.

LEASINGHAM

Clare Valley
❉ *Shiraz, Cabernet Sauvignon, Malbec*
❦ *Riesling, Semillon*

Leasingham was established in 1893, initially called Stanley, then Stanley Leasingham. It was acquired by HARDYS in 1987, and has since gone from strength to strength. There are a couple of particular points of interest with Leasingham. First, it has always been a champion of Malbec, a grape accorded little respect in Australia, but one which the great wine

Leasingham
The climate in the Clare Valley is able to produce those big, generous styles associated with Australia reds – this full-bodied wine has plenty of the characteristic minty Clare flavours.

popularizer, Wolf BLASS, realized was perfect for making full, fleshy, ripe red wines. He primarily used Langhorne Creek fruit, but Leasingham were the ones who established it in Clare and still give it full rein.

Second, despite being part of the giant Constellation Wine Group, HARDYS, through their senior winemakers, and particularly through Peter Dawson, have always been eager to give youth and talent its head. Kerri Thompson, chief of Leasingham, was only 25 and had been an assistant there for a mere four months, when the head winemaker left, just before 1999 harvest. Dawson could see she was good – so he said, the job's yours, get on with it. And she hasn't let him down.

Steely, citrus Riesling is by far the best white, particularly the Classic Clare label, but it is the reds that have the widest reputation. Bin 61 Shiraz, Classic Clare Shiraz, Bin 56 Cabernet/Malbec and Classic Clare Cabernet Sauvignon are hefty, big-boned wines, flooded with fruit, initially saturated with oak, but recent vintages show less wood and more fruit, but still enough tannin and extract to stop a runaway truck. They are expensive and do particularly well in wine shows but in the real world need 10 years or so to be broken in. Sparkling Shiraz is excellent.

Best years: (reds) 2002, '01, '99, '98, '97, '96, '95, '94, '91, '90, '88.

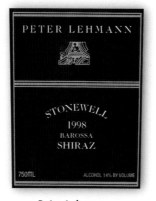

Peter Lehmann
Stonewell Shiraz, made by Barossa winemaker extraordinaire Peter Lehmann, shows rich, ripe fruit and lovely meaty complexity, finished off with 100 per cent new American oak which tests the fruit to its limit.

PETER LEHMANN

Barossa Valley
❉ *Cabernet Sauvignon, Shiraz, Grenache, Merlot*
❦ *Riesling, Chardonnay, Semillon, Chenin Blanc*

Peter Lehmann is a larger-than-life figure who has stood astride his beloved Barossa Valley for over 30 years and though he hasn't made the wines for some time now, they've never lost his imprint – proudly Barossa in nature, reflecting their vineyard character but also reflecting the indulgent, passionate and generous nature of Peter Lehmann himself. Though famous for reds, the whites are remarkably good, in particular Chenin Blanc and Semillon and the top wine, dry, long-lived Eden Valley Riesling – and all age well.

The reds are altogether more lush – happy-juice Grenache followed by rich, oaky Cabernet Sauvignon and Shiraz. The varietals are led by outstanding Stonewell Shiraz which since the early 1990s has achieved that rare feat of marrying power with beauty and is regularly one of Barossa's finest Shirazes, and the extremely serious Mentor Cabernet.

All the Lehmann wines feature beautiful artwork on the labels, often with a gambling, poker playing theme, with the Queen of Clubs a particular favourite. This is a reference to the gamble Peter took in 1978 of promising to take the grapes of Barossa growers whose contracts had been broken by bigger companies. Lehmann's contract was a hand shake. His now highly successful company was built on trust and handshakes. Those growers still don't have a written contract. With Lehmann they know they don't need one. Californian Donald Hess bought a controlling interest in 2003 and there's every sign the same level of integrity and quality will be maintained.

Best years: (Stonewell Shiraz) 2002, '01, '99, '98, '96, '94, '93, '92, '91, '90, '89.

LINDEMANS

Coonawarra
❉ *Cabernet Sauvignon, Shiraz, Merlot, Cabernet Franc, Malbec*

Lindemans
The Coonawarra vineyards are the quality end of the whole Lindemans operation and Limestone Ridge is one of three excellent long-lived reds that keep Lindemans' reputation high.

With the closure of their winemaking facilities in the Hunter, most of Lindemans' wines are now made at the mega winery at Karadoc in the Murray Darling region (see page 116), including the great value Lindemans Reserve reds sourced largely from Padthaway. The Coonawarra operation is very much the premium face of this famous wine company. Long-term winemaker, Greg Clayfield, produces three outstanding reds: the single-vineyard St George Cabernet Sauvignon, one of Australia's best examples of the Shiraz/Cabernet blend, Limestone Ridge, and Pyrus, a silky smooth blend of Cabernet Sauvignon, Merlot, Cabernet Franc and Malbec.
Best years: (Limestone Ridge Shiraz Cabernet) 2002, '01, '99, '98, '96.

MAJELLA

Coonawarra
❉ *Cabernet Sauvignon, Shiraz,*
❉ *Riesling*
The Lynn family, grape-growers in Coonawarra for more than 35 years, have been making wines under their own label for little over a decade – with remarkable success on the show circuit. While his brother Tony toils in the vineyard, Brian 'Prof' Lynn markets the wines brilliantly and steals all the glory. There is a trademark lush, sweet vanillin oakiness to the reds which is always balanced by dense, opulent fruit. The profound The Malleea Shiraz/Cabernet is the flagship wine while the Cabernet Sauvignon – a succulent, fleshy, cassis bomb – is among the region's best, yet remains modestly priced. The Shiraz is excellent with spicy, vanillin oak and fruitcake and concen-

trated dark plum flavours: the Sparkling Shiraz, too, is a helluva mouthful.
Best years: (Cabernet Sauvignon) 2002, '01, '00, '98, '96, '94.

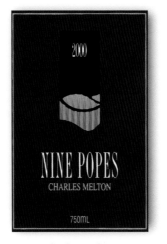

Charles Melton
Charlie Melton is one of the leaders of the revival of old-vine Grenache and other Rhône varieties in the Barossa Valley. 'Nine Popes' is a tongue-in-cheek reference to Châteauneuf-du-Pape in France's southern Rhône.

CHARLES MELTON

Barossa Valley
❉ *Shiraz, Grenache, Mourvedre, Cabernet Sauvignon*
There's a bunch of young turks who have followed the lead of Peter Lehmann in reviving the Barossa Valley's reputation as a tip-top producer of superripe, sensually scented reds – and as a consequence keeping the local growers in business and their marvellous ancient vines in the ground.
Twinkly-eyed 'Charlie' Melton is among the pace-setters with a rich, spicy mix of locally grown Shiraz, Grenache and Mourvedre called Nine Popes, that started out as a bit of a take-off of France's famous Châteauneuf-du-Pape wine, and would now stand shoulder to shoulder with the best of them. There is also a smashing juicy pink Rose of Virginia that's pretty pricey for a pink, but so gluggable you've already ordered the second bottle before you remembered who's paying. He makes rich, ripe Shiraz – particularly favouring the irresistible perfumed style of the southern part of the Valley – and good Cabernet. And then there's the sparkling Shiraz. Hah! A long day in the sun, a bench outside the winery and Charlie in a wicked, witty mood. Glug, glug. Hic. Am I always on the second bottle of Melton's wines before I wonder who's paying?
Best years: (Nine Popes) 2002, '01, '99, '98, '96, '95, '94, '93, '92, '91, '90.

GEOFF MERRILL

McLaren Vale
❉ *Cabernet Sauvignon, Shiraz, Merlot, Grenache, Sangiovese*
❉ *Chardonnay, Sauvignon Blanc, Semillon*
Because of his flamboyant handlebar moustache and easy friendship with many of the sporting greats of England and Australia, Geoff Merrill has got rather a 'showbiz' reputation, but in fact he is an extremely serious and committed McLaren Vale promoter and producer. He's also had extensive overseas experience, notably in South Africa and Italy, and this shows in his wines which are leaner, crisper than most McLaren Vale examples, yet the reds in particular, age superbly. And he's not a conformist. He was early into the 'no oak' style of Chardonnay and Sauvignon after his European ventures. He doesn't oak his Grenache either, and gaily reverses orthodoxy with his other reds. He uses lashings of new *French* oak in his Shiraz (American oak is the norm) and he happily uses well-seasoned American on Coonawarra Cabernet.
The result is a very interesting bunch of wines. His Sauvignon is truly tangy and refreshing. His Chardonnay is heavily oaked but acid too, slow maturing but worth the wait. I've had them at 10 years old and they're excellent. It is lean when young and nutty and rich when mature. The Cabernet Sauvignon reflects Merrill's European penchant for early picking – being zesty and crisp, with tart redcurrant flavours and low tannin but aging to a delicious blackcurrant maturity in 10–15 years. Bush Vine Grenache is delightfully peppery (he makes a juicy rosé too). Shiraz is ripe, but dry and top of the line Henley is richly scented and seductive. And in 2003 he had a baby boy. I would say he's been grinning from ear to ear ever since, except his moustache is so bushy, I'm not sure where his mouth stops and his ears start.

Majella
The flagship wine from Majella is The Malleea, an old-fashioned blend of Cabernet and Shiraz from vines planted on a fantastic piece of Coonawarra terroir. Aged for 2 ½ years in new French oak, the wine has very intense blackberry, blackcurrant, cedary oak and spice aromas.

Geoff Merrill
Geoff Merrill is a high-profile winemaker who combines the rare talents of an instinctive feel for wine with marketing ability. The wines are very accessible when young but will take a lot of aging too.

MITCHELL

Clare Valley

❉ *Shiraz, Cabernet Sauvignon, Grenache*
❉ *Riesling, Semillon*

You could call Jane and Andrew Mitchell Clare Valley old-timers – although they won't like it – because they set up their winery in an old stone apple store way back in 1975 and since then have been a considerable force in the valley. Their reds don't quite have the intensity they used to, and their now excellent Riesling is recovering from an unexplained dip in the late 1990s, but they are definitely among the leaders once again. The Watervale Riesling is steely, the Growers Semillon rich and oaky, Growers Grenache is a lively stew of herbs and fruit and Peppertree Shiraz and Sevenhill Cabernet Sauvignon are plump, chocolaty and able to age.

Mitchell
This Clare Valley producer makes beautifully focused Riesling with floral limy flavours and crisp piercing acidity which is now back on form again.

MOUNT HORROCKS

Clare Valley

❉ *Shiraz, Cabernet Sauvignon, Merlot*
❉ *Riesling, Semillon, Chardonnay*

Since purchasing the Mount Horrocks label in 1993, Stephanie Toole has transformed it into one of the Clare Valley's best producers. The Watervale Riesling shows zesty, pure lime juice flavours, taut structure and racy acidity. The Cordon Cut Riesling is a rare non-botrytis dessert wine that is made by cutting the cane (or cordon) of the vine and allowing the sugar to concentrate as the grapes hang on the vine. This is silky smooth, even lush, with honey and lime flavours: fine, beautifully balanced, and quite delicious. Both these wines are among the best example of their style in the whole country. The cedary oaked Semillon and fleshy, savoury Shiraz are also worth seeking out. The cellar door, at the renovated

Mount Horrocks
This wine from a single vineyard of unirrigated vines is yet more proof that the Clare Valley produces great Riesling. The wine is bone dry with incredible length and could easily be kept for 10 years or more.

Auburn Railway Station, is worth a visit at weekends, too.
Best years: (Riesling) 2003, '02, '01, '00, '99, '98.

MOUNTADAM

Eden Valley

❉ *Shiraz, Cabernet Sauvignon and others*
❉ *Chardonnay and others*

The superbly designed Mountadam winery, perched high in the hills above the Eden Valley, takes its grapes from the low-yielding estate vineyards. Wind and drought are constant foes but the concentration of flavour is more than enough recompense. The Chardonnay is complex and long-flavoured; the Pinot Noir, stylish and deep; both of these wines being especially renowned for their lush fat texture. The Cabernet Sauvignon and Merlot are similarly stylish and dark-fruited if less lush; and a complex, lees-aged sparkler is pretty serious stuff. Eden Ridge organic and David Wynn are excellent labels for non-estate grapes. Mountadam was bought in 2000 by the Margaret River winery, CAPE MENTELLE (itself owned by luxury megabrand LVMH).
Best years: (Patriarch) 2000, '99, '98, '97, '96, '95, '94, '93, '91, '90, '87; (Chardonnay) 2001, '00, '98, '97, '94, '93, '92, '91, '90.

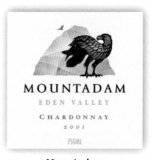

Mountadam
Eden Valley has become one of Australia's top white grape producing areas. This rich, buttery Chardonnay with ripe, tropical flavours has a worldwide reputation.

Nepenthe
Homer was said to have loved the magical Egyptian drink, Nepenthe, and if anyone could make it, it would be Peter Leske, Nepenthe's talented winemaker.

NEPENTHE

Adelaide Hills

❉ *Cabernet Sauvignon, Merlot, Pinot Noir, Zinfandel, Tempranillo, Cabernet Franc, Malbec*
❉ *Chardonnay, Sauvignon Blanc, Semillon, Pinot Gris, Riesling*

Nepenthe has made a substantial impact in its first decade well before any of its three vineyard blocks (totaling 102ha) – at Lenswood, near Charleston, and at Balhannah – have reached maturity. Having a winery – a rarity in the ecologically neurotic Adelaide Hills – helps. So, too, have the financial resources of the Tweddell family. And the lynch-pin has been talented winemaker, Peter Leske, who has had extensive overseas experience as well as working with the Australian Wine Research Institute and Grosset. Not only has the company grown (to produce 45,000 cases in 2003) but the quality across the range is outstanding: Riesling, Pinot Gris, Semillon, Chardonnay and Tryst Sauvignon/ Semillon or Cabernet/ Tempranillo and whatever else was lying around – are excellent, Pinot Noir is fine, deep and scented. Zinfandel has a deserved cult following – me, for a start – and Tempranillo and Cabernet Franc shows promise. Perhaps the best comment I can make is that the wines display a true sense of place, a character of where they come from.
Best years: (Pinot Noir) 2002, '01, '00.

ORLANDO

Barossa Valley

❉ *Shiraz, Cabernet Sauvignon, Merlot, Grenache, Pinot Noir and others*
❉ *Chardonnay, Semillon, Riesling, Verdelho, Viognier, Sauvignon Blanc*

Owned by the French Pernod-Ricard group,

Dirt road and gum trees high up in the Eden Valley on the Mountadam Estate. If you want to see the wildlife in Australia, dawn and dusk are the times to do it. And the gold of the setting sun on this lane in High Eden creates so many shadows and shapes I see a kangaroo behind every tree.

PARKER COONAWARRA ESTATE

Coonawarra

❊ *Cabernet Sauvignon, Merlot, Cabernet Franc, Petit Verdot*

Red wine specialist now run by Andrew Pirie (formerly of PIPERS BROOK) and bought by YERING STATION in 2004. The top wine, First Growth, can be one of the best – and most Bordeaux-like – reds in Australia. It is dark, rich, dry and released only in better years. The second label Terra Rossa Cabernet Sauvignon is tasty but lighter and leafier. The Merlot is one of Australia's best, too.

Best years: (First Growth) 2001, '99, '98, '96, '93, '91, '90.

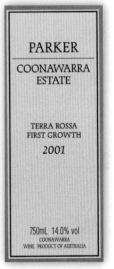

Parker
The top wine from Parker, with opulent berry-blackcurrant fruit and classy oak handling, is cheekily called First Growth in imitation of Bordeaux's top wines and is only released in selected years.

PENFOLDS

Barossa Valley

❊ *Cabernet Sauvignon, Shiraz, Merlot, Grenache and others*

❦ *Chardonnay, Riesling, Semillon and others*

For many, Penfolds and Grange, Australia's most famous red wine, are synonymous, but the modern Penfolds is actually more important for its budget-priced wines than for creating what was once called Australia's only 'First Growth'. Through a series of acquisitions, Penfolds, along with LINDEMANS, WYNNS, Seaview and many others all under the umbrella name of Southcorp Wines, now dominates Australian wine production, and

Orlando-Wyndham is Australia's third-biggest wine company and is responsible for some of the most valuable and well-known wine names in Australia – Coolabah boxed wines, Wyndham Estate and above all, the international superstar Jacob's Creek (see page 20). In 1993 Jacob's Creek became the UK's biggest brand of bottled wine – and is now a worldwide phenomenon, with annual sales of 78 million bottles.

And why the success? Wines of total consistency – consistently attractive and easy to drink, consistently reasonable in price. The basic Jacob's Creek red – loosely based on the Bordeaux varieties – and the basic white – a pleasant, soft, off-dry Semillon/Chardonnay blend – have now been supplemented by a pleasant-flavoured, pleasant-priced Chardonnay, a rather good spicy, limy Riesling, a Grenache and various Shiraz, Merlot and Cabernet permutations, as well as a sparkling Chardonnay/Pinot Noir and very classy Jacob's Creek Reserve and Limited Release wines.

There is a range of other Orlando labels – some traditional and high quality such as St Helga Rhine Riesling, St Hugo Cabernet Sauvignon and St Hilary Chardonnay, Steingarten Rhine Riesling, Lawson's Shiraz and Jacaranda Ridge Cabernet Sauvignon. Orlando also owns MORRIS (Rutherglen), Russet Ridge (Wrattonbully), Wickham Hill (New South Wales), Gramp's and Richmond Grove in the Barossa Valley and POET'S CORNER in Mudgee which also produces the Montrose and Henry Lawson brands. Wyndham Estate in the Hunter Valley is now showing some improvement.

Best years: (St Hugo Cabernet) 2002, '01, '00, '99, '98, '96, '94, '92, '91, '90, '88, '86.

Orlando
Steingarten Riesling is one of Orlando's top whites – small parcels of fruit from the Steingarten vineyard high up in the Eden Valley are used when possible in the blend.

Penfolds

Bin 707 is the closest thing to a Cabernet Sauvignon version of Grange, Penfolds' flagship Shiraz. It is very powerful, oaky and firmly structured with tremendous blackcurrant fruit richness.

is the leader in making full-flavoured reds at a fair price. However, it has good whites too; a series of Adelaide Hills-sourced Semillon and Chardonnay are first rate including the so-called 'White Grange' Yattarna.

Grange is still the flagship red (see also page 22). The secret lies in 50- to 100-year-old, low-yielding Shiraz vines picked at peak ripeness, and in the skilled use of new American oak: a heady profusion of black-berry, cherry and vanilla aromas and flavours is supported by a structure of exceptional strength and complexity. Cabernet Sauvignon Bin 707, St Henri Claret, Magill Estate, The Clare Estate and Cabernet/Shiraz Bin 389 are the other top-ranking reds, with ripe fruit and (excepting St Henri) lavish use of new or near-new oak as cornerstones.

But further down the range wines like Bins 28 and 128 don't have the same broad-fruited, packed-with-flavour style they used to, and Koonunga Hill and Rawson's Retreat are unrecognizable from the gutsy reds we cut and stained our teeth on. The 2002 vintage showed something of a return to form. Please, Penfolds, do get back to what you do best, because over the years, your reds have probably done more than any others to turn the rest of the world on to Aussie wines.
Best years: (top reds) 2002, '01, '99, '98, '96, '94, '93, '92, '91, '90, '88, '86, '84, '83, '82.

PENLEY ESTATE

Coonawarra

🍇 *Cabernet Sauvignon, Shiraz*

🍃 *Chardonnay*

Kym Tolley comes from two wine families – the famous Tolleys and the even more

famous PENFOLDS, so he was literally born with both wine and a silver spoon in his mouth. Penley Estate generated more publicity prior to producing its first wine than any other Australian winery, but after a few uncertain steps, the wine has well and truly lived up to the propaganda. Satin-smooth Cabernet Sauvignon, with highly skilled use of French and American oak, can show Coonawarra at or near its best, but he also makes Shiraz, Merlot and the traditional Coonawarra claret – a Shiraz/Cabernet. He also does fine Chardonnay and lovely fizz, and although he established his winery on land outside the traditional 'cigar'-shaped area of terra rossa soil, he has certainly done much to legitimize the less than classic mix of red and white soils to the east of the 'cigar'.
Best years: (Cabernet) 2001, '00, '99, '98, '96, '94, '93, '92, '91.

Penley Estate

Coonawarra is well known for its elegant Cabernet and this wine from a relatively new company is no exception – fine-structured but powerful with impressive fruit depth and weight.

PENNY'S HILL

McLaren Vale

🍇 *Shiraz, Cabernet Sauvignon, Grenache, Merlot*

🍃 *Chardonnay, Semillon*

This is one of McLaren Vale's newer producers (first vintage 1995) which makes all of its wines from the estate's three vineyards: the slightly elevated Penny's Hill (planted 1991–6), and Goss Corner (1996) and Malpas Road (1990) which are on the valley floor. I sort of realized they were a serious crew when I was tasting the excellent Footprint Shiraz and said – so where exactly do the grapes come from – and they said – rows 4–7 – look, it's on the label. And it is. Just four special rows out of the 7-ha Penny's Hill vineyard, kept apart simply because they're always the best. There's terroir for you. While the cellar door, art gallery and café attract tourists, the other wines are good

Penny's Hill

Planted in 1993, the Penny's Hill Chardonnay vineyard benefits from a slight elevation over the rest of McLaren Vale and avoids the worst of the summer heat. The wines are full-bodied with gentle tropical fruit and peachy aromas.

too – rich, smoothly textured Penny's Hill Shiraz, gutsy Grenache and the fresh, clean, intensely citrus Goss Corner Semillon – and they make tasty 'port' too.
Best years: (Shiraz) 2002, '01, '00, '98, '97.

PETALUMA

Adelaide Hills

🍇 *Cabernet Sauvignon, Merlot, Shiraz*

🍃 *Chardonnay, Riesling, Viognier*

Petaluma is the brainchild of the legendary Brian Croser, whose winemaking techniques have had the most influence on Australia's emergence as one of the world's leading wine nations.

Interestingly, Petaluma has taken many years to evolve its own wine style to the high level Croser demands. Recent vintages, in which he has finally been able to use exactly the grapes he wants from what he calls distinguished sites – in particular Adelaide Hills fruit for his Chardonnay, Mount Barker (a warm spot in Adelaide Hills) for Shiraz and Viognier and Coonawarra Cabernet and Merlot grapes for his red – have been stunningly good. Tiers Chardonnay rapidly became one of Australia's most expensive and impressive whites. Croser Champagne-method

Petaluma

From Hanlin Hill, one of Clare's higher, cooler vineyards, Petaluma's Riesling is lean, citrus, serious wine that will age for 10 years or so.

sparkling wine is much more approachable than it used to be, but still has a rather austere style. The Clare Valley Riesling is at the fuller end of the Australian spectrum and requires long aging. Other wines are made under the Sharefarmers and Bridgewater Mill labels. Sharefarmers has been at the heart of recent disputes over the Coonawarra boundary but its wine is never as good as Petaluma's traditional Coonawarra. Petaluma has acquired a number of significant producers, including MITCHELTON, KNAPPSTEIN, Smithbrook and STONIER. It was itself taken over by Lion Nathan Breweries in 2001, although Croser is still involved.

Best years: (Coonawarra) 2002, '01, '00, '99, '97, '94, '91, '90, '88.

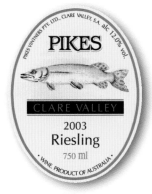

Pikes

This is a really good fresh Riesling, only 12 per cent alcohol, retaining an aggressive citrus grapefruit character.

PIKES

Clare Valley

❉ *Shiraz*

❉ *Riesling, Sauvignon Blanc, Viognier*

The Pike family made a name for itself in South Australia with the brewery they established in 1886. By the time the family sold it in 1972, Edgar Pike was well-established as vineyard manager for a large wine company. Both his sons followed him into wine: Andrew as viticulturist with Southcorp and Neil as winemaker at Mitchells. The brothers established this family winery in the Polish Hill River sub-region of Clare in 1984 and it now produces 35,000 cases a year from 40ha of their own vineyards supplemented by local growers.

Best of the very good range of regional wines are the vibrant, limy, minerally Rieslings, the beautifully textured, chocolaty Shiraz and the peppery, juicy Shiraz/Grenache/Mourvedre, while the Sangiovese is starting to turn some heads. Watch out, too, for their joint venture operation: Pike & Joyce from Lenswood, in the Adelaide Hills.

Best years: (Reserve Riesling) 2003, '02, '98, '97.

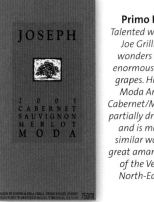

Primo Estate

Talented winemaker Joe Grilli works wonders with an enormous range of grapes. His Joseph Moda Amarone Cabernet/Merlot uses partially dried grapes and is made in a similar way to the great amarone wines of the Veneto in North-East Italy.

PRIMO ESTATE

Adelaide Plains

❉ *Shiraz, Cabernet Sauvignon, Sangiovese and others*

❉ *Colombard, Pinot Gris (Pinot Grigio), Riesling*

It doesn't sound promising when your driver turns off the road in the flat dusty nothing land just north of Adelaide and says 'here we are'. I've come looking for one of Australia's most talented and innovative winemakers and we've arrived on a patch of dust that looks as though it would be better growing tomatoes – which is what most of his neighbours do. But that's one reason why Joe Grilli of Primo Estate is so special.

The land around the winery isn't special, and it is very hot indeed, but Grilli coaxes marvellously lemony Colombard and spicy Shiraz/Sangiovese out of it. That's just the beginning. Under the Joseph label he produces waxy, honeyed Pinot Grigio, remarkable Cabernet/Merlot made like Italy's amarone from dried Cabernet grapes and a little cool climate Merlot, and a simply stunning sparkling red containing material up to 40 years old, called just Joseph.

Add in superb sweet Riesling and a thrilling fortified called 'The Fronti' that he ages as hot as possible in his vineyard shed rather like they age Madeira – and you've got one of Australia's – and the world's – great wine originals. Oh, olive oil. He makes sumptuous olive oil from 100-year-old trees that was recently voted Australia's best. Thank goodness he doesn't play cricket.

Best years: (Cabernet/Merlot Joseph) 2002, '01, '00, '99, '98, '97, '96, '95, '94, '93, '91, '90.

REYNELL

McLaren Vale

❉ *Shiraz, Cabernet Sauvignon, Merlot*

❉ *Chardonnay*

The beautiful buildings of Chateau Reynella, the old Reynell homestead about 20km

Reynell

The wine is made with traditional basket presses that delicately extract the juice from the skins without breaking the grape seeds and over-extracting the harsh tannins from the skins. However, it is still a fairly tannic style.

south of Adelaide, house the corporate headquarters of the HARDY WINE COMPANY.

A limited range of Basket Pressed Shiraz, Basket Pressed Merlot and Basket Pressed Cabernet Sauvignon are released under Reynell label (the Chateau Reynella label is used for export), all exhibiting awesome power, concentration and a good depth of blackberry/blackcurrant fruit. They're more tannic nowadays than they used to be, but the old vines, some dating back to the 1930s, give so much intensity to the fruit that a little tannin and a heavy hand with the oak doesn't do too much harm, if you can let the wines age a few years. Few of us can or do.

Best years: (reds) 2002, '01, '00, '98, '96, '95, '94.

ROCKFORD

Barossa Valley

❉ *Shiraz, Grenache, Cabernet Sauvignon, Mataro*

❉ *Semillon, Riesling, Muscat Blanc (White Frontignac)*

Wonderfully nostalgic wines from Robert O'Callaghan, a great respecter of the old vines so plentiful in the Barossa Valley and

Rockford

As well as sumptuous still Shiraz, 'Rocky' O'Callaghan makes irresistible but rich and complex sparklers, inspired by a sparkling Burgundy he found in his father's cellar.

supporter of the farmers who grow them. He also delights in using antique machinery. Masterful Basket Press Shiraz, Eden Valley Riesling, Moppa Springs (a Grenache/Shiraz/Mourvedre blend) and cult sparkling Black Shiraz, are all redolent of another age, not only in the way they are made, but, fancifully, in the way they taste. They are rarely blockbusters but always have a long, lingering flavour and gentle texture – now these are basket-pressed wines that really show the gentleness of the old methods.

Best years: (Basket Press Shiraz) 2002, '01, '99, '98, '96, '95, '92, '91, '90, '86.

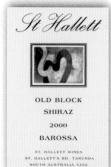

St Hallet
One of the Barossa Valley's best red wines is Old Block Shiraz from St Hallett. Made from wines that are always at least 60 years old, this is rich, chocolaty and intense, without ever going over the top.

ST HALLETT
Barossa Valley
❧ *Shiraz, Cabernet Sauvignon, Grenache*
❧ *Chardonnay, Semillon, Riesling*

St Hallett made its reputation in much the same way as Peter LEHMANN. When the Barossa wineries were all being taken over by multinationals whose accountants immediately said, 'These Barossa grapes are too expensive, let's use something cheaper', St Hallett, in the shape of larger-than-life boss Bob McLean, stood up and said, 'Barossa grapes may be expensive, but they're exceptional: we'll use nothing else.' In 1988 when McLean took over, this act of faith in the Barossa and its old vines was of massive significance.

Nowadays, everyone appreciates how good Barossa fruit is and they fall over themselves to pay top dollar for it. But then, McLean and Lehmann were offering a lifeline to grape-growing families who'd been in the valley since the 1850s. St Hallett makes a whole raft of reds and whites – good Semillon and excellent Eden Valley Riesling lead the whites – but the reds are St Hallett's best – especially its rich, proud, dense Shirazes: Faith, Blackwell, and, above all, one of Australia's most famous – Old Block – made from vines that are never younger than 60 years old and have often passed the century mark. Now owned by Lion Nathan

Breweries (as is PETALUMA), the general feeling is that things will be OK, although I was disappointed to see on my last visit that all the great old fermentation tanks had been removed.

Best years: (Old Block) 2002, '01, '99, '98, '96, '94, '93, '91, '90.

Seppelt
Para Liqueur Port is one of the finest fortifieds made at the historic Seppeltsfield winery in the Barossa. First established in 1867 it produced enormous quantities of table and fortified wines, and even today holds stocks of 12 million litres of maturing fortified wine.

SEPPELT
Barossa Valley
❧ *Shiraz, Pinot Noir, Cabernet Sauvignon*
❧ *Chardonnay, Riesling, Semillon*

Another member of the Southcorp family, Australia's most all-embracing wine company, Seppelt has headquarters at the historic Seppeltsfield winery in the Barossa – long the scene of its fortified wine production and at Great Western in Victoria where sparkling wine (and Australia's only underground drives) has a century-old tradition (see page 119).

Great Western is best known for red wines and fizz, while Seppeltsfield's greatest achievements are in fortifieds. They have produced fine reds from such vineyards as nearby Dorrien, but they pale beside such wonders as the great 'ports', 'sherries' and other fortifieds, 12 million litres of which lie quietly maturing at Seppeltsfield. Most famous of all is Para Liqueur Port – a tiny amount of which is released as an unblended 100-year-old wine of quite staggering intensity. Other 'ports', under the Para and DP labels, are also outstanding, as are the DP 'sherries', probably the best in Australia. Delicious Rutherglen Tokays and Muscats complete the range.

SHAW & SMITH
Adelaide Hills
❧ *Merlot, Shiraz*
❧ *Sauvignon Blanc, Chardonnay, Riesling*

Michael Hill-Smith MW (Australia's first Master of Wine) and his cousin, Martin Shaw, one of the original 'flying' winemakers to come and make wine in the northern

Shaw & Smith
This Adelaide Hills winery makes wines of great definition and flavour, including M3 Chardonnay. Unlike many Australian Chardonnays, this barrel-fermented wine is intended for serious aging.

hemisphere, founded a vibrant, internationally focused business in 1989 making one of Australia's first truly tangy Sauvignon Blancs, a trail-blazing unoaked Chardonnay, and an utterly convincing, complex pear, citrus, nut- and cream-influenced Reserve Chardonnay. Until 2000 wines were made at PETALUMA, but they now have an exciting new winery at Balhannah along with 40ha that is being planted with Riesling, Sauvignon and Pinot Noir. They have the 28-ha M3 vineyard at nearby Woodside, planted to Chardonnay, Sauvignon and Merlot. Excellent Shiraz is sourced from near Mount Barker in the southern part of Adelaide Hills.

Best years: (M3 Chardonnay) 2003, '02, '01, '00.

STONEHAVEN
Padthaway
❧ *Shiraz, Cabernet Sauvignon, Sangiovese, Merlot*
❧ *Chardonnay, Riesling, Viognier*

Even by Australian standards, Stonehaven's 10,000-tonne, state-of-the-art winery is remote, situated at Padthaway, in the hinterland of the Limestone Coast, but it's ideally positioned to handle fruit for the HARDY WINE COMPANY from all over the Limestone Coast. Each of the three Stonehaven labels offers varietal Chardonnay, Cabernet Sauvignon and Shiraz. The quaffing Stepping Stone label

Stonehaven
Chardonnay is one of the most successful wine styles to emerge from the large-scale plantings in the Limestone Coast zone.

has produced several of Australia's best value wines in recent years. The mid-priced Limestone Coast label also includes a promising Viognier while the Limited Vineyard Release trio are all sourced from Padthaway (where the company has 452ha). As the winemaker says, the good luck of Stonehaven is to have a brand new winery based on old-established vineyards (at Padthaway and Coonawarra). However, I'm not sure that Stonehaven's greatest triumphs won't be from the 160ha recently established at Wrattonbully, whose first crops have produced exceptional red flavours.
Best years: (Limited Release Cabernet) 2002, '01, '99, '98.

Taylors (Wakefield)
Family-owned Taylors is the largest producer in the Clare Valley and there has been a significant improvement in quality in recent years.

TAYLORS (WAKEFIELD)

Clare Valley
❦ *Cabernet Sauvignon, Shiraz, Merlot*
❦ *Riesling, Chardonnay*
Based near Auburn in the south of the Clare Valley, Taylors has over 500ha under vine and an annual production of 250,000 cases. The Wakefield name is used for exports. Significant investment in improved viticulture and better winemaking has lifted standards across the board. The Estate range (especially the Riesling, Shiraz and Merlot) represent good value for money, while the cheaper Promised Land range (notably the Shiraz/Cabernet and Cabernet/Merlot) are cheerful and tasty. The flagship St Andrews wines, introduced in 1999, are released with substantial bottle age. The Shiraz is given lavish American oak treatment while the mature, toasty flavours of the Riesling will appeal to lovers of this traditional style.
Best years: (Estate Riesling) 2003, '02, '01, '00, '99, '98, '97, '96.

TORBRECK

Barossa Valley
❦ *Shiraz, Grenache, Mataro*
❦ *Semillon, Viognier, Marsanne, Roussanne*

Torbreck
The Torbreck wines now have a cult following. In northern Rhône style, the RunRig is Shiraz blended with a tiny amount of Viognier to give the wine an extra dimension.

Luckily, every generation seems to produce a few heroes determined to 'save' the Barossa Valley. Dave Powell is such a one. He specializes in producing opulent, deeply flavoured and well-structured reds from 60 to 120-year-old Shiraz, Grenache and Mataro (Mourvedre) dry-grown vines – what one could fairly call the essence of the Barossa.

He took me to see some of the vineyards and they were often so overgrown and decrepit you'd hardly know they were there. Then you'd taste from the barrel or so of fabulous rich, red wine each plot of ancient vines had delivered – and you realized why these saviours of tradition are so important. Made in tiny quantities, the flagship RunRig, single-vineyard Descendant and Factor, and the Eden Valley/Barossa blend, the Struie, are all richly concentrated, powerful and complex Shirazes (the first two with a touch of added Viognier) that are the epitome of Powell's craft.

The business has been operating for 10 years with production dramatically increasing (to about 40,000 cases) in recent vintages thanks to sizeable quantities of The Steading and Juveniles – both Grenache/Mataro/Shiraz blends (the latter unoaked) – and the Woodcutters White (Semillon) and Red (Shiraz) – lightly oaked quaffers still bearing a little of the hallmark of a master.
Best years: (The Descendant Shiraz) 2002, '01.

TWO HANDS

Barossa Valley
This is essentially a negociant business set up in 1999 to specialize in producing regional Shiraz from around Australia, especially for the US market. There is a cellar door at Marananga in the Barossa Valley which will be the site of a micro-winery and barrel shed from the 2005 vintage. Two Hands has secured long-term contracts from growers in key regions. The core of the company's operation is the Garden Series which includes regional Shiraz from the Barossa, McLaren Vale, Clare, Padthaway, Langhorne Creek and Heathcote. The flagship Shiraz is the powerful, densely flavoured, oaky Ares –

the best expression of the variety they can make in a particular year. The wines I like best so far are the cheapest in the portfolio: 'Angel's Share' – an approachable, medium-bodied, wild berry McLaren Vale Shiraz – and 'Brave Faces' – a succulent Barossa Shiraz/Grenache. These won't get such high marks from American commentators, but then the best easy-drinkers rarely do.
Best years: (Angel's Share) 2003, '02, '01.

Two Hands
Super-concentrated Shiraz from Australia's prime Shiraz regions is the thinking behind Two Hands. Bad Impersonator comes from the Barossa.

VERITAS

Barossa Valley
❦ *Shiraz, Cabernet Sauvignon, Merlot, Mourvedre, Grenache*
❦ *Semillon, Riesling, Chardonnay*
In vino veritas (In wine there is truth), say the Binder family. There's certainly truth in the bottom of a bottle of Hanisch Vineyard Shiraz or Heysen Vineyard Shiraz, both blindingly good wines. The Shiraz/Mourvedre (known locally as Bulls' Blood as a reminder of Rolf Binder's Hungarian roots) and Shiraz/Grenache blends are lovely big reds; the Cabernet/Merlot is also good. Under the Christa-Rolf label, Shiraz/Grenache is good and spicy with attractive, forward black fruit. Rolf also makes wine for Magpie Estate – chunky, juicy, fair-priced reds.

Veritas
Massively proportioned, super-ripe and high in alcohol (14.5%), this wine is more subtly oaked than many big Barossa reds. Allow at least five years' aging before broaching.

Geoff Weaver
Geoff Weaver's small, high-quality vineyard produces Sauvignon Blanc jammed with intense varietal character and lovely fruit sweetness.

GEOFF WEAVER

Adelaide Hills

🍇 *Pinot Noir, Cabernet Sauvignon, Merlot*
🍷 *Sauvignon Blanc, Chardonnay, Riesling*

In a way you need to go up into the Adelaide Hills with Geoff Weaver in the bright early morning and sit with him idly, silently, contemplating his lovely vineyards to really understand him and his wines. He is now a winegrower and an artist – he creates his own labels – and someone who is truly content in his low-key calling, making excellent tangy Sauvignon Blanc and Riesling and smoothly honed Chardonnay and Pinot Noir. Then ask him for his history, and he'll tell you he was one of the most powerful winemakers in Australia in 1992, heading HARDYS' winemaking, responsible for 10 per cent of all Australia's grapes. And I knew him then too. He wasn't happy then. He is now.

WENDOUREE

Clare Valley

🍇 *Shiraz, Cabernet Sauvignon, Mourvedre, Malbec*
🍷 *Muscat of Alexandria*

Wendouree must rank at the very top of the

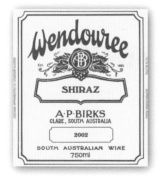

Wendouree
This Clare winery has a cult following for its tiny output of massively extracted, ageworthy reds from tiny yields and old-fashioned winemaking.

vinous national treasures of Australia. You walk down a track through the scented gum forest and find the stone winery constructed by A P Birks in 1895, and much of the second-hand equipment he obtained for the winery is still in use. You head out into the vineyards and you're walking through history – the 1898 Malbec block, the 1892–93 Shiraz plantings – still producing 3 tons to the acre in a magic Clare mesoclimate.

And for the past 20 years there has been the fierce guardianship of Tony and Lita Brady. When I last visited Tony said, 'Do you want to taste young or old?' Panic! Wendouree wines are so rare – they're all sold privately, bar three cases sold to 'historic' merchants – you long to taste the old. But I said young, and it was the right decision. Tony fastidiously drew wine from old barrel after old barrel, expounding his preservationist philosophy as he went. I'd walked the vines, felt the tanks, weighed the berries in my hand – and now – 'Shiraz, Central Block, 1923' – yes, I remember from half an hour ago. God, it's good. 'Central Block 1893' – 'Cabernet Eastern Block 1919', 'Malbec 1898'. And the flavours swirl about you but each patch of vines seems to rise from the glass to explain itself. And you really feel you understand this rarest and most excellent of wines.

You don't, of course. This is just the first step. You need to follow them for 25, even 50 years as they gradually unfold their brilliance. Maybe then I'd understand. Or would I? I'm not sure you need to understand great wine. You just have to revel in it. And be grateful. And the actual wines – blends or varietals – including Muscat and an inspired vintage 'port' – vary every year according to what Tony thinks best expresses Wendouree in that vintage. As I said, let's just be grateful.

Best years: (reds) 2002, '01, '99, '98, '96, '95, '94, '92, '91, '90, '86, '83, '82, '81, '80, '78, '76, '75.

WIRRA WIRRA

McLaren Vale

🍇 *Shiraz, Cabernet Sauvignon, Grenache, Petit Verdot, Merlot*
🍷 *Chardonnay, Riesling, Semillon, Sauvignon Blanc, Semillon, Viognier*

The modern-day Wirra Wirra winery was not established until 1969, but the viticultural and winemaking links of the family of proprietor Greg Trott – a wonderfully eccentric and much-loved figure, usually called 'Trottie' – go back to the 19th century.

Recent years have seen rapid expansion of this already impressive winery. Its best white wines are tropical gooseberry Sauvignon Blanc and sculpted Chardonnay, but its stellar acts are the Church Block

Wirra Wirra
This is big, ripe and spicy Shiraz from the McLaren Vale with rich, blackberry fruit and a touch of ripe black pepper and very well-balanced and integrated oak.

Cabernet blend and the superpremium, chocolaty RSW Shiraz and The Angelus Cabernet Sauvignon, whose blackcurrant, berry, cedary aroma and impressive depth of fruit are partly due to an addition of Coonawarra grapes to the blend. The Cousins is a pretty decent fizz.

Best years: (The Angelus) 2002, '01, '00, '99, '98, '97, '96, '95, '92, '91, '90.

WYNNS COONAWARRA ESTATE

Coonawarra

🍇 *Cabernet Sauvignon, Shiraz, Pinot Noir*
🍷 *Chardonnay, Riesling and others*

Wynns is not only the largest Coonawarra producer but also one of Coonawarra's best, despite being owned by the giant Southcorp, whose track record on quality is not thrilling. Its personality seems to have suffered less than most of Southcorp's other brands and, except at the top end, prices have remained fair.

Aromatic, limy Riesling sells for a song, yet performs like a thoroughbred in the cellar, building complexity for five years at least. Chardonnay is becoming increasingly subtle and complex. However, Wynns is best known for reds. The Shiraz and Black Label Cabernet Sauvignon are both good.

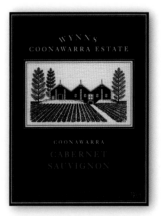

Wynns Coonawarra Estate
As well as making some of Coonawarra's most famous reds, Wynns produces a range of excellent-value standard Shiraz and Cabernet.

Top of the line are John Riddoch Cabernet (see page 53) and Michael Shiraz. John Riddoch has been astonishingly consistent since being launched in 1982 and shows the black-fruited intensity and weight of top Coonawarra Cab. It isn't made in poor years – no 1995 and '99, for instance. Michael is less consistent – but at best is a rich, oaky, chocolaty Shiraz.
Best years: (John Riddoch) 2001, '98, '96, '94, '91, '90, '88, '86, '82.

YALUMBA

Barossa Valley
❉ *Cabernet Sauvignon, Shiraz, Pinot Noir, Merlot, Petit Verdot, Sangiovese*
❦ *Riesling, Chardonnay, Sauvignon Blanc, Semillon, Viognier, Pinot Gris*
Owned by the Hill-Smith family, Yalumba is one of the most successful of Australia's

Yalumba
Despite many new directions at the lower end of the market, Yalumba still turns out high-quality premium reds such as The Signature, a distinctive Australian blend of Barossa Cabernet Sauvignon and old-vine Shiraz first made in 1962.

independent wine companies and manages to operate on several levels, all with considerable success. In particular, it has managed to have a smash hit with its sparkling wine portfolio, led by huge-selling, enjoyable Angas Brut. Oxford Landing has developed a good reputation as a keenly priced range of varietal wines and the new 'Y' series of varietals is good, as are the high-quality 'hand-picked' labels. The Signature, The Menzies and Octavius embody a rather more traditional but high-quality approach.

Yalumba also operates three separate estates – Hill-Smith Estate, Pewsey Vale and Heggies – all producing good, single-vineyard wines from the northern end of the Eden Valley with particular emphasis on slow-maturing wines from Riesling, Semillon and Chardonnay. They also own Nautilus in Marlborough, New Zealand, and Jansz in Tasmania.

It's crucially important that these independent family firms prosper in Australia and Yalumba's determination and commitment to quality, tradition and useful innovation on all levels shows how to do it.
Best years: (The Signature red) 2001, '00, '99, '98, '97, '96, '95, '93, '92, '91, '90, '88.

ZEMA ESTATE

Coonawarra
❉ *Cabernet Sauvignon, Shiraz, Merlot, Cabernet Franc, Malbec*
❦ *Sauvignon Blanc*
Coonawarra is largely the province of the big company wineries and so the Zema story is refreshingly heart-warming. After working as a painter in Penola for more than 20 years, an Italian immigrant,

Demetrio Zema and his wife Francesca were able to fulfil a lifelong dream of owning their own vineyard. In 1982, Demetrio purchased a central Coonawarra block already planted with 3ha of Shiraz: 5ha of Cabernet were soon added.

Another 20 years on and Zema is a thriving family business run by sons Nick and Matt (and winemaker Tom Simons) with 61ha under vine – almost exclusively Cabernet and Shiraz. Zema first made an impact because of the success of its traditional viticultural and winemaking approaches and because of the modest prices they asked for their wines. The Cabernet and Shiraz are excellent examples of the regional styles while the Family Selection reds have a degree of complexity as well as greater richness and depth of flavour.
Best years: (Cabernet Sauvignon) 2002, '01, '00, '98, '96.

Zema Estate
Zema is one of the few producers in Coonawarra still to carry out hand-pruning and dry-farming. Family Selection Cabernet Sauvignon is classic Coonawarra, combining deep black plum fruit with herb dryness and a hint of perfume.

Quick guide ◆ Best producers

Adelaide Hills Ashton Hills, Chain of Ponds, Henschke, Knappstein/Lenswood Vineyards, Nepenthe, Petaluma, Pike & Joyce, Shaw & Smith, Geoff Weaver.
Adelaide Plains Primo Estate.
Barossa & Eden Valleys (Shiraz-based reds) Barossa Valley Estate, Bethany, Burge Family, Grant Burge, Elderton, Glaetzer, Greenock Creek, Henschke, Hewitson, Jenke, Trevor Jones, Peter Lehmann, Charles Melton, Miranda, Mountadam, Orlando, Penfolds, Rockford, St Hallett, Saltram, Schild Estate, Thorn-Clarke, Three Rivers, Torbreck, Turkey Flat, Two Hands, Veritas, The Willows, Yalumba; (Cabernet Sauvignon-based reds) Grant Burge, Greenock Creek, Henschke, Peter Lehmann, St Hallett, Veritas; (Grenache, Mourvedre, Shiraz) Burge Family, Grant Burge, Charles

Cimicky, Elderton, Henschke, Jenke, Peter Lehmann, Charles Melton, Penfolds, Torbreck , Turkey Flat, Two Hands, Veritas; (Riesling) Bethany, Grant Burge, Leo Buring, Henschke, Hewitson, Peter Lehmann, Orlando, Ross Estate, St Hallett, Yalumba, Grosset, Pewsey Vale; (Semillon) Grant Burge, Henschke, Heritage, Jenke, Peter Lehmann, Rockford, Turkey Flat, The Willows.
Clare Valley (whites) Tim Adams, Jim Barry, Wolf Blass, Leo Buring, Crabtree, Grosset, Knappstein, Leasingham, Mitchell, Mount Horrocks, O'Leary Walker, Petaluma, Pikes, Taylors (Wakefield); (reds) Tim Adams, Jim Barry, Grosset, Kilikanoon, Leasingham, Mitchell, Mount Horrocks, Pikes, Taylors (Wakefield), Wendouree.
Coonawarra Balnaves, Bowen, Brand's,

Hollick, Katnook, Lindemans, Majella, Orlando, Parker, Penfolds, Penley, Petaluma, Wynns, Zema.
Langhorne Creek Bleasdale, Bremerton, Glaetzer/Heartland.
Limestone Coast Beringer Blass, Hardys, Heartland, Orlando, Southcorp, Yalumba.
McLaren Vale Cascabel, Chapel Hill, Clarendon Hills, Coriole, D'Arenberg, Fox Creek, Hardys, Kangarilla Road, Maxwell, Geoff Merrill, Mitolo, Penny's Hill, Pirramimma, Reynell, Rosemount, Tatachilla, Wirra Wirra.
Padthaway Browns of Padthaway, Henry's Drive, Lindemans, Orlando, Padthaway Estate, Seppelt, Stonehaven.
Riverland Angove's, Hardys (Banrock Station, Renmano), Kingston Estate, Yalumba (Oxford Landing).

NEW SOUTH WALES

FOR THE FIRST 170 OR SO years of viticulture and winemaking in New South Wales, the wine map was dominated by the Hunter Valley, albeit with a sideways glance at the vast sprawl of bulk production in the Riverina. But since the early part of the 1990s, the small, premium quality regions hugging the western side of the Great Dividing Range have assumed rapidly growing importance. The long-term resident was Mudgee, but it has now been joined by cool climate Orange (at a significantly higher elevation), by Cowra, a distinctly warm region, by Hilltops, the Canberra District and finally, well into the foothills of the Australian Alps, the decidedly chilly Tumbarumba. Of these Mudgee, Cowra and Hilltops already stand as major producers in terms of volume, and as significant contributors to the pool of Australian premium wine. Orange, Canberra District and Tumbarumba have great quality potential, although site selection is essential.

Australian winemakers – including some in the Hunter itself – have been quoted as saying that, with the level of knowledge we now have about climate, soil and grape vines, no-one in their right mind would ever plant a vineyard in the Hunter because sub-tropical weather patterns make the ripening of grapes fraught with risk, but somehow it has produced some of Australia's greatest wines; and as tourism has flourished so the Hunter has duly blossomed.

Travelling west out into the hinterland you come to the Riverina. An area of irrigation, high yield and virtually any grape variety you care to mention. But even here the quality message is hitting home. Several companies are bottling premium lines and even trying their hand at Estate labels, and one of the world's greatest sweet wines – De Bortoli's Noble One – comes from Riverina fruit.

Tyrrell's Vat 47 Chardonnay from the Long Flat Vineyard in the famous Hunter Valley was the first Australian Chardonnay I tasted. My wine-drinking world would never be the same again.

SPOTLIGHT ON
New South Wales

Water pumps and dams are integral parts of water conservation, one of the most important factors in vineyard management in Australia. Companies such as Orlando-Wyndham now use the latest technology in an effort to conserve water more efficiently. This is Orlando Wyndham's Montrose estate in Mudgee where most of the vineyards are drip-irrigated using water from such dams.

NEW SOUTH WALES is where I started my Australian wine odyssey. And I have to admit my first Australian hangover was in New South Wales, though it was the result of beer, not wine, but I wouldn't vouch for the genesis of numerous subsequent ones. It's where Australian wine started its journey, too. The very first vines to reach Australia sailed into Sydney Harbour with the First Fleet in 1788. They had been picked up in Rio de Janeiro and in the Cape of Good Hope on the long voyage out from England, and in no time the settlers had cleared some scrub by the harbour and planted vines. They weren't a great success – the humid atmosphere encouraged black spot disease, knocking out any grapes before they had a chance to ripen – but the scene had been set. All the main Australian settlements took the same line, establishing vineyards at the same time as establishing a community. And the reason usually given was to encourage sobriety. In a new, savage country where rough men became more savage and wild under the influence of fiery high-strength spirits, wine was seen as a moderating influence, a weapon against drunkenness and disorder.

These attempts in New South Wales to promote a benevolent, rosy-cheeked, wine-sipping society didn't work out too well, because there were very few places near Sydney suitable for vines. Close to the sea, the climate is too sub-tropical and vines routinely rotted. Further inland, around Bathurst, the cooler, high-altitude terrain looked promising, but harsh spring frosts simply made vine-growing economically unviable.

Although a few vineyards did survive near Sydney until modern times – at Camden, Rooty Hill and Smithfield – the story of wine in New South Wales is one of establishing vineyards well away from the main consumer market-place, with quality acting as the magnet drawing the attention of Sydney. This movement still continues today.

The crucial factors in New South Wales are excessive heat from the relatively northerly latitude; the presence of the sea close by; and the Great Dividing Range of mountains which separates the humid, populated seaboard from the parched, empty interior. The Great Dividing Range provides cool vineyard sites in some of its high hill passes, as well as the springs from which enough rivers flow inwards to irrigate some of the largest agro-industrial vineyards in Australia. Indeed, without the irrigation water provided by the Lachlan, Darling, Macquarie, Murrumbidgee and Murray Rivers that all end up in the great Murray-Darling river system, the majority of vineyards in Victoria and South Australia simply couldn't survive. Proximity to the sea brings with it advantages and disadvantages: the priceless bounty of cooling breezes but also the seasonal curse of cyclonic cloudbursts, frequently around vintage time.

Quick guide ◆ New South Wales

Location Lower and Upper Hunter Valley, Mudgee, Cowra, Orange and Riverina are the major wine regions. Newer high-altitude regions have been planted in a quest for cool climate fruit.

Grapes The state's mainly warm climate doesn't suit every grape, but can produce some unique styles.
❋ Shiraz is widely grown: leathery in the Hunter, rather solid in Mudgee and light and fruity in Riverina. Cabernet Sauvignon does best in Mudgee, where it's intensely blackcurranty and rather earthy, and the Hunter, where it can be rich and chunky. There are also a number of other reds, of which Merlot and Pinot Noir are the most significant.
❋ Semillon is the great grape of the Hunter, reaching its highest quality in the unoaked examples. But when aged in new oak it is ripe and toasty, full of lemon and lime fruit. It's grown in Riverina for soft, light everyday whites, and in smaller quantities for top-quality, botrytized wine. Chardonnay is fat and rich, full of lush, creamy, tropical fruit in the Hunter and Cowra, and leaner and nuttier in Orange. There is a small amount of Sauvignon Blanc which can be pungent in cool Orange. In Riverina there are also substantial plantings of Trebbiano, Muscat Gordo, Verdelho and Colombard used for oceans of everyday whites.

Climate The latitude is relatively northerly and it is hot, even by Australian standards, particularly in the Hunter Valley and Riverina. Proximity to the sea brings with it priceless cooling breezes but also seasonal

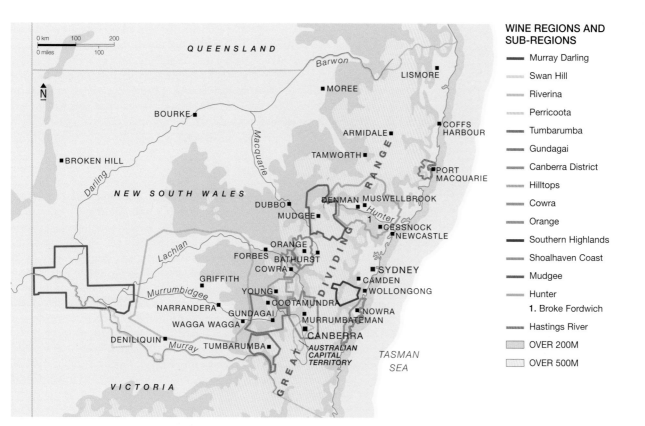

WINE REGIONS AND SUB-REGIONS

- ▬ Murray Darling
- ▬ Swan Hill
- ▬ Riverina
- ▬ Perricoota
- ▬ Tumbarumba
- ▬ Gundagai
- ▬ Canberra District
- ▬ Hilltops
- ▬ Cowra
- ▬ Orange
- ▬ Southern Highlands
- ▬ Shoalhaven Coast
- ▬ Mudgee
- ▬ Hunter
  1. Broke Fordwich
- ▬ Hastings River
- ▨ OVER 200M
- ▨ OVER 500M

HUNTER VALLEY

The first real success came with the Hunter Valley, which is about 130 kilometres north of Sydney and just inland from the major industrial city of Newcastle. Vineyards were being planted there as early as the 1820s, but it wasn't until the 1860s that the areas now thought of as the best – those around the mining town of Cessnock – were planted. I cover the Hunter Valley more fully on page 86.

Because the Hunter Valley so dominated the headlines in any tale about New South Wales, and because the vast Riverina area, also called the Murrumbidgee Irrigation Area, might have provided the great majority of the grape harvest in New South Wales, but virtually never appeared on the label, you could be forgiven for thinking that New South Wales as a state lacked the variety of rivals like Victoria and South Australia. But in the twenty-first century, that isn't entirely fair. She has vineyards that range from ice cold to oven hot and from desert dry to jungle damp. She has vineyard regions that go back 200

cyclonic outbursts. Wet, humid autumns encourage the development of rot.

Soil Sandy and clay loams predominate, along with some red-brown volcanic loams, granite and alluvial soils.

Aspect Vines are planted on the gently undulating valley floors (Cowra, Riverina and Upper Hunter Valley), or in the foothills of the Brokenback and Great Dividing Ranges (Lower Hunter Valley, Mudgee, Hilltops and Orange).

Do regions matter? They do, but the producer usually matters more. Unoaked Semillon from the Hunter is a unique style.

Do vintages matter? It depends which region you are talking about. For reds and the top Semillons from the Hunter Valley, the vintage is incredibly important, often veering between hopeless and brilliant. Mudgee is also prone to rains at the wrong time and Orange is high and cool and is definitely susceptible to cool weather conditions for its red wines.

Organization Some wineries here are boutique operations, others are owned by large corporations and but as all over Australia, the grip of the large companies is strengthening.

A few facts 37,039ha of vineyards, 24 per cent of Australia's total plantings; 33 per cent of total production; 392 wineries.

years, and others that are hardly established as I write. Yet I have to say that many of these areas are pitting themselves against nature and are far less able to offer a reliable crop of ripe, healthy grapes than, say, most of the wine regions of South Australia or Western Australia. Which is fair enough. But one of the joys of wine that keeps me eternally fascinated by it, is how men and women willingly throw themselves into the battle with nature, and, perhaps precisely because conditions are so difficult, come up with new and exciting flavours and styles that stop our wine world from ever becoming boring. And the 'lesser' regions of New South Wales certainly fit into that category. But let's have a look first at the regions that do make a significant contribution.

MUDGEE

It's not exactly a great wine name, is it? Well, maybe not in English, but in the local Aboriginal language Mudgee means 'a nest in the hills' – and suddenly it's much more attractive. Because that's just what Mudgee is. As the plane lands at the tiny airport you do feel as though you have been dropped into a basket nested between hills close up to the western side of the Great Dividing Range. Begun by German settlers and fuelled by its own gold rush, Mudgee has had an up and down wine existence, and its greatest contribution to Australia has been the isolation of a top quality Chardonnay clone during the 1960s, which became the source for the lush, fruit- and flavour-laden Aussie Chardonnays that shocked and excited the wine world in the 1970s and 1980s. But the wines didn't have Mudgee labels on them and Hunter Valley was the region that garnered most of the plaudits, Despite the presence of some big national companies and despite some very feisty local growers, a lack of identity for Mudgee's wineries is still a problem, and only Rosemount with Mountain Blue and Hill of Gold have made much of a reputation for their Mudgee wines.

Cowra is a recent, but well-established wine region with a reliably warm climate, lots of sun, hardly any rain and good water supplies for irrigation. Vines are not yet dominant here – green swathes of grazing land still carpet the landscape, but on the gentle slopes of the Lachlan and Belubula rivers, there are now some sizeable slabs of vineyard too.

Soft, peachy Chardonnay, archetypal Aussie Chardonnay in fact, and spicy, cool-tasting Shiraz are its two main wine styles and Cowra fruit is used to flesh out many big brands. These vineyards belong to Richmond Grove, owned by Orlando-Wyndham.

There are now about 4500 hectares of vines with the majority of estates to the north and north-east of the town of Mudgee. Although unlikely to get dumped on by cyclonic storms as happens in the Hunter, rain does fall all year round (vineyards in the west have drier summers with most of their rain falling in the winter). Despite fairly warm days, a mixture of cold nights, some very high vineyards (up to 1050 metres, though most are closer to 500 metres) and fairly heavy clay soils means vintage is usually a month later than in the Hunter, with rather solid, sometimes tough-edged Cabernet and Shiraz and broad, fleshy Chardonnay and Semillon. And despite the occasional remarkable wine like Rosemount's Mountain Blue, I think Mudgee is still searching for a personality of its own.

COWRA

Cowra really is a story of Chardonnay above all else. To look at, it would seem to be just one more slab of land lucky enough to have a couple of rivers draining out of the Great Dividing Range which give enough water to raise a few crops as we head towards the harsh interior of Australia. But it's better than that.

There were some grape vines in the nineteenth century, but Cowra did nothing of note until the 1970s. The first modern wines went in on the banks of the Lachlan in 1972, but the seachange in Cowra's fortunes came in 1973 when Tony Gray, a Sydney businessman, sensing the first stirrings of the great Australian Chardonnay revolution in the Hunter Valley, thought he'd plant some himself – out at Cowra. He'd picked a good place, and a good time. From the very first crop his Cowra Chardonnay exhibited a lushness, a tropical sensuality, a sun-soaked super-ripeness that was absolutely perfect for the 1970s. This was Chardonnay in the grand manner that owed nothing to the lean European classic styles of Burgundy and everything to an 'up and at 'em' Aussie bravado that the world would become increasingly accustomed to drinking in the 1980s and 1990s.

There were a couple of very famous Chardonnays made from Cowra fruit: Petaluma, one of Australia's foremost labels, made its first Chardonnays from Cowra fruit in the late 1970s, and this gave Len Evans at Rothbury Estate the idea in 1981 to buy the Cowra Vineyard and make a series of mouth-filling Cowra Chardonnays. But most Cowra Chardonnay has been employed to add a bit of weight and character to big national brands. The character has always been the same – fat, lush, rich, unmistakably Australian, so even if we've never seen Cowra on the label, I'll bet most of us who've drunk big name Aussie Chardonnay over the years have been getting a taste of Cowra in the blend without even knowing it. As for other grapes – well, they do grow them. A fair amount of Semillon and Verdelho appear, and there's a pretty substantial harvest of Shiraz and Cabernet Sauvignon. But none of them shine like Chardonnay.

Which shows that such large, irrigated 'agro-industrial' vineyard areas can have different strengths. Riverina, further west in the Murrumbidgee River Flats, has made a speciality of Semillon and Durif – they really do taste different. South Australia's Riverland produces sensational Petit Verdot. And here in Cowra, it's Chardonnay. Given that it's fairly hot you'd expect reds to be better, but while the generally alluvial or sandy, free-draining soils give conditions of relentless reliability, reds do perform better on more compact soils in dry areas. And a majority of what rain there is falls in the growing season. Chardonnay can actually benefit from a little rain-induced rot appearing late in the season. Red varieties can't.

ORANGE

It's worth considering for just a moment how daunting the mountains of the Great Dividing Range must have seemed to early explorers, trying to find a way west from the cramped confines of Sydney. It might help if you look at a road map. If you want to head west over the mountains, there is just one main road – the Great Western Highway – heading through the Blue Mountains National Park to Lithgow, Bathurst and Orange, and there is one lesser road that clambers west to Lithgow past Richmond and beneath Mount Wilson. And that's it. You need to go 150 kilometres north past Newcastle or 150 kilometres south-west to Goulburn before you find another road braving the tangled twisted slopes of the Great Dividing Range. And visiting the wine region of Orange, you

Quick guide ◆ Gold and immigration

There are two great founding influences that I have come across again and again when researching the creation of Australia's wine regions.

First, the discovery of gold. The merest suggestion that someone has stumbled on a nugget of gold brings hordes of panting opportunists descending upon a place. Few of them would find much to get excited about, but the distant chance would keep them hard at their weary task of digging and panning and sluicing for years. And they would get thirsty. Very thirsty. Which is why wherever gold was found, land would rapidly be cleared and vines planted by those canny enough to realize that there was more gold to be had in providing thirsty miners with drink than sifting through the unforgiving earth in the pursuit of fortune.

Second, immigration from areas of Europe which knew all about vines and cultivating them. Right from the start the English colonizers seem to have wanted vines planted, and realized that they had absolutely no knowledge of how to do it. So they looked to the European mainland for their skilled workforce.

Understandably important among the groups they encouraged out to Australia are the Italians – though early Queensland was once offered a thousand Italians well versed in everything to do with vine cultivation by a bishop in northern Italy and turned them down for a band of Irishmen who may have done a good deal for the consumption of wine but did little towards establishing vineyards.

The Greeks and the Yugoslavs, the French and the Swiss have also been of considerable importance, especially in Victoria and Western Australia.

But the most influential group of all would have to be the Germans. South Australia's vast and highly influential wine industry would never have got started without them. But New South Wales, too, should be grateful for German help, ever since a guy called Schaffer from the Rhine Valley established a vineyard at Parramatta near Sydney in 1791, and by way of the Hunter Valley, Germans also established Mudgee's vineyards, just before the Gold Rush hit town.

Riverina, centred on the town of Griffith, owes its existence 100 per cent to irrigation. These vineyards belong to De Bortoli.

Quick guide ◆ Riverina stickies

One special product of the Riverina, a huge, warm inland area with vast fertile vineyards dependent on irrigation, is the remarkable botrytis-affected sweet Semillon or 'stickies' which the De Bortoli winery pioneered, with its internationally famous wine called Noble One, and others have followed. The quality usually matches that of a top Sauternes from Bordeaux.

The climate is hot and dry resulting in reliable grape-growing. The grapes are left to hang on the vine for up to two months after the normal vintage date – autumn rains and fog in April, with humid mornings and dry afternoons, mean that botrytis or noble rot forms easily and consistently on the Semillon grapes. No other part of Australia is able to work the same magic on such a regular basis.

Tasting note
The wines are deep, bronze gold in colour with intense, peach and barleysugar aromas. Very rich, sweet and increasingly complex with age. Drink between 3 and 10 years.

might first consider taking the extra time to go by train or car rather than fly. It's a fair distance – a good 200 kilometres – but it's worth it, because not only will you climb up through the imposing and intriguing Blue Mountains with their dense forest of scented eucalypts and their endless nooks and crannies defying early settlers' attempts to create a pathway through, but you'll appreciate something that came as a shock to me the first time I did it. The other side of the mountains isn't outback. It's high tableland, fertile, well watered and heavily settled, prosperous and remarkably attractive as a place to live. It just shows you can spend too long in the city.

Oh, the harsh country does start. You just head west through Parkes and Forbes and it gets tough and dry alright. But here on the western side of the Great Dividing Range, spreading right up to the Queensland border and beyond, is good country. It's high country, but it's good for grapes – some time ago Tasmanian pioneer Dr Andrew Pirie identified the 'New England' ridge, running north from Tamworth at about 1000 metres above sea level, as top vineyard country. Yet so far the only two regions over here that have made any real reputation are Orange and, 90 kilometres to the north, Mudgee.

By the way, Orange isn't a citrus producer – the town was named after one of history's numerous Prince Williams of Orange in 1828. And it certainly isn't a community that has a crying need for a wine industry. It's hale and prosperous on income from a variety of agricultural pursuits – its cherries are famous, and it produces more apples than Tasmania – and was once considered as a possible site for the national capital. And, of course, it had its own Gold Rush – in 1851 – but this one wasn't a seven-day wonder. Orange now has Australia's largest open-cut gold mine fully operational at nearby Cadia.

As for wine, its rise to prominence is recent – it was 1983 when Stephen Doyle of Bloodwood planted vines and began producing remarkable cool climate Chardonnay, Riesling, Pinot Noir and Shiraz, and 1986 when Canobolas-Smith started – somehow they manage to squeeze alcohol levels way over 14 per cent from their lush grapes. In 1988, Philip Shaw and Rosemount planted their vineyard that has produced exciting, oh so cool reds and whites. Most operations have been small scale until Cabonne initiated vast plantings led by the 505-hectare Little Boomey vineyard in the north of the region.

It is definitely a cool region. I stood outside in the brilliant February sunshine at 3pm and felt pleasantly warm, no more. This is mostly to do with height. Although some of the Boomey vineyards are around 600 metres high, most of the vineyards are between 800 and 900 metres and Habitat, on the slopes of the mighty Mount Canobolas, is at 1050 metres, one of the highest vineyards in Australia, and likely to get snow or sleet at any time of the year. There's a fair amount of rain – which is important because Orange lies at the head of tributary streams for the Murray-Darling river system and irrigation is tightly controlled. And its cool reputation is enhanced by having very few days over 30°C during the summer, as well as having frost risks in spring and autumn and, with the bulk of Mount Canobolas looming over the area you really can get a snowstorm in high summer! White wines so far have been exceptional, but Bloodwood, Rosemount, Belgravia and Canobolas-Smith have produced remarkable reds too, and Orange really is an area to check out for those who feel too many Australian wines have started to taste the same.

RIVERINA

Riverina, in the new zone of Big Rivers, centred on the town of Griffith, way down in the scorched flatlands, is the most significant wine region in New South Wales in terms of the volume of wine it produces. Previously known as the Murrumbidgee Irrigation Area, it taps into the river system of the Murrumbidgee, a tributary of the Murray, to produce well over 100,000 tonnes of grapes a year from about 5500 hectares of featureless land. It adjoins the large Sunraysia area which straddles the state of Victoria.

I remember approaching the Riverina the first time with a certain amount of trepidation. I knew it was important. I knew it produced far more wine than anywhere else in New South Wales. But what were the wines like? What was the place like? *Where* was the place? Well, much as I love taking the car or the train when I'm visiting wine regions, this time I took the plane, headed rapidly over the Blue Mountains west of Sydney and then seemed to traverse bleached, dun-coloured pasture for an eternity, until suddenly great blocks of green appeared out of the bleak nothingness. In Australia, that's always a sign of irrigation at work. And it sure was.

Riverina did OK for grazing and grain during the nineteenth century, but it wasn't until 1912 that they managed to channel the bountiful and crystal clear waters of the Murrimbidgee into irrigation schemes. That's when the vineyards started. They struggled through the inter-war years, but flourished, largely on the back of Italian immigration, after the Second World War. Riverina's first reputation had been for fortified wines – and McWilliam's still makes small amounts of outstanding fortifieds. With the Italian influence came a greater increase in table wine, but with no local markets, no well-established names, but a considerable demand for cheap red, white and fizz, Riverina, with its broad, flat vineyards, its ample irrigation water and its high temperature, low humidity, sun-soaked climate became the master of low cost, high volume, anonymous wines.

Certainly Riverina is as good at that as anywhere in Australia but quality is possible as the Westend Estate shows, and Cranswick proves with its Pioneer Old Vine releases. Some grapes really do excel here. Petit Verdot and Durif reds, maybe the Italian and Spanish varieties too. And especially Semillon whites. The dry ones are cheap and very tasty. But the sweet ones are world class (see box left). A very different world famous brand is Casella's [yellowtail] and another Riverina hit.

OTHER VINEYARD AREAS

Although Sunraysia on the Murray River does have substantial vineyards, most of the action is across the river in Victoria. Other developments in New South Wales have been more concerned with trying to locate high-quality sites, despite challenging climatic conditions. The most successful attempts at cool climate fruit so far have been in Tumbarumba, Hilltops and Orange. Tumbarumba in the Snowy Mountains, way down south near the border with Victoria, is producing some outstanding Sauvignon Blanc and Chardonnay, and Pinot Noir has great potential and Hilltops near Young has been established by McWilliam's Barwang wines (see page 92).

(see page 92)

Quick guide ◆ Irrigation

If you're in the Riverina, there really isn't a lot to catch your eye. But I'd suggest one local sight – the channels full of bubbling, lively, crystal clear water that cascade along the sides of the vineyards and citrus orchards. These are the 'in' irrigation channels and they are packed with prime, untainted water direct from the mountain springs that feed the Murrumbidgee River. These are the lifeblood for this hot, parched flatland that sits in the narrowing triangle where the Lachlan, Murrumbidgee and Murray all converge.

And this is some of the purest irrigation water in Australia, because it has never been used. If that sounds strange, ask a local to show you the 'out' channels. These are full of the runoff from what is frequently still flood irrigation. Full of mud and chemicals, these channels are sluggish and stale, their water turbid and lifeless. All this is going back into the Murrumbidgee and thence into the great Murray, which waters so much of Victoria's and South Australia's crops, and which even provides drinking water for much of South Australia.

It will be used again and again and again, perhaps at Mildura, perhaps at Renmark, perhaps even in the Clare or Barossa valleys, maybe at Langhorne Creek right down towards the mouth of the Murray, where with all the use and re-use, a mere 5 per cent of the flow survives to reach the sea, a river that began bright and optimistic in the mountains of the Great Dividing Range, and ends broken, wheezing, polluted and exhausted creeping into the Southern Ocean carrying over 5000 tonnes of salt a day, and goodness knows what else, to be dispersed among the rolling ocean waves.

These are the old-style irrigation channels that crisscross the Riverina vineyards. They are gradually being replaced by more efficient drip-irrigation systems.

Mudgee has a more reliable climate than its more famous neighbour, the Hunter Valley, just over the mountains. A lack of identity for Mudgee's wineries is still a problem as a lot of its fruit gets blended away by the big Hunter wineries, as it always has done.

HUNTER VALLEY

AUSTRALIA'S GREAT WINE ODYSSEY started on the shores of Sydney Harbour, and it didn't take long for the centre of winemaking to head up to the captivatingly beautiful but seriously challenging conditions of the Hunter Valley, about 160 kilometres north of Sydney. And my Australian wine odyssey started in a rehearsal room near the waters of Sydney Harbour and it took me about 25 minutes to locate a bottle shop, buy a bottle of Hunter Valley Burgundy – I could have had Hunter Valley Chablis or Riesling for the same price, and for all I know it would have tasted the same – i.e. not a bit like Chablis or Riesling – and ease out the cork with my thespian friends. Revelation? Well, yes, definitely.

In Europe, they didn't have wines the colour of wheat that tasted like the grapes had been brushed in your armpit after a rather enjoyable game of beach volleyball. And then splashed with custard. And squeezed with lime juice. Hunter Valley Burgundy eh? Bin, what was it? Four figures anyway. Well, French Burgundy has had a thousand years to produce a wine like this if it wanted. But who *would* want to? Yes, and as I later discovered, who but a madman would want to plant grapes in the hellhole that the Hunter, through reason of drought or flood or cyclone, turns into more vintage times than not.

And yet, and yet. All these years on, I still remember the taste of that first shocking bottle of Hunter Burgundy – made, as I later discovered, from the Semillon grape, which has never been planted anywhere near France's Burgundy. I've had a lot more examples since, I've travelled the world of wine round and round again – and I've *never* discovered any wine that tastes like Hunter Burgundy – or Semillon as perhaps I should call it.

And that's not the only shock. Hunter Chardonnay. All day-glo yellow-green and viscous as heavenly engine oil. I once described Tyrrell's VAT 47 Chardonnay as having a sensual, clinging texture that swirled lazily round the glass like a courtesan interrupted during her siesta. Not that I knew the details, of course. A friend of a friend told me. And it had a flavour that sent stars bursting over my palate, of peaches and honey, hazelnuts, woodsmoke and lime. Now we should have been calling *this* wine Hunter Burgundy because it was made from Burgundy's Chardonnay grape, yet it had nothing to do with the fascinating, if intellectual pleasures of those pale oatmeal and mineral-scented whites from the centre of France.

We think of Chardonnay as an Australian classic nowadays. But it's very recent. There was hardly any Chardonnay in Australia until the 1980s and it was only through the inspired

It all seems so idyllic here at the Broke Estate Vineyards in the Hunter Valley. The grapes ripen in the summer sun, the Brokenback mountains look on under a perfect azure sky. But the Hunter is subtropical and, more often than not, cyclonic storms will rage down the east coast and drench the vines – normally just before harvest. However, the rain, the humidity, the afternoon cloud cover and weak sea breezes all operate to reduce the impact of the heat which would otherwise make the production of quality table wine almost impossible.

SELECTED WINERIES

1. Wyndham Estate
2. Pendarves Estate
3. Tempus Two
4. Keith Tulloch
5. Rothvale
6. Bimbadgen
7. Kulkunbulla
8. Tyrrell's
9. Lowe Family Wines
10. Scarborough
11. McGuigan Cellars
12. Brokenwood
13. Tamburlaine
14. Glenguin
15. Meerea Park
16. Rothbury Estate
17. Pepper Tree
18. Evans Family
19. Lake's Folly
20. De Bortoli
21. Allandale
22. Lindemans
23. Drayton's Family Wines
24. McWilliam's Mount Pleasant
25. Petersons
26. Saddler's Creek

LOWER HUNTER VALLEY

TOTAL DISTANCE NORTH TO SOUTH 25KM

 VINEYARDS

N

BROKENBACK RANGE

MOUNT VIEW RANGE

0 km ———— 1 ———— 2
0 miles ———— 1

WHERE THE VINEYARDS ARE

The Hunter River is just visible on the map, snaking briefly in and out of the top righthand corner. It continues to run from the west, just above the top of the map. All the original important vineyards were established on these fertile river flats. You can see just one remaining example on the bend of the river at Wyndham Estate. However, from the 1860s onwards, plantings shifted south and west, towards the slopes of the Brokenback Range, an isolated ridge west of Cessnock, where rich, red, volcanic loams provide that unusual combination – high quality and high volume. Occasional outcrops of red volcanic soil in the Valley also offer these conditions, as at Lake's Folly and Evans Family vineyards. The south-facing aspect also helps by reducing exposure to the hot sun. The little Mount View Range, which lies directly to the west of Cessnock, is also particularly suited to vines.

Rosemount Estate's Roxburgh Vineyard in the Upper Hunter Valley where a great swathe of vineyards was planted in the boom time of the 1970s and which very soon established a reputation for top quality Chardonnay.

Red grapes Mainly Shiraz and Cabernet Sauvignon, with some Merlot, Pinot Noir and Malbec.

White grapes Chardonnay and Semillon are the most important grapes, but there is some decent Verdelho and Traminer.

Climate The summer heat is tempered by cloudy skies. Autumn is often wet. The Upper Hunter Valley needs irrigation.

Soil The rich, red volcanic loams and the alluvial soils near the Goulburn River in the Upper Hunter are the best. The poor-draining, heavy clay subsoils are tough going.

Aspect In the Upper Hunter vines are planted next to the Goulburn River. Lower Hunter vineyards are on the lower slopes of the Brokenback Range, or on the valley floor.

farsightedness of men like Murray Tyrrell at Tyrrell's and Bob Oatley at Rosemount that Australia's Chardonnay boom began, after they'd located some old clone Chardonnay vines in nearby Mudgee, sniffed which way the wind was blowing, and then planted Chardonnay as if their lives depended on it.

My TV career may have depended on it too. I was an actor then, not a wine writer – but I knew about wine, and the word got around, especially since I was in a wonderful outfit called the English Winetasting Team. We used to throw down challenges to any country that would listen – France, Germany, the USA and so on. We'd clash antlers – usually at their place: much more fun – and we'd win. Since I was always doing some kind of a West End show – I was playing General Peron in *Evita* when we took on the Americans – I always got my picture in the papers and become known as 'the actor who knew about wine'. So when a new BBC show called 'Food and Drink' was starting up they said – let's get that actor bloke to do a blind tasting on TV. What, really blind? With millions of people watching? Yup. So I went out in front of the cameras – and I saw this glass of day-glo yellow-green liquid. I swirled it, and the wine clung lazily, sensuously to the sides, like a courtesan… Tyrrell's VAT 47. It had to be. I knew it without even tasting. I knew the vintage, the price, where to get it. And in the space of a couple of lucky minutes on TV, with the help of a wine like no other in the world – I was suddenly a winetasting expert. And suddenly part of the BBC Food and Drink team. I'm not sure any other wine could have done it. That day-glo yellow, that viscous texture… because I had a stinking cold that day! I admit no other wine in the world tasted like Hunter Valley Chardonnay. But, that day, the important thing was no other wine looked like it either.

The Hunter specializes in wines that taste like no other. Although I think the majority of her greatest wines are white, her reds are equally famous, led by Hunter Shiraz. This gained a fearsome reputation for its 'sweaty saddle' character that came to dominate the wine with a little bit of age. For those of us who don't ride, let's just imagine a saddle soaked in the sweat of a cowboy who has spent a hundred days glued to his seat herding cattle in the sweltering outback heat. Do you get the message? Mmm. Not really a very nice drink. And frequently it wasn't. That 'sweat' was sulphides developing in the wine that had probably been made in conditions even the cowboy would scarcely have regarded as palatial. There were a few superbly meaty Shirazes, which, by the way, were also called 'Burgundy' or 'Hermitage' in the old days – but most Hunter reds were instantly recognizable for their faults rather than for their virtues.

So why is the Hunter so famous? Well, it's near Sydney. That's the main reason it was developed. And on the coastal side of New South Wales there are precious few sites that suit grapes, so you make the best of what you've got. And Sydney's proximity means you will attract some geniuses. The Hunter had just enough – people like Maurice O'Shea of McWilliam's in the old days, people like Len Evans, founder of Rothbury, and Max Lake, founder of Lake's Folly in modern times – to somehow force this capricious valley to create supreme wines. But it's not easy. Neither the soil, nor the climate are in general likely to give you an easy time.

UPPER HUNTER VALLEY

From a wine point of view, there are two principal parts to the Hunter Valley as it snakes inland from Newcastle. The Upper is in the north around Denman. Although initially planted with vines in the nineteenth century, it only achieved any prominence in the 1970s. Its most famous winery is Rosemount, whose reputation was built on whites, particularly Chardonnay. This makes sense. The soils are rich and alluvial. It's very hot, and the significant rainfall is most likely to come during the ripening period or at harvest, just when you don't want it. The white grapes can often survive, the red ones can't. Only one vineyard here has proved to be worldclass – Rosemount's Roxburgh, a weathered limestone and basalt outcrop in the middle of pastureland between Denman and Muswellbrook.

LOWER HUNTER VALLEY

So let's head south, past the open cast coal mines that make up a vital part of the local economy, to the Lower Hunter, pausing only near Broke to look at the relatively new region of Broke Fordwich that is producing very good whites – and for which I have a special fondness because I had my first ever pint of beer at the George and Dragon pub at Fordwich in Kent.

And then we're in the Lower Hunter and suddenly we're not in a world of large lonely vineyards and infrequent wineries. We're in a region of wineries at every turn in the road and, generally, rather fewer vineyards than you'd expect. The wineries are there because wine tourism is now massive business in the Lower Hunter – more people are employed in tourism than in wine. The relative lack of vineyards except on the south-west side is because the centre of the Valley is mostly infertile, pallid pug clays – pretty useless for vines – though some sandy soil runs near the creeks, and you can at least grow good whites on that. But it is the deep, fertile and reassuringly red soils all along the south-western side, up the slopes of the Brokenback, along the Marrowbone Ridge, huddled in below Mount View – along with the odd volcanic pimple like Lake's Folly – that provides the necessary conditions for quality – fertile, but well-drained soil ready for flood and ready for drought, because you'll get both in the Lower Hunter.

Water – well, there's usually not enough rain when you want it – in the winter and spring – and too much when you don't – just when the grapes are ripening and about to be harvested. Shiraz, in particular, often gets ruined. And then some years it doesn't rain at all. This is OK if you've got a good supply of irrigation water, but disastrous if you haven't. Because it *is* hot – the Hunter is one of Australia's warmest and most humid vineyard regions – and if it wasn't for regular afternoon cloud cover and some cool sea breezes sucked in up the valley, you really couldn't grow decent grapes here. But they do, and against all the odds they make some of the most remarkable white wines in the world.

Tyrrell's Vat 1
This is the wine against which all other Hunter Semillons are judged and is the only Semillon with a proven track record in the auction market. When young it shows fresh, lemony aromas and a lively palate. Over time it becomes extremely complex, with waxy texture, golden colour, honeyed straw-like aromas and it will continue to improve for a generation. A real wine lover's wine.

Bloodwood
Stephen Doyle thinks that the Orange region is ideally suited to growing Riesling. In suitable vintages he makes a luscious, late-picked dessert wine from botrytized grapes that have been left on the vine after the first frosts in early May.

BLOODWOOD

Orange
☆ *Cabernet Sauvignon, Merlot, Shiraz, Cabernet Franc, Malbec, Pinot Noir*
⧫ *Chardonnay, Riesling*

A glance at the excellent website, www.bloodwood.com.au, or a begging email asking to be put on the mailing list for Australia's most idiosyncratic winery newsletter reveals Stephen Doyle as a straight-talking vigneron who knows how to turn a phrase. With his wife, Rhonda, Doyle planted the first vineyard in Orange in 1983. Now its 8ha are (as Doyle says) home to 21,274 vines at just over 800m above sea level. For the Doyles the 20 years of hard toil have not subdued their sense of fun. The wines are good to excellent with the best being the Riesling, the two Chardonnays – the Bloodwood and the Schubert – and the Shiraz. And if you're really up for it and are in elliptical enough in a mood to cope with the inspired back label notes, the pink Big Men in Tights is a must-buy.
Best years: (Riesling) 2003, '02, '01, '98.

BROKENWOOD

Hunter Valley
☆ *Shiraz, Cabernet Sauvignon, Merlot, Pinot Noir*
⧫ *Semillon, Sauvignon Blanc, Chardonnay*

Until 1982 only reds were produced here, but since that time Brokenwood's success has allowed it to spread its wings in many

Brokenwood
The appropriately dark and brooding Graveyard Vineyard Shiraz is an exciting, intense, well-structured wine from low-yielding fruit.

directions. Winemaker Iain Riggs produces classically delicate yet ageworthy, unoaked Hunter Valley Semillon (with a Reserve version), a grassy, subtly oaked regional blend Semillon/Sauvignon Blanc and, more recently, a Verdelho sourced from Cowra vineyards in which ROTHBURY had an interest since the very early days of planting there. The appropriately dark and brooding Graveyard Shiraz is one of the top half-dozen Shirazes in Australia, but Riggs also produces other single-vineyard Shirazes, a regionally blended Shiraz and powerful Cabernet Sauvignon. Cricket Pitch reds and whites are cheerful, fruity easy-drinkers.

Riggs used to oversee the winemaking at Seville Estate in the Yarra Valley, adding supple Pinot Noir to his large repertoire, and also Chardonnay, Shiraz and Cabernet Sauvignon in a very different style. But after buying land in the high potential Beechworth area in North-East Victoria, Brokenwood has sold its Yarra interests.
Best years: (Graveyard Vineyard Shiraz) 2002, '00, '99, '98, '96, '95, '94, '93, '91, '90.

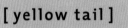

Casella
Launched in the early 2000s, [yellow tail] has been one of the fastest growing wine brands in the history of Australian wine. Although the quality is fine and the price is right, there's no doubt that artist Barbara Harkness' inspired label design has a lot to do with the brand's success.

CASELLA

Riverina
☆ *Shiraz, Merlot, Cabernet Sauvignon*
⧫ *Chardonnay, Semillon, Marsanne, Verdelho, Colombard, Caverdella*

The Casella story is that of the most remarkable export success in the history of the Australian wine industry. The family established their winery at Yenda in 1969 where three generations of Casellas are now

involved. The seeds of the current success were sown when John Casella returned to the family company in 1994 and Casella built the region's most impressive winery to process fruit from growers and 218ha of their own vineyards. At that time, they sold in bulk and under labels such as Carramar Estate, Cottlers Bridge, Yenda Vale and [yellow tail]. In 1998, Casella began exporting to the USA and in 2001 sold 500,000 cases of [yellow tail] (against initial forecasts of 25,000 cases). Sales rose to 2.2 million cases in 2002. In 2003 they exceeded 5 million cases, crushed 85,000 tonnes of grapes and expanded production yet again to meet the unprecedented demand. And the wine's not bad. It would be easy to decry the quality of such a phenomenal success story, but the wine Casella has put out under [yellow tail] is of better quality than the 'me-toos' and more traditional labels at this low price point. One thing that does worry me is that this is partially achieved by sweetening the reds as well as the whites, and, sadly, retailers are now beginning to demand higher sugar levels in their cheaper wines – a process that will mask the use of poor quality grapes and, in the long term, will harm Australia's image abroad.

DE BORTOLI

Riverina, Hunter Valley; also Victoria (Yarra Valley)
☆ *Shiraz, Merlot, Cabernet Sauvignon, Durif*
⧫ *Semillon, Chardonnay, Riesling, Sauvignon Blanc*

This large, family-owned winery owes its world reputation to one wine first made in 1982 and then largely fortuitously. What is more, the wine – a magnificent, luscious botrytis Semillon called Noble One that has even upstaged Ch. d'Yquem in some tastings – represents less than 3 per cent of De Bortoli's production, but it was of great significance, since it proved that the inland area of Riverina was not just a faceless bulk producer, but could achieve world class in this ultra-sweet 'Sauternes' style.

De Bortoli
In 2002 De Bortoli expanded into the Hunter Valley by purchasing an existing winery and vineyard in a prime location just off Broke Road. The aim is to make classic, traditional Hunter wines.

De Bortoli now also owns an extremely smart winery in the Yarra Valley (see page 114) and a new Hunter Valley operation as well as significant vineyards in Victoria's King Valley. The other Riverina wines are adequate, good value and user-friendly. Well, most of them are; one or two are exceptional. In particular they've shown that Petit Verdot and Durif are two varieties marvellously suited to Riverina. They even make a sparkling Durif, which really kicks arse. Best years: (Botrytis Semillon) 2002, '00, '99, 98, '97, '96, '95, '94, '93, '90, '88, '87, '84, '82.

Huntington Estate
One of the oldest and largest wineries in Mudgee specializes in full-flavoured red wines which are usually oak-aged for three years followed by another two in bottle before release.

HUNTINGTON ESTATE

Mudgee
❊ *Shiraz, Cabernet Sauvignon, Pinot Noir, Merlot, Grenache*
❧ *Chardonnay, Semillon*
Established by Bob and Wendy Roberts in 1969 and run by them with their winemaker daughter, Susie, Huntington Estate is one of Mudgee's best. All wines are sourced from the 42-ha estate vineyard where most of the vines are 30 years old. Apart from its Chamber Music Festival, Huntington is best known for its ageworthy reds. The Reserve Shiraz is fruit-driven, has complex meaty, chocolaty flavours and fleshy texture although recent vintages have seen more new oak. The Cabernet Sauvignon and Cabernet/Merlot, too, are robust reds full of character and complexity. Semillon is the best white: it is fragrant, vibrant and bursting with fruit flavours. Best years: (Reserve Shiraz) 2000, '99, '97, '94.

LAKE'S FOLLY

Hunter Valley
❊ *Cabernet Sauvignon, Petit Verdot, Shiraz, Merlot*
❧ *Chardonnay*
Charismatic founder Dr Max Lake sold out

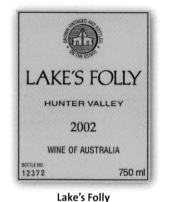

Lake's Folly
Lake's Folly is best known for its austere, long-lived Chardonnay, which is barrel-fermented and aged on its yeast lees for several months in French oak.

to Perth businessman Peter Fogarty in 2000, the vineyard has been revitalized and the wines, under Rodney Kempe, look likely to regain levels of excellence and consistency that they used to enjoy. In best years, austere Chardonnay ages slowly to a masterly antipodean yet Burgundy-like peak. Max Lake used to carry bottles around in his briefcase when he visited Europe and get wine experts to taste it blind. 'Meursault' was the word Max wanted to hear and surprisingly often, that's exactly what he heard. The red is a harder ask. Only time will tell, because they have always needed a few years in bottle to show whether or not the winemaking and the ripeness of the grapes were in harmony. Best years: (Cabernet Blend) 2003, '02, '01, '00, '99, '98, '97, '96, '93, '91, '89; (Chardonnay) 2003, '02, '01, '99, '98, '97, '96, '94.

MCGUIGAN WINES

Hunter Valley
Brian and Fay McGuigan spent 15 years building up Wyndham Estate before floating it as a public company in 1985. They launched Brian McGuigan Wines in 1992 and, over the next decade, built up sales of close to 1.2 million cases. The merger with Simeon in 2002 gives the new company nearly 6000ha under vine (second only to Southcorp), a larger grape intake than anyone except HARDYS and Southcorp, two of the four largest production facilities in the country, and makes it the fifth-largest producer of branded wine. Two years ago, it was not even ranked in the top 20 in any of these categories.

McGuigan makes wine under the budget priced Black Label and Bin Range as well as the more expensive Personal Reserve Range. The 2003 takeover of MIRANDA will enable the company to grow further. It certainly looks as though

McGuigan
Black Label Red is one of McGuigan's top-selling wines worldwide. Made from a blend of different grape varieties from all over South-East Australia, its soft, fruity flavour is a typical McGuigan crowd pleaser.

McGuigan's influence on Simeon is working. Simeon's wine quality left a lot to be desired a couple of years ago and has smartened up dramatically. But then Brian McGuigan always knew how to give the people what they wanted.
Best years: (Personal Reserve Hunter Valley Shiraz) 2000, '99, '98.

MCWILLIAM'S

Riverina
❊ *Shiraz, Cabernet Sauvignon, Merlot*
❧ *Chardonnay, Semillon, Colombard, Riesling*
It's difficult to generalize about McWilliam's as a company because it does so many things, generally at a high level of quality. What is undeniable, however, is that McWilliam's is still family owned, a famous old name whose fortunes are still directed by various family members when so many

McWilliam's Hanwood
The Hanwood range of wines, made in the Riverina region, proves that high-volume 'brands' can deliver good flavours at a fair price. They're all good – a nice citrus Verdelho and serious reds from Merlot, Cabernet and Shiraz.

of the other historical wine companies of Australia are merely anonymous parts of some vast corporation. Long may they remain independent. They are based at Yenda in the Riverina, a hot fertile region that still provides the bulk of the fruit for their wines, and which still grows great fortifieds. Last time I was there I tasted a 1962 Port and an ancient Liqueur Muscat which were quite superb. They're still making these styles. What's changed is the table wine emphasis. They have vineyards at Lillydale in Victoria's cool climate Yarra Valley. They have bought and greatly

The vast Barwang Estate in the cool climate Hilltops region now belongs to McWilliam's. There are over 100 hectares of vines which are planted along the ridges and contours to protect them from the spring frosts. It is warm enough here for most of the New South Wales varieties, but the higher altitude and the well-drained soils encourage a slow, regular ripening season with consequently intensified fruit flavours. Initially thought of as a sparkling wine region that wouldn't ever really ripen the grapes, the estate now produces excellent Chardonnay and intense, finely focused Shiraz and Cabernet.

expanded BRAND'S OF COONAWARRA in South Australia, a winery with great potential which had been underachieving for a generation and they pioneered the super cool but high quality Hilltops area of New South Wales on their Barwang Estate. Their most famous vineyards are in the Hunter Valley at MOUNT PLEASANT (see right).

In 2002 McWilliam's formed a joint venture with California's giant E & J Gallo winery for the Hanwood Estate brand. This is a commendable effort to take on the big boys like ORLANDO and LINDEMANS with their expensively promoted brands. But let's hope it stops at a joint venture and McWilliam's don't get swallowed. As one of Australia's great family firms, whose quality has kept on improving over the last decade, they're too good to lose.
Best years: (Elizabeth Semillon) 2001, '00, '99, '97, '95, '94, '93, '91, '89, '86, '83, '82, '81, '79.

MIRANDA
Riverina
❄ *Cabernet Sauvignon, Merlot, Shiraz, Petit Verdot, Durif*
❄ *Semillon, Chardonnay, Colombard, Verdelho*
This family company, established in Griffith in 1939, is one of Australia's largest wine

Miranda
This luscious botrytized Semillon comes from the Riverina, an area becoming increasingly known for this Sauternes-style of wine. No other area of Australia is able to make botrytized wines with such success.

producers – ranked eighth in 2003 for sales of branded wine. It was originally a bulk winemaker but saw the need to diversify before most of the other bulk producers and moved into the premium area with the purchase of the Barossa's Rovalley Estate in 1992. A third winery and vineyards in the King Valley was established in 1998 for their High Country label and this began to break the stranglehold BROWN BROTHERS had on this increasingly high quality King Valley fruit – to the eventual benefit of everybody! A little bit

of competition never did any harm. Most of the wines from the Riverina (under the Mirrool Creek, Firefly and Somerton labels) are budget priced but they've always tasted pretty decent: the exception is the flagship, Miranda Golden Botrytis Semillon, an unctuous, lush sticky. There has been a substantial improvement in quality in recent years. The company was taken over by McGuigan in 2003 but will continue to be run as a separate entity with the Miranda family very much involved.

Best years: (Family Reserve Old Vine Shiraz) 2002, '01, '98, '96.

MOUNT PLEASANT

Hunter Valley

❉ Shiraz, Merlot, Pinot Noir, Tyrian

❋ Semillon, Chardonnay, Verdelho

It's a slugging match between Mount Pleasant (the Hunter arm of McWilliam's) and Tyrrell's for the title of top producer of that uniquely Australian white: Hunter Semillon. Supporting the Mount Pleasant case are the fine, delicate, lemondrop citrus intensity of the single-vineyard Lovedale Semillon – released with six years of bottle age – and the large volume but absolutely classic Elizabeth Semillon (released at four years), a bigger, richer, more powerful, toast and honey-flavoured marvel. There's also a museum-release Elizabeth with about nine years' bottle age. Given that these Semillons are world classics, they are extremely attractively priced.

The reds, too, have heaps of regional character, especially the three Shirazes: Old Paddock & Old Hill, Rosehill and the Maurice O'Shea. But you don't always want too much regional character in a Hunter red – it can get a bit too tarry and horsey. Most of these Mount Pleasant reds stay just about on the right side of the fence.

Best years: (Lovedale Semillon) 2000, '98, '97, '96, '95, '86, '84.

McWilliam's Mount Pleasant
Mount Pleasant Elizabeth and Lovedale are classic, bottle-aged Semillons from the Lower Hunter Valley. Best years show a wonderful, warm, toasty richness of flavour and aroma with superb texture and a very long finish.

Poet's Corner
Poet's Corner, named after the local bush balladeer, Henry Lawson, is one of the names used by Orlando-Wyndham for their Mudgee wines. This one is a blend you'd only find in Australia – Bordeaux and Burgundy grapes mixed together – and it works.

POET'S CORNER

Mudgee

❉ Shiraz, Cabernet Sauvignon, Sangiovese, Barbera, Merlot

❋ Chardonnay, Semillon, Sauvignon Blanc

Poet's Corner is the reincarnation of two of Mudgee's most historic wineries: Craigmoor (established 1858) which is now the venue for the cellar door and Montrose (established in 1974) where the modern winery is situated. New owners, Orlando-Wyndham established the brand in 1989 as Montrose could not be sold on the export market – because of the clash with the Bordeaux château of the same name.

There are three labels: Poet's Corner, Henry Lawson and Montrose. Under the Montrose label is the flagship, Black Shiraz, as well as two interesting examples of Italian varietals in Australia – the Sangiovese and the Barbera. These were planted by winemaker Carlo Corino in the 1970s and made into blends until 1997. Great value for money at all price points. However, Poet's Corner is also used as a 'brand' label for South Eastern Australia – i.e. the fruit can come from virtually anywhere. Add to that the fact that the wineries have been undergoing a painful modernization, and Poet's Corner is a bit of a curate's egg – good in parts.

Best years: (Montrose Black Shiraz) 2002, '99, '98, '97, '96.

ROSEMOUNT ESTATE

Hunter Valley, Mudgee; also South Australia (Coonawarra, McLaren Vale, Adelaide Hills)

❉ Shiraz, Cabernet Sauvignon, Merlot, Pinot Noir

❋ Chardonnay, Semillon, Sauvignon Blanc, Riesling

Rosemount first challenged Australia, and then took on the world, with a small but very talented winemaking and management team, and with success following success. Its vineyard holdings now include prime land in the Upper Hunter Valley and Mudgee and in South Australia, while its grape-purchasing tentacles extend into every worthwhile nook and cranny of South Eastern Australia.

All of this has meant a proliferation of labels and for a time seemed to defy the usual logic of increasing demand meaning declining quality by maintaining their character and individuality. In 2001 the business merged with Southcorp and since then ambitious plans for rapid expansion have led to the inevitable loss of personality in the wines and a fear that the vast Rosemount/Southcorp giant has become too big for anybody's good. Too big, but also too impersonal. Rosemount had always thrived on the personalities of the founder, Bob Oatley, the CEO, Chris Hancock and the chief winemaker, Philip Shaw. Until the Southcorp mega merger you felt you could still taste the hopes and aspirations and talents of these men in the wines. And then it all went kaput.

Rosemount Estate – and what's the word 'Estate' doing on the label: most of the wines are now blends from here, there and everywhere – became a byword of heavily promoted, sugared-up blandness. Wines that had revolutionized the world's view of high quality being compatible with commercial success and immediate drinkability now looked leaden and forgettable against the opposition. Well, I do detect a change for the better. For instance the Rosemount Diamond Cabernets henceforth will be made with 80% of the fruit coming from quality regions rather than the vast agro-industrial

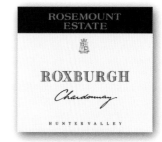

Rosemount Estate
Rosemount's flagship Roxburgh Chardonnay is very rich and powerful and redefined the world's view of this grape variety during the 1980s. It is still a fine wine, but has struggled to express itself in a more restrained way when it's been used to carry its all before it by sheer force of personality.

spreads along the Murray and Murrumbidgee rivers that fuelled their growth. Let's see. A bit less sugar would be welcome, too. In the meantime Roxburgh Chardonnay (Hunter), Mountain Blue and Hill of Gold (Mudgee), Balmoral Syrah (McLaren Vale), and Show Reserve Cabernet Sauvignon (Coonawarra) have more responsibility than ever to uphold the reputation of the company.

Best years: (Balmoral Syrah) 2002, '01, '00, '98, '97, '96, '94, '92, '91, '90.

The Rothbury Estate
The Rothbury Estate series of wines, made from specified parcels of vines in the Hunter, Cowra, Mudgee and Orange, is named after the chief winemaker, Neil McGuigan.

THE ROTHBURY ESTATE

Hunter Valley
❉ *Shiraz, Cabernet Sauvignon, Merlot, Pinot Noir*
❊ *Chardonnay, Verdelho, Semillon, Sauvignon Blanc*

The king is dead, and neither queen, prince or princess to follow him. Following its acrimonious acquisition by Beringer Blass, the wine division of Fosters, Len Evans has left Rothbury for good, but is busily creating a new, multi-faceted empire in the Hunter Valley (see TOWER ESTATE). Rothbury meanwhile is making some effort to redefine and reposition itself and its products, with modest success. The imposing winery is still there, and the Fosters Group now owns one of the largest direct mail wine businesses in the world, into which the Rothbury Estate Society direct mail club naturally fits. Soulless stuff, perhaps, but properly handled, keeps shareholders happy.

TOWER ESTATE

Hunter Valley
❉ *Pinot Noir, Merlot, Shiraz, Cabernet Sauvignon*
❊ *Semillon, Verdelho, Sauvignon Blanc, Riesling, Chardonnay*

Len Evans is a flamboyant, irrepressible Welshman-cum-Australian who virtually

Tower Estate
Tower Estate concentrates on producing small amounts of premium classically styled wines from grapes sourced from South Australia as well as from the Hunter.

created the Australian wine boom of the 1960s and '70s single-handed. Or that's what he says. He was certainly Australia's best known wine man and for many years ran The ROTHBURY ESTATE in the Hunter Valley with tremendous verve and a self belief that you could only gasp at and admire.

His latest venture, in partnership with a syndicate that includes British superchef Rick Stein, focuses on sourcing top-notch grapes from their ideal regions. So, there is powerful, stylish Coonawarra Cabernet, top-flight Barossa Shiraz, fine floral Clare Riesling, fruity Adelaide Hills Sauvignon Blanc and Chardonnay and classic Semillon, Shiraz, Verdelho and Chardonnay from the Hunter Valley. Volume is limited to 1000 cases per wine. Len, old chum, these wines had better be good.

TRENTHAM ESTATE

Murray Darling
❉ *Shiraz, Merlot, Cabernet Sauvignon, Petit Verdot, Nebbiolo, Ruby Cabernet, Pinot Noir*

Trentham
Tropical fruit-flavoured Chardonnay is one of a wide range of good-value varietal wines from this small family winery in the Murray River Valley.

❊ *Sauvignon Blanc, Chardonnay, Viognier, Semillon, Pinot Gris, Taminga*

Even though the Murphy family's winery produces 65,000 cases of wine each year, it is tiny by comparison with the mega wineries in the surrounding area. Almost all of the wine produced in the Murray Darling finds its way into anonymous large company blends and so Trentham Estate is one of the few who produce wines from the region.

At this stage, they're a bit coy: it would be great to see their labelling proudly proclaiming the wine's regional status. As it is, all of the Trentham wines are consistently good to very good and all represent excellent value for money. Aromatic, fruity Viognier, savoury, tarry Nebbiolo, earthy, jammy Petit Verdot all impress. In the best years, lush yet fine Noble Taminga is a delicious sticky.

Keith Tulloch
The Semillon, made from both early picked and fully ripe grapes, and part barrel-fermented and part whole bunch pressed, is one of the best in the Hunter Valley but sadly only a few hundred cases are made each year.

KEITH TULLOCH

Hunter Valley
❉ *Shiraz, Merlot, Cabernet*
❊ *Semillon, Chardonnay*

The Tullochs have been one of the Hunter's most important families for more than a century. Keith Tulloch worked as a winemaker for LINDEMANS and ROTHBURY, before establishing his own 3000-case boutique winery in 1997.

Since then, painstaking attention to detail and intellectual rigour have enabled him to produce highly individual wines of the finest quality from unirrigated, old-vine vineyards that he leases or contracts in the Pokolbin area. The complex, balanced Semillon has intense, lemon rind flavours with bracing acidity but just a touch of barrel fermentation for complexity and the Chardonnay has good, vaguely Burgundian savoury nuttiness. The Kestler Shiraz with a splash of Viognier (influenced, says Tulloch, by the vintage he spent with Jaboulet in France's Rhône Valley) is richly textured and deeply flavoured.

Best years: (Semillon) 2003, '02, '00.

Tyrrell's Wines
Tyrrell's top wines, the Winemaker's Selection Range, follow a vat numbering system, traditionally representing the cask in which the wine was either fermented or aged.

TYRRELL'S

Hunter Valley

🍷 *Shiraz, Pinot Noir, Cabernet Sauvignon*
🍷 *Semillon, Chardonnay, Verdelho, Sauvignon Blanc*

Tyrrell's has changed out of all recognition since the first time I bowled up as a cub reporter and asked the famously curmudgeonly Murray Tyrrell, 'What's your most successful wine?'. 'Blackberry nip,' he growled before lurching off to do something more important than talk to me. That gruff exterior masked one of the great innovative characters of the Hunter Valley, the man who introduced Chardonnay to the valley – his 1971 Vat 47 revolutionized attitudes to Chardonnay with its magnificent golden waxy depth – whose Pinot Noir had prime ministers of Australia on their knees begging for a case, and whose Shiraz and Semillon were – and still are – some of Australia's classics.

Murray's gone now – though happily the higgledy piggledy old winery building is still there – but son Bruce has transformed a great classic wine company into a highly successful modern winery, offloading the 'Long Flat' brand but keeping up the big-volume 'Old Winery' label, adding vineyards in South Australia (McLaren Vale and Limestone Coast) and Victoria (Heathcote) and yet maintaining the standard of the great old, numbered Vat Tyrrell classics of Semillon, Chardonnay and Shiraz. It's not often one can unequivocally applaud modernization – too often the character that made a place famous in the first place gets diluted or discarded in the name of efficiency or rationalization or goodness knows what.

But at Tyrrell's, Bruce seems to have preserved everything that was good – if anything improving the quality of the great Hunter wines, yet creating several lower cost Hunter wines that are delicious and affordable – as well as becoming a quality leader in new areas like Heathcote. He even seems willing to take on some of Murray's role as 'The Mouth of the Hunter', though in a less curmudgeonly and more urbane style.

My only complaint is that last time I visited I couldn't get anyone to give me any blackberry nip.
Best wines: (Vat 1 Semillon) 2003, '02, '01, '00, '99, '98, '97, '96, '95, '94, '93, '92, '91, '90, '89, '87, '86, '77, '76, '75; (Vat 47 Chardonnay) 2003, '02, '01, '00, '99, '98, '97, '96, '95, '94, '91, '89.

WESTEND ESTATE

Riverina

🍷 *Shiraz, Cabernet Sauvignon, Merlot, Durif, Petit Verdot*
🍷 *Semillon, Chardonnay, Sauvignon Blanc, Trebbiano*

There are other Australian winery owners who are teetotal but Bill Calabria must be the only winemaker who is unable to drink, except for tasting and spitting at the time of making the wine: in his case, because of a rare allergy to the acid in wine.

The family winery was established by Calabria's parents in 1945 and renamed Westend in 1974 when Bill took over. The 3 Bridges label, launched in the mid-1990s, is restricted to wines which have won at least one gold medal in a wine show. It is available in relatively small volumes and has helped lift the status of the region. About 120,000 cases are released under the 3 Bridges and the budget-priced Richland and Outback labels with the rest of the Westend production being sold off in bulk. All the wines represent excellent value for money. The whites are remarkably good considering the hot vineyard conditions, but the reds are genuinely exciting with the Durif in particular showing real class. In common with other Riverina producers he also makes excellent sweet botrytis Semillon.
Best years: (3 Bridges Botrytis Semillon) 2002, '99.

Westend
This is another successful example of luscious sweet wine from the Riverina. The Semillon grapes are left on the vine for two months or so after the normal harvest and then if the weather conditions are favourable botrytis attacks the grapes.

Quick guide ◆ Best producers

Cowra Charles Sturt University, Cowra Estate, Hamiltons Bluff, Richmond Grove, Rothbury, Windowrie.

Hilltops Demondrille, Grove Estate, McWilliam's Barwang, Woodonga Hill.

Lower Hunter Valley Allandale, Brokenwood, De Bortoli, De Iuliis, Hope Estate, Kulkunbulla, Lake's Folly, Lowe Family, Margan Family, McWilliam's Mount Pleasant, Meerea Park, Pendarves, Poole's Rock, Rothbury, Scarborough, Andrew Thomas, Tower, Keith Tulloch, Tyrrell's.

Mudgee Farmer's Daughter, Andrew Harris, Huntington Estate, Miramar, Orlando/Poet's Corner, Rosemount, Thistle Hill.

Murray Darling Trentham Estate.

Orange Belgravia, Bloodwood, Brangayne of Orange, Canobolas-Smith, Cumulus Wines, Highland Heritage Estate, Indigo Ridge, Logan, Rosemount, Philip Shaw Wines.

Riverina Beelgara, Casella, Cranswick Estate, De Bortoli, Gramp's, Lillypilly, McWilliam's, Miranda, Riverina Estate, Westend.

Upper Hunter Valley Rosemount.

SPOTLIGHT ON
Canberra District

These grapes are being picked on Hardys' vast new Kamberra development. If you think they still look green in their buckets – I'd agree with you. But that's what Hardys want from Kamberra – the fresh, green liveliness of cool climate fruit.

I WONDER WHETHER CANBERRA DISTRICT should change its name. The trouble is, Canberra and the Australian Capital Territory were created out of nothing during the 1920s, halfway between Sydney and Melbourne as a compromise capital when it was clear that neither of those two great cities would let the other be capital of the new Australian Federation of States. That mutual antipathy exists, albeit muted, to this day – and so, stuck between these two is poor old Canberra – home of politicians, bureaucrats, state academics – and tax gatherers. But Canberra wine? Except in the capital itself and in the very local surrounding area, the wine is not at all easy to find. I'd tasted the odd sample and thought some of the whites, particularly Riesling, were rather good in a very cool climate way, but I didn't look at Canberra as a 'must visit' region until I'd been tasting wine in South Africa in 1996. It was a South Africa versus Australia tasting test match that Australia won without breaking sweat. And the Shiraz class – which included giants like Grange and Henschke Hill of Grace and various Barossa titans – was won by a wine called Clonakilla. It was fabulously scented, full of ripe damson fruit, yet cool and peppery at the same time. I'd never had an Aussie Shiraz like it. And it came from Canberra. It was time to change 'might visit' in my diary, to 'must visit'.

Several things quickly became apparent. The wine region *is* dominated by the capital, indeed many of the winery people are refugees from government life – and their independent, rebellious view on life makes their company and their wines an excellent antidote to taxes. Second, it *is* small scale. With one stark exception. The giant Hardy Wine Company has built the region's largest winery – called Kamberra – and a state of the art visitor centre just to the north of the city by the racecourse, and have planted 270 hectares of vines – pretty much doubling Canberra's vineyard area at a stroke. This was a shrewd move by both the local government and Hardys. Hardys liked the cool climate character of Canberra fruit and wanted to ensure supplies. The government wanted to promote its wines elsewhere in Australia and abroad but had no critical mass to allow them to do so. And Hardys did like the idea of having their winery tied in with the region's visitor centre and 400,000 willing consumers on their doorstep. So Hardys end up with a massive vineyard and Canberra at last has a producer big enough to progress past cellar door sales and a few local restaurants. Outside the city – on the New South Wales border mostly – are spread about 150 growers and 30 wineries, for whom 8 hectares of vines is regarded as a fair size.

But is it a cool area? Parts of it certainly are. If you head north-east towards Lake George, perched on high cliffs at 860 metres, you'll find Lark Hill, where the grapes sometimes ripen even more slowly than in Tasmania, but that's why those Rieslings can be so good. Yet just a few kilometres north, huddled under the lee of the escarpment on Lake George's western banks, the protection and lower altitude already allows fine Chardonnay and Pinot Noir to flourish. However, the main vineyard area is among the paddocks and the grazing meadows around Murrumbateman. That's where Clonakilla grows lovely Shiraz and Viognier, but it's also where Helm, Brindabella Hills, Doonkuna and others make tangy Riesling; good Bordeaux reds; Shiraz and serious fizz. Some patches are cool. Some are obviously as warm as Bordeaux or the Rhône Valley in France. And that's just *so* Australian. And have all the good vineyard sites been discovered yet? I doubt it. Take the 'treeless plain', for example. This is a considerable spread of land north of Murrumbateman towards Yass, a few volcanic plugs – but treeless! It's the soil – deep, orange red, clay-rich soil. The irrepressible Ken Helm, one of the District's pioneers, reckons that if Canberra would send up some of its 'grey' waste water for irrigation, this could produce some of the best wine in Canberra. But with evaporation twice as high as rainfall in Canberra, it'll never be planted without government action to provide irrigation. And if the 'treeless plain' doesn't turn you on – what about around Hall just north of Canberra? Out of the wind, a 'heat sink', water available, warm climate, maybe, just down the road from cool? And *that* is so Australian.

CLONAKILLA

❄ *Shiraz, Cabernet Sauvignon, Pinot Noir*
❋ *Viognier, Riesling, Chardonnay*

It has been primarily the stellar quality of the Shiraz Viognier that has brought Clonakilla to prominence. The vineyard was established by CSIRO scientist, Dr John Kirk, in 1971 and remains in the family. He made the Canberra region's first commercial wines (a Riesling and Cabernet Shiraz) in 1976. The red blend was made until 1990 when it was decided to bottle two varietal wines. The success of the 1990 Shiraz led to more general recognition of the variety's potential in the region.

John Kirk's fourth son, Tim, became increasingly involved in the winery (he took over as winemaker in 1996) and learnt much from a trip to the Rhône in 1991. Viognier was added to the Shiraz wine from 1992, just as is traditionally done in the Côte-Rôtie in the northern Rhône; further experimentation has evolved the style to the point where the Shiraz Viognier is recognized as one of the country's best

Clonakilla
Clonakilla, a small family winery that has achieved international fame, makes increasingly sublime Shiraz (with a dollop of Viognier in the blend). The graphics on the label are a tribute to the Kirk family's Irish roots.

Shirazes. The Riesling and Viognier are also impressive and Tim is convinced that Canberra is going to be Australia's top region for Viognier.

Best years: (Shiraz Viognier) 2002, '01, '00, '99, '98, '97, '95.

Vineyards at Brindabella Hills 10km north of Canberra. A cool dry climate and high altitude may sound good but can pose problems with frost damage, flowering and lack of ripeness for later ripening varieties.

Quick guide ◆ Best producers

WINES TO TRY
Clonakilla Shiraz Viognier, Riesling, Viognier
Brindabella Hills Cabernet
Doonkuna Estate Chardonnay, Cian sparkler
Helm Wines Riesling, especially Late-Harvest
Kamberra Riesling, Shiraz
Lark Hill Pinot Noir; Riesling; Shiraz
Madew Riesling, Chardonnay, Pinot Noir
Best producers Brindabella Hills, Clonakilla, Doonkuna, Helm, Kamberra (Hardys), Lake George, Lark Hill, Madew.

VICTORIA

IN 1890 VICTORIA'S VINEYARDS produced well over half of Australia's wine, yet by 1960 there were only four wineries in the state outside North-East Victoria. Today, there are more than 521 licensed winemakers. From being on its knees, Victoria is now bursting with new wineries and new regions.

Most of Victoria's wine regions are grouped within a radius of 200 kilometres from Melbourne. The outposts are the distinctly chilly Henty near Portland in the far west, the bountifully mass-producing Murray Darling extending around Mildura in the north-west corner, and Rutherglen and Beechworth in the north-east. In between, virtually every kind of wine style and climate is covered, though the majority of Victoria's most famous wines are from relatively small wineries, in relatively cool areas.

The small wineries are primarily red wine producers, though there is exciting Chardonnay, Sauvignon Blanc, Riesling and Gewurztraminer, and even Marsanne in small quantities. Red wine production, mainly Shiraz and Cabernet Sauvignon, is focused on the Grampians-Pyrenees-Bendigo-Heathcote-Goulburn Valley belt of Central Victoria. Nearer Melbourne, Yarra Valley, Mornington and Geelong are all cool regions, with a maritime climate. Here Chardonnay, Pinot Noir and the Cabernet family are the centre of attention. The rambling Gippsland zone is cool but with very dry growing conditions. Cooler still is the Strathbogie Ranges region where grapes can actually struggle to ripen. The North-East, centred on Rutherglen and Glenrowan, produces Australia's distinctive fortified Muscats and Tokays but these days the region's most interesting table wines are more likely to be those from the slopes of the King and Alpine Valleys regions.

It really is magic up here as this picture suggests. Brown Brothers' Whitlands Vineyard was developed at an altitude of 765 metres way up in the Great Dividing Range to provide cool climate fruit, and it's done that triumphantly. But when I visit, I just want to sit under a tree and gaze at the captivating blue mountains yonder until the sun goes down.

SPOTLIGHT ON
Victoria

The Mornington Peninsula is a super-trendy, fast-growing region near Melbourne where many of the 50 or so small wineries make high quality wine but in minute quantities. Many of the original vineyards were established up in the hills above Dromana and over Red Hill towards the towns of Shoreham and Flinders on Western Port Bay. Traditionally these sites have struggled to ripen their fruit in cooler years, but have survived on reputation. Now even the well-established, higher-altitude wineries realize they must go to lower sites if they are to secure supplies of consistently ripe fruit, and areas around the Moorooduc Flats and Devilbend Reservoir are increasingly favoured.

I USED TO BE A JUDGE for the Victorian Wine Export Awards. This was during the 1980s when the vast volumes of wines now exported from Australia were not even a dream. But the Victorian Government decided that in view of sheer variety, sheer brilliance of flavours, they could beat the other states hands down. And in those days, when it came to their delicate, silky Pinot Noirs, their sensuous Shirazes and eucalyptus-scented Cabernets, their savoury, satisfying Chardonnays and gorgeous head-spinning fortified Muscats and Tokays – I suspect they could. The trouble was, there was often just a single outstanding performer showing the thrilling potential of an area, and then there might be a gap of 100 kilometres or more before the next vineyard. And the winery whose wines so excited the panel of judges was quite likely to say – actually, we haven't made enough for export this vintage – try again next year.

Most of the vineyards were remnants of the days when Victoria had been Australia's leading vineyard state with the largest area under vine and indeed, Victoria was named 'John Bull's Vineyard' in honour of its exports to Britain. Early settlement, European immigration, and then, of course, the Gold Rush of the 1850s gave Victoria pride of place in wine production. Wines were made that were judged world class in European competitions. But it wasn't to last. So let's look at a little of the rollercoaster history of Victoria's wine.

FIRST PLANTINGS

The vine arrived in 1834 from Tasmania, of all places. Melbourne itself, at the north of Port Phillip Bay, proved ideally suited to vine-growing: not too hot, with an attractive maritime climate easing the grape towards ripeness. But the city's expansion was, obviously, always going to push out the vineyards, and the two areas that thrived were out of town at Geelong and the Yarra Valley.

Geelong is to the west of Port Phillip Bay, and is challenging vineyard land. The best sites are on outcrops of deep, crumbly, black volcanic soil, and are water-retentive but not prone to waterlogging. Although it isn't that wet, it's rarely that hot either and the cold Antarctic gales haven't crossed any landmass to reduce their chilly force when they hit Geelong. The reason Geelong did well – by 1861 it was the most important vineyard area in the state – was largely due to the settlement of Swiss vignerons who knew how to coax good flavour out of cool surroundings. They did the same in the Yarra Valley and I look at that in more depth later (see page 108).

The next wave of vineyards was established not because the land was thought suitable, but because gold was discovered there in 1851 (see box page 103). Eventually the Gold

Quick guide ◆ Victoria

Location In the search for cool climates most of Victoria's modern wine regions are tucked in the foothills of the Great Dividing Range or down on the windy coast. In arid North-West Victoria the great Murray River provides irrigation for the vast vineyards of Murray Darling and Swan Hill.

Grapes Shiraz and Cabernet Sauvignon are the main varieties and come in varying styles (Central Victoria produces dense and peppery Shiraz and the best mint-and-eucalyptus Cabernet), followed some way behind by Merlot and elegant and perfumed Pinot Noir, especially from the Yarra and other cool climate regions. There are tiny plantings of Cabernet Franc and Sangiovese and even a few hectares of Tempranillo. The main quality variety is Chardonnay (the finest examples come from the cool climate regions), followed by Muscat Gordo Blanco, Colombard, Sauvignon Blanc, Semillon and Riesling. There are small amounts of Chenin Blanc, Verdelho, Viognier, Marsanne and for the fortified wines Muscadelle (known locally as Tokay) and Muscat Blanc à Petits Grains (better known as Brown Muscat in Australia).

Climate This ranges from cool climate regions down on the coast, through the hot, dry regions north of Melbourne where the altitude moderates the heat, to the north-east and north-west of the state where conditions are even hotter and drier, ideal for producing fortified wines.

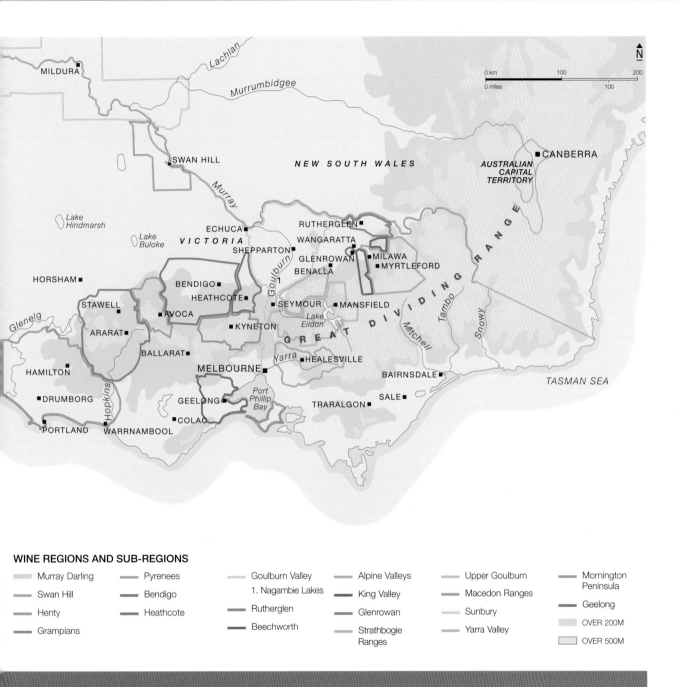

WINE REGIONS AND SUB-REGIONS

- Murray Darling
- Swan Hill
- Henty
- Grampians
- Pyrenees
- Bendigo
- Heathcote
- Goulburn Valley
  1. Nagambie Lakes
- Rutherglen
- Beechworth
- Alpine Valleys
- King Valley
- Glenrowan
- Strathbogie Ranges
- Upper Goulburn
- Macedon Ranges
- Sunbury
- Yarra Valley
- Mornington Peninsula
- Geelong
- OVER 200M
- OVER 500M

Soil There is red loam in the north, quartzose alluvial soils in the Goulburn Valley and crumbly black volcanic soil at Geelong.

Aspect Steep, sloping, north-facing vineyards in cool climate areas allow extended ripening. Most of the interior is pretty flat and featureless.

Do regions matter? There are various small cool climate regions scattered around Melbourne (Mornington Peninsula and Geelong), but the climate gets warmer as you head north and the wines are correspondingly richer and beefier in the Goulburn Valley and Bendigo.

Do vintages matter? Victoria's wine regions have such different climates that what is good in the north-east may not be good at all in the Yarra Valley.

Organization Victoria has far more boutique wineries than any other state and over half have a cellar door facility. Many are very small but the sheer number creates a hugely diverse and exciting wine industry.

A few facts 38,284ha of vineyards, 24 per cent of Australia's total plantings; 15 per cent of total production; 521 wineries. Interesting fact: with almost the same area of vineyards as New South Wales, Victoria produces less than half as much wine.

Rush died, and with it most, though not all, of the vines. But far worse was to come. Phylloxera arrived in Australia via Geelong in 1875. Geelong's vines were uprooted by government order, and so were those of Bendigo, but to no avail. Phylloxera spread through most of Victoria and by 1910 the state that was once the jewel in Australia's winemaking crown had seen her wine industry reduced to a withered rump centred on Glenrowan and Rutherglen in North-East Victoria, the Murray vineyards (whose founders, the Chaffey brothers, were paupered by the combination of the Great Bank Crash of 1893 and the Murray River inexplicably drying up) – plus a few vines at the Tahbilk winery in the Goulburn Valley and at Great Western.

A COOL CLIMATE?

Australian vineyards were always established initially near the local main city, and Melbourne was no exception. All the vineyard areas around Melbourne are cool, and they have enjoyed mixed fortunes. To be honest, after a good half century when southern Victoria had virtually no vines, it wasn't until the 1980s that the modern wine revival really got going. Geelong however, Victoria's most important vineyard area way back in the 1860s, was revived by Idyll Vineyard in 1966. Yet Geelong is no easier a place to grow vines than it was 150 years ago.

Spring frosts, too much wind, hail, and a shortage of rain all make life tough. One or two vineyards have made a name for themselves, like Bannockburn and Scotchman's Hill and there is a trickle of serious Pinot Noir, dark-hearted Shiraz and attractive whites, but the region has not really shared in the New Wave success of Victorian Wines.

The other two main areas close to Melbourne have not only shared in the success; they've led it. Yarra Valley, to the north-east (I look at it in more detail on page 108), has established itself as an international player. Mornington Peninsula, to the south-east, hasn't. The chief reason is – it's really nice down there. Well, think about it. You've got Melbourne, a prosperous city of over 3 million people – and its nearest area of great

Mount Langi Ghiran's vineyards near Ararat in the Grampians region are located in a spectacular setting at an altitude of 450 metres at the base of the Mount Langi Ghiran. The growing season is long with warm days and cool nights and picking can be as late as June. Slow berry development produces wines with intense fruit flavours, one of Mount Langi's hallmarks. Given the quality, one might ask – why aren't there more vineyards here? Well, it is very remote, and things like water supply are really tough to secure. I'd love to see more wines with a character like Langi Ghiran's but I doubt they'll ever be thick on the ground.

beaches and gentle hillsides and tranquillity is – the Mornington Peninsula, running south of the city along the shores of Port Phillip Bay. Vines and holiday homes? So far, they've managed both, but the vineyards are mostly fairly small – with the exception of the new Dromana development near Moorooduc – and they really only manage to prosper by having a large, well-heeled, and tolerably thirsty recreational community on their doorstep. Though there were vineyards here in the nineteenth century, like the rest of southern Victoria's vines they faded away, and current vineyards date from 1971 at Elgee Park – still a source of tasty Chardonnay and Riesling.

This is pretty cool country – cooler by a degree or two even than Geelong – but its maritime position on the Bay minimizes frost risk. Most of the traditional names established their vineyards on hilly sites – Red Hill in particular, has lots of vines – but the newer outfits realize it's far too cold up there to ripen a crop every year, and recent developments are increasingly on the undulating flatlands around Moorooduc. There are now about 180 vineyards – usually in blocks of less than 8 hectares or so – and the whites, particularly the Chardonnays, have a real intensity. So long as the sun shines, so do the Pinot Noirs. But to really understand why people planted Mornington Peninsula you need to sit in the evening sun at somewhere like Stonier, gazing out past the vineyards, to the bright blue water at the mouth of Western Port Bay and watch the sailboats gallantly dodging the white horses of waves breaking on the reef. And you sip a little more Chardonnay. And then it makes sense.

There are further cool climate vineyards whose fruit intensity is remarkable in the Henty region near Portland in the south-west and at Gippsland in the south-east. Sunbury, a flat to undulating region barely past the airport, is cold and windy but has produced some startling Shiraz. Macedon, just further north but much hillier, combines fine sparkling wine with stunning lean but concentrated reds and whites.

THE GOLDFIELDS

There's an arc of vineyard land running through Central Victoria from Ballarat, west of Melbourne, sweeping on to Ararat and Great Western to the north-west and then cutting back through Bendigo, Heathcote and Rutherglen before ending perched high above the Ovens Valley at Beechworth. These are the Goldfield vineyards.

Let's first look at the western end, where the vineyards have survived but fitfully, yet where some rare beauties are made. Mostly the soils are poor, the rainfall is low and good irrigation water is hard to find. Those conditions mean there won't be many survivors, but they are also the conditions that favour production of small amounts of intensely concentrated wines – usually red. That's not what all these rump goldfield vineyards do – there's a lot of sparkling wine made in Great Western and near Ballarat for a start – but it's rich, scented reds that sing of the fabulous flavours of Victoria's hinterland. Around Avoca the area is called the Pyrenees. It's a lovely rolling area of pasture and gums, but the European Pyrenees it ain't. Even so, remarkable, dense wines are made at wineries like Dalwhinnie and Taltarni.

To the west, centred on Ararat, we've got the Grampians region – presumably some Scottish gold miner wanted to be reminded of home, though sunny Ararat is a bit more hospitable than the grey Scottish Grampians. Although vineyards are still scattered, there are some real stars like Mount Langi Ghiran, and there's the town of Great Western. This is a great region for fabulously scented, succulent Shiraz, but the fame of the area is based on fizz. When the gold ran out, miners were employed to dig long 'drives' into the rock, just like the storage caves in Champagne. By the beginning of the twentieth century Great Western bubbly was famous – probably because this was the only place in Australia with proper cool caves to mature the wine, and the wines needed maturing – they were often made from the unspeakably severe Ondenc grape. Even I have found my lips puckering at examples of Ondenc 10 years old or more. Seppelt took over the 'champagne drives' in 1918 and have made superb white – and red – fizz here, but even they have realized top reds are the thing. Recent twenty-first-century releases are the best Seppelt Shirazes for a generation.

Gold was discovered in Victoria in 1851. From all over the world men flocked to the heartland of Victoria, their minds giddy with dreams of untold wealth from these extensive, easily dug lodes of precious metal. And, boy, they were thirsty too.

Avoca established vineyards in 1848, Bendigo followed suit in 1855, Great Western in 1858 and Ballarat in 1859. North-East Victoria already had vines near the little township of Rutherglen, but was equally boosted by the mad-house prosperity brought by gold. Wine could be sold for as much as £5 a gallon in the goldfields – twenty times the price it would fetch in New South Wales, southern Victoria or South Australia.

Vineyards prospered mightily while gold was there to be dug, but faded as gold was exhausted. Some like Avoca faded right away before revival in the 1960s. Others, like Glenrowan and Rutherglen, for much of the twentieth century had to wave the banner for Victoria's quality wines almost single-handed. But even they have a mere fraction of the vineyards that used to cover whatever land was not being mined in the glory days of gold.

The elegant buildings in Rutherglen's Main Street are reminders that Victoria's gold rush of the 1850s ushered in an era of great prosperity for Central and North-East Victoria. Many small towns such as Rutherglen were founded on this sudden new wealth. Rutherglen's population grew suddenly within a few months to over 20,000, men outnumbering women 20 to one. Now there are a mere 1850 residents.

These ungrafted, pre-phylloxera vines at Tahbilk, Victoria's oldest family-owned winery and vineyard in the Goulburn Valley, were planted on the property in 1860 and are among the oldest Shiraz vines in the world (Barossa has some even older). They produce just 400 cases a year of very fine full-bodied Shiraz, '1860s Vines Shiraz'. But it's not a wine that reveals its charms without a struggle. Tahbilk wines from the 1970s can still be closed up and severe. They're a little more forthcoming nowadays, but I'd still recommend a 10-year-wait for the 1860s stuff.

Bendigo, 120 kilometres north of Ballarat, suffered a more abrupt decline in vineyards after the Gold Rush than most because, when the devastating phylloxera aphid was discovered there in 1893, the government ordered all the vines be uprooted, and it wasn't until 1969 that anyone dared to try again. There are now a fair number of producers, around 25, but most are fairly small-scale – excepting the very good Water Wheel – and the wines are tasty, especially the eucalyptus-scented Shiraz.

But there's an area to the east called Heathcote around the eponymous town which used to be thought of as just another bit of Bendigo, but just taste a Heathcote Shiraz and you'll say – this isn't a sub-region of anywhere. This is a starry piece of dirt. The Shirazes have fabulous depth, richness of fruit and power, but they're also wonderfully fresh and balanced. Drinking them is like watching a fat man with twinkletoes excel at the Blue Danube Waltz. The secret seems to be the oldest soil in Australia – a streak of red Cambrian pulverized rock that's 500 million years old and which surfaces briefly on both sides of the Mount Carmel Range before gradually petering out southwards just north of the town of Heathcote. This isn't the only soil in Heathcote – to the south there's granite soil much the same as that of Macedon, further south towards Melbourne; and there are grey-yellow gravels and deep, silty riverbed gravels that give remarkable results from Viognier and Shiraz – but the star turn is the deep red Cambrian soil, soils so red that even the sheep look red. Big companies like Tyrrell's and Brown Brothers as well as locals like Jasper Hill and Heathcote Winery are already making thrilling Heathcote red wines here.

Let's sweep right across to the north-east now, to Glenrowan and Rutherglen; Glenrowan crouched between the Warby Range and Lake Mokoan and Rutherglen nestled right up against the Murray River on the border of New South Wales. Ballarat may be the grandest of the remaining Gold Rush towns, but Rutherglen is where the vineyards were at their most mighty, three being over 250 hectares each in size and surviving into the 1950s, producing vast amounts of fortifieds and thick-textured red table wines for the British market. Although the North-East's main fame is now for its fortifieds, it does make some spanking good reds that used to have about as much subtlety as an iron girder, but the modern Shirazes and Durifs, in particular, marry muscle with scented succulence surprisingly well.

But gold is and was what the North-East is all about. The golden brilliance of its fortified Muscats and Tokays (they also make some excellent, super-sweet vintage 'ports' quite unlike the Portuguese originals) has never been dimmed except by lack of public interest and even during periods in the twentieth century when no-one seemed to want these gems, hoary-headed family chieftains kept on making them. Look at when these companies were founded. Chambers Rosewood 1858, Morris 1859, Campbells 1870, Stanton and Killeen 1875. And who's running them now? Bill Chambers, David Morris, Chris Campbell, Chris Killeen. Even the Rutherglen Classification is entirely and successfully self-regulating. Rutherglen Muscat is the basic level and the freshest style; Classic Rutherglen Muscat is older and richer; Grand Rutherglen Muscat is still more intense; and Rare Rutherglen Muscat is the very finest and oldest. There are no precise criteria for any of these categories – Muscats at different quality levels are tasted together by all the producers, and when one producer doesn't seem to be getting the quality and character quite right, they all sit round and talk about it, and, if necessary, make visits to the cellars to help things back on track. Rutherglen Muscat and Tokay is pure, precious gold indeed.

There's just one more Gold Rush vineyard to visit – Beechworth. Head south from Rutherglen, past the heaps of sad, sandy soil that still mark the gold diggings now sucked dry of whatever precious metal was in them, through Chiltern and suddenly the road rises steeply through stringy bark forest. It doesn't seem at all like promising vineyard land, but, once again – blame the lure of gold. Beechworth perches just behind a magnificent escarpment and its vineyards run right to the rim, overlooking the Ovens Valley far below. In fact, more vines were planted down in the Ovens which also had substantial gold reserves, but Beechworth has managed to create a real frisson of excitement in modern times because it is high and cool. Vineyards go as high as 880 metres up the mountainside at Stanley, and the escarpment is more like 550-600 metres, producing anything from sparkling wine to Pinot Noir and Chardonnay to exceptional Shiraz at the lower end of the escarpment at the 350-metre mark. Except for the new 48-hectare Indigo vineyard, the 22 producers are all small-scale and delightfully idiosyncratic, led by Rick Kinzbrunner at Giaconda and his world class Chardonnays, Pinot Noirs and Shirazes.

And there's still more to Victoria. First, the valleys that run up into the Victorian Alps. The Great Alpine Road runs up the Ovens Valley and spans several side valleys like the Buckland and the Buffalo. Add to these the Kiewa, a mountain ridge further east and you've got the Alpine Valleys wine region. Everything here depends on how high you go up the valleys towards the snowfields, as the mountains close in and you lose sun and heat and can find yourself doing the vintage in April while snow covers the ground. That's why people like Annapurna Estate specialize in pale dry whites and fizz. But the Ovens Valley, in particular, offers more diversity. It's dotted with old corrugated iron sheds – these are the drying sheds for hops and tobacco which still grow in the valley. Vines occur on the river flats, but ideally they are located on the relatively rare north-facing slopes, and as we head north down the valley it broadens out and the sun starts burning on my brow.

There's a reason to keep heading north, however, and that's the tiny hamlet of Milawa. This is where Brown Brothers, one of Australia's most important family-owned wineries, operates. The grapes at Milawa aren't that special, but Brown Brothers was crucial in creating a focus for the whole area of North-East Victoria, using grapes from all the different regions right down the Murray to Swan Hill, over to Rutherglen and Beechworth, and up the Alpine Valleys, particularly up the King Valley.

The King runs parallel to the Ovens, just to the west, and again, is a land of tobacco-farming and polyculture dominated by Italian immigrants. Until the 1990s this meant high yields of not very exciting grapes, mostly bought by Brown Brothers. But the Browns underwent a seachange towards higher quality in the late 1990s and the King Valley, denied its market for dull, high yield fruit, has responded magnificently. The valley floor is still often used for tobacco and other crops, but the valley sides, and even the plateau land, either at Myrrhee to the west or on the high windswept fields of Whitlands at 800 metres high, are producing some of Victoria's finest wines. You only have to taste something like Brown Brothers' Patricia Cabernet – a mix of King and Myrrhee fruit – or the thrilling Sangiovese and Nebbiolos that Fred Pizzini coaxes from his King Valley hillside vines, to know that these Alpine Valleys, and the King in particular, are something special.

In a state so magnificently diverse as Victoria, and where vineyards have been established for so many different reasons, it's easy for some fine producers not to fit into any overall pattern. At Mansfield, just to the south of the King Valley, Delatite makes delicate whites and scented reds under the baleful eye of the snowfields of Mount Buller. This is the eastern end of what is loosely termed the Central Victorian High Country. To its north are the Strathbogie Ranges, running north-east of Seymour, and through Seymour, the beautiful and substantial Goulburn River runs north towards the Murray. Just south of the Nagambie Lakes, in warm conditions near a river bank crowded by the waving limbs of pale gum trees and calmed by the eerie, bell-like song of magpies, is Tahbilk – founded in 1860 and still producing palate-crunching reds and honey-scented Marsanne to this day.

THE MURRAY RIVER

The Murray River marks the northern border of Victoria. The majority of Victoria's wine comes from the vast, irrigated fields that fan out from the lefthand banks of the river. An increasing amount is made to a remarkably high standard. Lindemans' Karadoc, the biggest winery in Australia, processes much of the fruit grown here, and the giant Mildara plant at Merbein, just north of the small town of Mildura, does a similar job.

The Yarra Valley has a calming, tranquil quality like few other wine regions of Australia – or, indeed, the world. Ringed by mountains, traversed by the lazy Yarra River and knitted together into a patchwork of orchard, pasture and vines, it's a little splash of paradise on earth, yet just half an hour away is the hurly-burly of big city Melbourne.

High up in the valley's southern hills, the beautiful Hoddles Creek Vineyard is prized as a source of quality fruit for sparkling wine.

YARRA VALLEY

I'm beginning to wonder whether the most beautiful vineyard in Australia could be hidden in deep forest only an hour or so's drive outside Melbourne. Not only the vineyard itself, but the road to this vineyard is dramatic, breathtaking and lovely. Bastard Hill is the vineyard. I mean it. That's its name, and when you try to stand upright on its giddy slopes and then imagine being a vine pruner or a grape-picker without mountain goat in your DNA, you'll know who christened it and why.

Bastard Hill is part of the Hardy Wine Company's Hoddles Creek Vineyard, hidden high in the hills on the south-eastern edge of the Yarra Valley. You drive up a twisting logger's road through the tallest, straightest gum trees I know in Australia. They grow so thick and stout, it's like being in a rainforest of gums and as the sun dapples the road in front of you, your human self is humbled by their grand beauty. So you'll be in the right frame of mind when you do get to Hoddles Creek and as you drive out into the open air from the forest you can gaze in amazement on this gash of red soil and green vines, on a slope so shocking it's like a wedge cut from a wheel of cheddar cheese. Hoddles Creek isn't all so severe as Bastard Hill, but, locked into this verdant woodland, on steep slopes running south, west and north, it really is like a glade in a fairy forest.

SELECTED WINERIES

1. Arthurs Creek Estate
2. Diamond Valley
3. Yarra Yarra
4. Shantell
5. De Bortoli
6. Fergusson
7. Yarra Ridge
8. Mount Mary
9. Yering Station/Yarra Bank
10. St Huberts
11. Domaine Chandon
12. Yeringberg
13. Oakridge
14. Metier Wines
15. Long Gully
16. TarraWarra
17. Rochford's Eyton
18. Yarra Yering
19. Coldstream Hills
20. Five Oaks Vineyard
21. Seville Estate
22. Lillydale Estate Vineyards (McWilliam's)
23. Yarra Burn/Hoddles Creek

YARRA VALLEY

TOTAL DISTANCE NORTH TO SOUTH
27.5KM

▓▓▓ VINEYARDS

0 km   1   2
0 miles   1

WHERE THE VINEYARDS ARE

That's the outskirts of Melbourne in the lower left-hand corner, and the Great Dividing Range of mountains is over on the right. The Yarra Valley is beautiful, and it's only a short journey via electric train from Lilydale to the city centre. Pressure from property developers is the biggest threat to face the Yarra Valley, and a flourishing wine industry is one of the best ways to combat it. Vineyard planting here has exploded, tripling in size between 1995 and 2003 to 2500 hectares, with more vines still being planted. This is great news to halt urban development, but such rapid expansion in a cool area brings poor wine as well as good.

The vineyards originally stretched north-east of Coldstream across the grey loam soils at St Huberts and Yeringberg, and a little further west towards Yarra Glen at Yering Station. Only well-drained banks are suitable for grapes on the valley floor. There has been a great deal of development around Dixons Creek in the north of the valley, but again only on the raised ground. The land around the Warramate Hills is high enough, and as is the case in the Coldstream Hills, it is steep enough for drainage not to be a problem.

East and south of the Warramate Hills, away from the flood plain, the soil changes to a highly fertile, deep red terra rossa, where red grapes struggle to ripen, but occasional super sweet wines are made, notably by Seville Estate. This continues into the wooded hills to the south (off the map) where large developments at locations like Hoddles Creek are producing high-quality grapes, used primarily for sparkling wine.

The Yarra Valley, with its endless variations of conditions all packed into this tight river basin, surrounded by mountains and National Park forests, is showing the way by offering what is often perfect balance between coolish and ever so slightly warm conditions.

Red grapes Pinot Noir is the leading red, with some Cabernet Sauvignon and small amounts of Shiraz, Merlot, Pinot Meunier and Cabernet Franc.

White grapes Chardonnay dominates, but Sauvignon Blanc is also important.

Climate The cool climate allows extended ripening. Wind and rain can interfere with flowering and fruit-set in December and January.

Soil There are two main types of soil: grey, sandy clays or clay loams and deep, fertile, red volcanic soil.

Aspect The angle of slope and height above sea level vary greatly, with vineyards planted at 50–400 metres.

The eastern end of the Yarra Valley provides a perfect climate for growing high quality Pinot Noir and Chardonnay. There are myriad planting sites in the valley, each with a different combination of site, aspect and soil, but vines planted in rows running up and down the hillsides – such as these ones belonging to TarraWarra between Yarra Glen and Healesville – enjoy maximum exposure to the sun in this cool climate region, and hillside vineyards are less prone to frost than those on the valley floor.

Hoddles Creek may well be my favourite view of the Yarra, but the whole valley is beautiful; it exudes a tranquillity, a bucolic gentleness that belies the fact that Melbourne's eastern suburbs and greedy developers menace its peace at any opportunity. They'd probably have managed to turn many of its tranquil paddocks into subdivisions, were it not for the spectacular success of its wine industry. Its *new* wine industry that is, because between 1921 and the end of the 1960s, there wasn't a vine left in the Yarra Valley. Every vineyard had been uprooted and given over mainly to pastureland for cows. Even today, boasting more than 2500 hectares of vineyards, the vine can often seem like an interloper among areas of pasture and orchards.

Yet in the nineteenth century, the Yarra Valley probably came closer to rivalling the great wines of Europe than any other vineyards in the New World. Proximity to Melbourne helped, since Melbourne was Australia's most prosperous and sophisticated city through most of the nineteenth century. And settlement by Swiss emigrés played a large part. The settlers weren't necessarily grape-growers themselves, but they came from a wine-drinking culture, and they came from a country of cool climate vineyards. Yarra wines rapidly developed a reputation as the most delicate, fragrant, refined wines in Australia, winning trophies in Europe and appreciation from connoisseurs worldwide.

Australia's lurch away from light-bodied table wines towards heavy fortified wines, and the election of a Victorian government bent on teetotalism in the early twentieth century meant that in the space of 30 years the Yarra went from star wine status in 1889, winning gold medals in the Paris International Exhibition, to the last commercial harvest and wine wilderness in 1921. But winefolk have long memories, and, first in the 1960s with Mount Mary, St Huberts, Yarra Yering and Yeringberg, and then in the 1980s as a new wine boom in Australia led by warm climate vineyards caused many radical thinkers to say – hey, but we did great *cool* climate wines in the old days – people began seeking out those old nineteenth-century records of Yarra's brilliance. Once again, this lovely valley became the magnet for anyone searching after elegance and delicacy and investment.

But if this makes it sound as though the Yarra Valley is a homogeneous whole, that's far from the truth. Those early pioneers of the 1960s like Yarra Yering and St Mary's were much happier with varieties like Shiraz and Cabernet Sauvignon, which require a serious amount of sun and a fair amount of heat to ripen. It was the 1980s influx – enthusiastically led by such persuasive visionaries as James Halliday at Coldstream Hills and Tony Jordan at Domaine Chandon – who preached the gospel of cool. Halliday established vineyards on the slopes of the Warramate Hills designed to produce great Chardonnay and Pinot Noir – but right below him were the Shiraz and Cabernet vines of Yarra Yering, It was clear they could coexist. Jordan's objective was to make Australia's finest sparkling wine, and he planted just about as low down as the centre of the valley as you can go before you get to the floodplain and frost traps of the river. Yet on the other side of the road historic Yeringberg is famous for its Marsanne and Roussanne – two varieties from the distinctly warm climate southern Rhône Valley in France, So it was not as simple as it seems.

In the 1980s there was a tremendous need for Australia to prove that it could produce high quality cool climate wines – wine in the mould of the French cool climate classic Champagne, Burgundy and Bordeaux. The warm climate styles of big size reds and whites from South Australia and New South Wales were already making waves around the world, but sniffy commentators were able to lift their aquiline noses into the stratosphere and mutter 'but they're not French'. As if that meant they were inferior! Try making Barossa Shiraz or a Hunter Valley Chardonnay in France! Even so, the challenge was there and the new wave of savvy Aussie winemakers who understood the nuances and subtleties of French classics were determined to meet it.

If you look at statistics – well, Yarra Valley seems to be bang in the middle between Bordeaux and Burgundy – just a little cooler than Bordeaux, the Cabernet and Merlot homeland, and just a little bit warmer than Burgundy, the home of Pinot Noir and Chardonnay. Rainfall during the growing season is almost identical for Yarra, Bordeaux and Burgundy. But how meaningful are these statistics? Bordeaux and Burgundy are big places, rainfall in Bordeaux is notoriously localized, especially during late summer and autumn. And as for warmth, in a marginal climate things like altitude are crucial. The Romanée-Conti *grand cru* vineyard, capable of giving the most sensuous and complex of all red Burgundies, lies at 275 metres but directly above, at 350 metres, you can't ripen any grapes at all.

And it's just like that in the Yarra Valley. These beautiful vines up at Hoddles Creek are at a height of 400 metres and take six to eight weeks longer to ripen than vines down at 100 metres on the valley floor. Yet the warmest vineyards seem to be on the north side of the valley around Dixons Creek – and that's nearer 200 metres in height. In fact, some people are now saying that most of the Yarra Valley is too warm for Pinot Noir, even though the holy grail of great Pinot Noir was what drew the New Wave there in the first place.

Well, I think that as soon as we stop trying to compare Yarra with Bordeaux and Burgundy it becomes obvious that it's a really special place in its own right. The acid, barely ripe Hoddles Creek fruit is some of the most prized in Australia for making sparkling wine. There *is* great Pinot Noir made – up in the north-west, from small yields on difficult mudstone soils and at a height of around 200 metres – by people like Diamond Valley – as well as by the producers like Coldstream Hills with grey loam soils and with sites nicely angled northwards towards the sun – and they need to be: it's only 20 kilometres to Diamond Valley, but it can be 2° warmer on average up there than in the centre of the valley. And the Pinots don't taste like Burgundy. Coldstream Hills makes great, dense Cabernet Sauvignon Reserves in warm years, but they're totally different from the elegant, restrained but mouthwateringly drinkable Cabernet-based reds of Yeringberg and Mount Mary just down the road. And they don't taste like Bordeaux. Head to the north side of the valley at Dixon's Creek and taste De Bortoli's fantastic Shiraz and Viognier. You're less than 10 kilometres from Domaine Chandon's sparkling wine vineyards directly to the south over the river plain.

If the Yarra proves anything it is that grape yields do matter. If you keep the crop low on your vines, you can get fantastic fully ripe flavours and yet not have to wait until the sugars get so high that an impossibly alcoholic wine is the result. This is a dilemma for winemakers worldwide.

Quick guide ◆
Yarra Valley Pinot

Classic wine style Not at all hot by Australian standards, the Yarra Valley is emerging as a new classic region for the finicky, cool climate Pinot Noir. Producers such as Coldstream Hills led by James Halliday in the 1980s and 1990s have played an important role in the development of Pinot Noir as an Australian success story.

Tasting note
Often gentle and restrained in style with subtle strawberry and cherry fruit that gets deeper and richer with age.

When to drink
You can certainly drink these wines at one or two years old, especially the examples from the warmest zones in the valley like Dixons Creek but the best wines gain character by aging for up to five years.

Best years
2002, '01, '99, '98, '97, '94, '92, '91, '90, '88.

CLASSIC WINES TO TRY
Coldstream Hills Reserve Pinot Noir and Pinot Noir
De Bortoli Pinot Noir
Diamond Valley Estate Pinot Noir
Evelyn County Estate Pinot Noir
Mount Mary Pinot Noir
TarraWarra Pinot Noir
Yarra Burn Bastard Hill Pinot Noir
Yarra Ridge Reserve Pinot Noir
Yarra Yering Pinot Noir
Yering Station Pinot Noir and Barak's Bridge Pinot Noir
Yeringberg Pinot Noir

Coldstream Hills
Reserve Pinot Noir
This is one of Australia's finest examples of Pinot Noir – sappy and smoky with a fragrant cherry fruit that is distinctly richer than the fruit of the general release Pinot Noir and helped along with a clever use of oak. The grapes are sourced mainly from the Amphitheatre Block planted in 1985, which is about as steep a vineyard as you'll find anywhere in Australia.

All Saints
The Muscadelle grape reaches its apogee in North-East Victoria where it is called Tokay. All the wines at All Saints are good but what really counts are the luscious old Muscats and Tokays. This Rare Rutherglen Tokay is a light gold tawny colour with complex tealeaf and malty, barleysugar flavours.

ALL SAINTS

Rutherglen
❋ *Shiraz, Durif, Cabernet Sauvignon and others*
❋ *Riesling, Chardonnay, Marsanne and others*

You have to rub your eyes and think – hang on, which country am I in? There you are in the middle of the sunbaked paddocks and vineyards of Rutherglen in upstate Victoria, and yet you've just driven through ancient wrought-iron gates and are now standing on a lush green lawn gazing at what seems to be a Scottish castle! Well, it sort of is.

This magnificent red brick castellated edifice was built with misty-eyed zeal by George Sutherland Smith in 1864 to remind him of the Castle of Mey in Scotland where his family had worked for generations as carpenters. It had become something of a faded dowager waiting forlornly for a suitor by the time Peter Brown of BROWN BROTHERS bought it in 1998, but he has quickly brought lustre back to the grand old dame with a string of super Rare Tokay and Rare Muscat releases, delicious though younger stickies under the Grand label, some powerful reds, including the Rutherglen speciality Durif, and some fair whites. All Saints is not quite yet back on the top of the Rutherglen Stickies tree – after all, the greater Tokays and Muscats rely on a bank of old blending wine that stretches back generations but they're on the right track.

BAILEYS

Glenrowan
❋ *Shiraz, Cabernet Sauvignon*
❋ *Muscat, Muscadelle*

This is one of the great names of North-East Victoria, long famous for its sweet fortified wines or 'stickies', making Muscat and Muscadelle (labelled Tokay in Australia) in an inimitably rich, perfumed and treacly style. Now part of the Beringer Blass empire, Baileys did not initially benefit from the change of ownership. You couldn't improve on Bailey's great stickies, but you might at least try to maintain standards. After all, this is a wine dear to my heart.

When I was playing General Perón in *Evita* in London's West End, my mother and I would repair to Leicester Square after the show and drink a bottle of Founders Muscat between us. Straight down. No nonsense. It was that good. Stickies are once again good but no longer at 'me and my mum' standards. However, the dry Shiraz reds – especially 1920s Block – are big, rich, perfumed, impressive reds, though I sense even here a certain 'big company' meddling with their rare concoction of brute power and scent.

Baileys
Fortified wines have been a speciality at this very traditional Glenrowan winery for over 130 years. This is where Australia's most famous bush bandit, Ned Kelly, made his last stand.

BANNOCKBURN

Geelong
❋ *Pinot Noir, Cabernet Sauvignon, Shiraz, Merlot*
❋ *Chardonnay, Sauvignon Blanc, Riesling*

From low-yielding vineyards in the cool climate region of Geelong, this small winery makes one of Australia's most famous Pinot Noirs, enormously rich Chardonnay, good Cabernet Sauvignon and idiosyncratic Shiraz, influenced by the Rhône's Alain Graillot of Crozes-Hermitage. Gary Farr has been the winemaker here for over 27 years. He has also worked harvests at Domaine Dujac in Morey-St-Denis since 1983 and is wholly committed to adapting Burgundian viticulture and winemaking practices to Bannockburn. He creates wines of concentration, power and structure, with unmistakable varietal character.

The Pinot Noirs are impressive, though personally I'd like a little less emphasis on 'Burgundian' gaminess and a bit more expression of his own vineyards. Despite using Burgundian techniques, their flavour is far more muscular and rich than any

Bannockburn
All Gary Farr's wines are highly individual and not typically Australian in style. The Shiraz is ripe and intense with an elegance more reminiscent of the northern Rhône. Rich, chocolate and licorice fruit character are finely interwoven with subtle oak.

Burgundy you're likely to come across. All in all, I prefer the Shiraz. Best years: (Shiraz) 2002, '01, '00, '99, '98, '97, 96, '95, '92, '91, '90, '89, '88, '86.

BASS PHILLIP

South Gippsland
❋ *Pinot Noir, Gamay*
❋ *Chardonnay*

We must thank the good lord for Phillip Jones still being around to make these lovely wines after he narrowly escaped mutilation in an accident during the 2004 vintage. But he's still here and still producing tiny quantities (around 1500 cases per year) of Australia's most eagerly sought and stylish Pinot Noirs under the standard, Premium and occasional Reserve labels, together with a hatful of Gamay and Chardonnay for home consumption. The flavour is subtle yet penetrating and incredibly long-lasting, rapidly taking on the forest undergrowth character of high-class red Burgundy. The Village is a new, less expensive Pinot Noir, but still with plenty of Bass Phillip charm and mellow texture to soothe the palate.
Best years: 2002, '01, '00, '98, '97, '96, '95, '94, '93, '92, '91, '89, '85.

Bass Phillip
Pinot Noir is many Australian winemakers' holy grail. This small dedicated producer has risked everything for this enigmatic grape variety.

Best's

The Thomson Family Shiraz, from the historic Concongella Vineyard, has real old-vine complexity – 80 per cent of the wine comes from vines planted in the 1860s. Rich and concentrated, the tannin is finely structured and balanced to allow for 15–20 years' aging.

BEST'S

Grampians

Shiraz, Merlot, Cabernet Sauvignon, Pinot Noir

Chardonnay, Riesling

This small winery, now run by Viv Thomson and his extended family, was established in western Victoria in 1866, and is the last survivor, along with Seppelt, of the wineries established in the region, formerly known as Great Western, to slake the thirst of a society crazed by gold. Its priceless old vineyards are some of the few historic plantings left in the area, and contribute, in particular, to the wonderful, silky smooth, cherry and mint Shiraz (especially in the Thomson Family Shiraz from 130-year-old vines) which is deceptively long-lived. Tasty, clear-fruited Great Western Bin No. 0 Shiraz and Great Western Cabernet are good and the Riesling shows flashes of brilliance. Tropical fruity, finely balanced Chardonnay is variable, delicious at best.

Best years: (Thomson Family Reserve) 2001, '99, '98, '97, '96, '95, '94, '92.

BINDI WINE GROWERS

Macedon Ranges

Pinot Noir

Chardonnay

Bill Dhillon and his talented, imaginative son, Michael, have fashioned some superlative wines from the inhospitable, infertile soils of their 6-ha vineyard in the Macedon Ranges. The tiny production – 1200 cases a year – is made by Michael Dhillon with long-time consultant, Stuart Anderson. Each of the wines is among the best examples of the style or variety produced in Australia. The non-vintage Chardonnay/Pinot Noir bubbly is yeasty, boldly flavoured and tautly structured. As well as the restrained, austere Original Vineyard Chardonnay and the sleek, pure, savoury Original Vineyard Pinot Noir, there are rarer single-block varietals – steely Quartz Chardonnay and herb-scented,

gamy, inspired 'Block 5' Pinot Noir.

Best years: ('Original Vineyard' Pinot) 2002, '01, '00, '99, '98.

Bindi Wine Growers

In Macedon, one of Australia's coolest wine regions, Pinot Noir and Chardonnay are the leading varieties, making excellent sparkling and varietal wines. Bindi makes tiny quantities of both varieties.

BROWN BROTHERS

King Valley

Cabernet Sauvignon, Shiraz, Tarrango, Graciano, Merlot, Barbera and others

Chardonnay, Riesling, Pinot Gris (Pinot Grigio), Sauvignon Blanc, Chenin Blanc, Muscat of Alexandria and others

This is a remarkable family company with the third and fourth generations of Browns now involved in producing and selling over half a million cases of wine per year.

Brown Brothers draws on fruit from a number of vineyards in Victoria, in both warm and cooler, upland sites in the King Valley, at nearby Banksdale, at the mountain-top Whitlands site, and from significant new plantings at Heathcote. They use both familiar and unusual grapes to produce a wide choice of styles, including superb fortifieds (especially the Very Old Muscat and Tokay range) and consistently good vintage fizz. Perhaps partly due to the Kindergarten Winery, a 35,000-case 'winery within a winery', Brown Brothers has been able to upgrade what was a rather ordinary

Brown Brothers

Brown Brothers is well known for its experiments with a wide range of grape varieties – currently over 50. This light golden colour dessert wine is a blend of Muscat and Flora.

range of dry table wines into an impressive selection of good quality wines, both from well-known varietals, and such Aussie oddballs as Graciano, Dolcetto, Barbera and Tarrango. The patriarchal John Brown Senior, who had taken over the winery in 1934 and was actively involved into the 21st century, died in May 2004. The new premium 'Patricia' named after John Brown Senior's widow is an inspiring range that will set new standards for what the local vineyards can achieve.

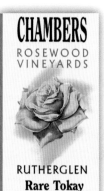

Chambers

Bill Chambers is one of the characters of the Australian wine industry. His speciality is remarkably powerful Liqueur Muscat and Tokay which draw upon ancient stocks of wine put down in wood by earlier generations of his family.

CHAMBERS

Rutherglen

Shiraz, Cabernet Sauvignon, Cinsaut, Touriga

Muscat, Muscadelle, Riesling, Gouais

Bill Chambers is a paradox. He'd almost rather sell you plastic flagons – bring your own if you want – of dull, dry, basic white for a buck or two a litre than let you give him 50, 60, 80 dollars for just a half-bottle of his Rare or Special Old Liqueur Muscats and Tokays which are among the greatest sweet wines in the world. Indeed, whenever someone has the temerity to buy some, Chambers puts the price up. But it's worth persisting. These great 'stickies' come in three grades – Rare is the top – and they are as viscous, as intense, as erotic as any wine you have ever put in your mouth and the flavour will linger for minutes, hours, days or years, depending on your mood. The Cabernet and Shiraz are good, the whites rather pedestrian.

COLDSTREAM HILLS

Yarra Valley

Pinot Noir, Cabernet Sauvignon, Merlot, Cabernet Franc, Shiraz

Chardonnay, Pinot Gris, Sauvignon Blanc

Famous Australian wine writer James Halliday founded Coldstream Hills, set in one of the

Coldstream Hills
James Halliday may have settled in Yarra to try to make great Burgundian Pinot Noir but Burgundy's white grape is Chardonnay and Coldstream Hills makes a lean, tasty, and just slightly Burgundian example.

loveliest corners of the Yarra, in 1985. In 1996 it was acquired by Southcorp, but Halliday's philosophy of understated, genuinely cool climate flavours still holds sway and he is still involved in the winemaking. Indeed I met him there this year just before vintage as passionately, opinionatedly eager to get his hands dirty as ever.

The most famous wine is the Pinot Noir which almost obsessively avoids any hint of overripeness, followed by a cool, restrained but attractive Chardonnay. Reserve versions are significantly fuller-bodied, Cabernet, Merlot and Shiraz all proudly showing their cool climate credentials. Best years: 2002, '01, '00, '99, '98, '97, '96, '94.

CURLY FLAT

Macedon Ranges
✳ *Pinot Noir*
✳ *Chardonnay, Pinot Gris*
Phillip Moraghan learnt about wine in the vineyard with his mentor, Laurie Williams, and by doing the vintage locally and in

Curly Flat
Sleek velvety Pinot Noir is the main wine produced at this boutique winery near Launcefield in cool-climate Macedon Ranges.

places such as Oregon and Long Island in the USA. The 14-ha vineyard (established in 1992) contains five clones of Pinot Noir and four of Chardonnay. Initial plantings use the labour-intensive Lyre trellis system to maximize sunlight in this cool climate region. It is rigorously maintained to yield a miserly 2500 cases a year. Since 2002 the wines have been made at the new winery by Moraghan under the guidance of Gary Farr (the winemaker at BANNOCKBURN). The complex, cool Chardonnay has a creamy, honeyed texture while the ripe, perfumed and deeply flavoured Pinot Noir has a long, satiny mid-palate.
Best years: (Pinot Noir) 2002, '01, '99, '98.

Dalwhinnie
Lovingly tended vineyards and low yields are the key to Dalwhinnie's extraordinarily intense, full-bodied reds which often seem to have been carved out the granite of the hillsides.

DALWHINNIE

Pyrenees
✳ *Shiraz, Cabernet Sauvignon, Pinot Noir*
✳ *Chardonnay*
Dalwhinnie is consistently the best producer in the Pyrenees region, drawing upon 25-year-old, low-yielding, unirrigated estate vineyards which are immaculately maintained. The quality of the grapes shines through in the carefully made wines: complex, melon and grapefruit-accented Chardonnay, almost as impressive in its way as the black cherry, berry and mint Shiraz and the sweet cassis and chocolate Cabernet Sauvignon. Pinot Noir, made with assistance from Rick Kinzbrunner of GIACONDA, has also made its mark in minute quantities. Best years: (reds) 2001, '00, '99, '98, '97, '96, '95, '94, '92, '91, '90, '88, '86.

DE BORTOLI

Yarra Valley
✳ *Pinot Noir, Merlot, Shiraz, Cabernet Sauvignon*
✳ *Riesling, Sauvignon Blanc, Semillon, Chardonnay, Viognier*
Following the successful introduction of Australia's best dessert wine – Noble One – the Riverina-based De Bortoli (see page 90)

De Bortoli
De Bortoli's top Yarra wine is named after Dame Nellie Melba whose home was in the Yarra Valley. Melba is generally a blend of Cabernet Sauvignon, Shiraz, Cabernet Franc and Merlot and spends two years in French oak. It is produced in tiny quantities at a high price.

decided to make a more substantial move into the premium market by purchasing the Yarra Valley property, Chateau Yaringa, in 1987. Windy Peak (sourced from throughout Victoria) has been the fighting brand behind the expansion from a 35-tonne crush in 1985 to 5000 tonnes in 2004. In recent vintages, Windy Peak and the slightly more expensive Yarra Valley label, Gulf Station, have been consistently among Australia's best value quaffing wines.

However, it has been the Yarra Valley label – Chardonnay, Pinot Noir, Cabernet Sauvignon and lately stunning Shiraz and Shiraz/Viognier – that has forged De Bortoli's reputation as a producer of very good to outstanding Yarra Valley varietals.
Best years (Yarra Valley Pinot Noir) 2002, '01, '00, '97.

Delatite
Bucking the Australian trend, Delatite makes two-thirds white to one-third red wine. Delicate, aromatic Riesling with cool climate floral and lime aromas is one of their best whites.

DELATITE

Strathbogie Ranges
✳ *Merlot, Cabernet Sauvignon, Shiraz, Pinot Noir*

🌿 *Riesling, Gewurztraminer, Sauvignon Blanc, Chardonnay, Pinot Gris*

If you need convincing about cool climate vineyards in Australia, Delatite should do the trick. Even in high summer you can be standing in the middle of the ripening vines and still see the glistening snow of the Mount Buller skifields in the distance. So you'll want the wines to taste cool as well. But what does cool taste like?

Delatite Riesling, for a start, delicate as spring water, scented with flowers. Delatite Gewurztraminer, all the heady aromas of the grape intact but tasted through a filter of bride-white muslin. Or the Pinot Noir and Devil's River red Bordeaux blend with their finely focused fruit, cut glass clarity and a sneak of minty perfume so fresh you'd never find it where the sun bakes down. A cool climate classic – if you still need persuading. Best years: (Riesling) 2000, '99, '97, '96, '94, '93, '87, '86, '82.

DIAMOND VALLEY VINEYARDS

Yarra Valley

🌿 *Pinot Noir, Cabernet Sauvignon*
🌿 *Chardonnay*

It's the quality of their sublime Pinot Noir for which this tiny, 5000-case winery is best known but I have to thank them for something else. As we nibbled on the Pinot Noir grapes one sunny early morning, a mob of kangaroos roused itself on the other side of the track, took little notice of us, but paired off and began boxing. Mothers teaching sons? Young males beginning to prove themselves? Or just magic in the grass next to one of Victoria's best little vineyards. Diamond Valley was established in 1975 when David and Catherine Lance planted a 3.5-ha vineyard at St Andrews. Wines appear under the impossible-to-obtain Black Label (notably the powerfully concentrated and succulent Close Planted Pinot) and the estate White Label (aromatic, varietally pure yet complex Pinot Noir, characterful Chardonnay and earthy Cabernet). The Blue Label wines

Diamond Valley Vineyards
This is an outstanding producer of silky, strawberry and cherry-style Pinot Noir. The Close Planted Pinot is a marvellously rich, savoury red. .

(Chardonnay, Sauvignon Blanc, Cabernet/ Merlot and Pinot) are sourced from Yarra Valley growers. After a 10-year apprenticeship with his father, James Lance has now taken over day-to-day winemaking responsibilities. The Lances also produce small quantities of very good wine from their permanently-netted 2.5-ha vineyard on the southern coast of Phillip Island 120km south-east of Melbourne.
Best years: (Estate Pinot Noir) 2003, '02, '01, '99, '98, '96.

Domaine Chandon
Moet & Chandon's showcase winery in the Yarra Valley makes top-quality Champagne-method sparklers, including vintage, Blanc de Blancs and rosé.

DOMAINE CHANDON

Yarra Valley

🌿 *Pinot Noir, Pinot Meunier, Shiraz*
🌿 *Chardonnay*

'Anything you can do, I can do better' might well be the song sung by this Domaine Chandon to the Champagne house Moët & Chandon's other overseas subsidiaries, and in particular to the Napa Valley. Since 1986 it has established itself as one of Australia's top sparkling wine producers, succeeding handsomely both in the domestic and export trade (in the latter being known as Green Point, so called because the spur of land running down from the Yeringberg Hill to the Yarra River stays green longer than any other part of the valley).

Its various vintage sparkling wines are united by their finesse and elegance, typically with a gentle creamy texture and flavours of citrus and ripe pear; there is also a popular non-vintage Brut and sparkling Pinot/Shiraz. Its Green Point Chardonnay, Pinot Noir and Shiraz table wines are starting to match the best in the valley. The showcase winery is one of the Yarra Valley's architectural joys.

DROMANA ESTATE

Mornington Peninsula

🌿 *Cabernet Sauvignon, Merlot, Pinot Noir, Shiraz, Nebbiolo, Sangiovese, Barbera, Dolcetto*
🌿 *Chardonnay, Sauvignon Blanc, Arneis*

The ever-restless Garry Crittenden, who started this model winery in 1982, is a unique combination of viticulturist,

Dromana Estate
The Garry Crittenden 'i' range of Italian varietal wines, including Sangiovese, Barbera, Dolcetto, Nebbiolo and Arneis, is based on fruit produced by growers of Italian origin in North-East Victoria's King Valley.

winemaker and marketeer extraordinaire. After 20 years at the helm, Garry and Margaret Crittendon have left to start Crittenden at Dromana using the original vineyard, winery and restaurant which they still own. Dromana Estate Ltd is now a publicly listed company that owns Dromana Estate, Mornington Estate, Yarra Valley Hills and the David Traeger and Garry Crittenden 'i' range. Son Rollo is now chief winemaker. Dromana Estate Chardonnay and Pinot Noir from Mornington fruit are delightful but Rollo is an innovator and his Nebbiolo, Sangiovese, Barbera and Arneis from Heathcote and King Valley will be Dromana's best yet. For a real thrill try his dried grapes 'Amarone' style 2003 Cabernet! Best years: (Reserve Chardonnay) 2003, '02, '01, '00, '99, '98, '97.

GIACONDA

Beechworth

🌿 *Shiraz, Pinot Noir, Cabernet Sauvignon*
🌿 *Chardonnay, Roussanne*

The shy, quietly spoken Rick Kinzbrunner has achieved vinous rock-star status since establishing his Giaconda winery in North-East Victoria in 1985. Part of the hysteria may be due to the tiny total annual production – although the vineyard has gradually doubled in size to 6ha – but it is also the

Giaconda
Beautifully balanced and packed with fruit sweetness, this wine nevertheless clearly has Burgundy as its role model.

character of the man. Like the hermit on the hill he has gradually assumed the manner of 'sage' – not only for Beechworth but for all North-East Victorian producers who aspire to make great table wines. When he doesn't talk, his wines do. Sublimely balanced oatmeal and nut Chardonnay, scented Pinot tasting as much of the minerals in the soil as the fruit on the vine, and growling, feral, rock-wracked Shiraz with a sweetness deep hidden by boulders.

Best years: (Chardonnay) 2002, '01, '00, '99, '98, '97, '96, '93, '92.

Hanging Rock
The grassy and herbaceous Jim Jim Sauvignon Blanc is named after the eponymous rock, a six-million-year-old extinct volcano facing the winery.

HANGING ROCK

Macedon Ranges
❋ *Pinot Noir, Shiraz*
❋ *Chardonnay, Sauvignon Blanc, Pinot Gris*

I don't know whether John and Ann Ellis went to see Peter Weir's classic 1975 film *Picnic at Hanging Rock* – one of the all time great atmospheric films. Even if they had, I'm not sure that spectacularly unsuccessful picnic would have had me trying to establish a vineyard on the extinct Jim Jim volcano nearby. If you stand among the vines facing south there's the Hanging Rock dead ahead.

And you won't be very warm. The Macedon Ranges are just about as cold as vineyards get on mainland Australia. And it's windy. And irrigation water is hard to come by. But if you're after an ice-cool character in your wines, and don't mind yields often being close to pathetic since sometimes the grapes are hardly ripe by June – wow, the Macedon guys can make some hairy wines. The cool conditions make for great sparkling wine grapes – their Macedon is a thrilling, dense, yeasty sparkler. Jim Jim Sauvignon is simply unequaled for verve and rapier-thrust in Australia. I had the 1994 this Easter – still a stunner even if the knees were a bit wobbly. They also make excellent Heathcote Shiraz and good wines from bought-in Victorian grapes – including their 'Rock' red and white gluggers.

Jasper Hill
Highly regarded and eagerly sought after, these Shiraz wines have immense richness and structure.

JASPER HILL

Heathcote
❋ *Shiraz, Nebbiolo*
❋ *Riesling, Semillon*

If Heathcote has leapt to the forefront as one of the supreme Shiraz regions of Australia in the last 10 years, you can hand a fair wodge of the blame to Jasper Hill. And the Laughton family, the owners, only planted their first grapes in 1975. Since then, however, the low-yield crop grown on 500 million-year-old pulverized Cambrian rock-based soil that goes to make up the 100 per cent Shiraz Georgia's Paddock, and the 95 per cent Shiraz Emily's Paddock (the names are those of the Laughtons' two daughters, by the way) have thrilled the relatively few wine lovers who've managed to get their hands on a bottle. What sets them apart is the startling purity of fruit, absence of intrusive oak, and enormous depth and ripeness – but it's a ripeness which, unlike some of the great Shirazes from places like Barossa or McLaren Vale, never topples into the stewy, raisiny world of overripeness. And that's why Heathcote and Jasper Hill are so special.

To be honest, in a warm, very dry area like Heathcote, I'm surprised Ron Laughton gets a crop sometimes, because he doesn't irrigate his vines and he employs non-interventionist organic principles in his vineyard. His winemaking, too, is non-interventionist, and these two 'Paddock' wines are profound and beautiful expressions of their place. Oh, I almost forgot. Jasper Hill makes a nice Riesling too.

KOOYONG

Mornington Peninsula
❋ *Pinot Noir*
❋ *Chardonnay*

Because of its proximity to the sizeable Melbourne market, the vast majority of Mornington vignerons produce a reasonably extensive range of wines to sell at the cellar door. Kooyong (established in 1995) is on a much larger scale than most and has focused its attention solely on the two varieties which the region does best.

Kooyong
Vineyard site selection is crucial in the Mornington Peninsula and Kooyong is planted on one of the warmer, more inland sites.

All their wines are sourced from five discrete estate vineyards, 20ha planted to 20 clones of Pinot Noir and 12ha of Chardonnay (10 clones). Increased complexity results from vinifying each of the clonal parcels separately. The winemaker, Sandro Mosele, has been involved from the outset in the development of the vineyard and winery. Both the intensely grapefruity Chardonnay and sweet, spicely oaked Pinot Noir are classy wines which show finesse and complexity. A range of single-vineyard varietals is planned: so far these are the Mosaic and Faultline Chardonnays and the Haven Pinot Noir.

Best years: (Pinot Noir) 2002, '01, '00.

LINDEMANS

Murray Darling
❋ *Shiraz, Cabernet Sauvignon, Merlot*
❋ *Chardonnay, Sauvignon Blanc, Semillon, Colombard*

Lindemans – a large, historic company and key component of the Southcorp corporation – produces around seven million cases of wine a year. Much of this will come from the vast Karadoc winery that sprawls along the banks of the Murray River at Karadoc, in the far northern tip of Victoria. But very little of the famous stuff will. Lindemans' flagship wines come from long-established vineyards

Lindemans
Supremely consistent with ripe, peachy-melony fruit, this wine has probably introduced more drinkers to Australia than any other.

in New South Wales' Hunter Valley, where they are one of the prime producers of Hunter Semillon and Shiraz. They also come from some of the best vineyards in South Australia's Coonawarra and Padthaway regions (see page 66). But their volume business is based in Victoria, in Karadoc – an enormous industrial complex that is one of the biggest winery operations in Australia. This is where the Cawarra cheapos – remember the Sydney Olympics: this was the official wine – the Bin 65 Chardonnay and the Bin 45, 50 and so on reds come from.

However, though there are serious plantations of vines around Karadoc and all along the Victorian side of the Murray, right down to Rutherglen near Albury, the wines that come out of Karadoc are rarely based purely on Victorian fruit. If you look at the label of these Lindemans wines, they will almost without exception sport the 'South Eastern Australia' badge. This means grapes are trucked to Karadoc from virtually anywhere except Western Australia to be processed into wine. To be honest, when we're talking about high volume wines, this isn't a bad thing. If you can draw your grapes from South Australia and New South Wales as well as Victoria, then vinify them in one of the most up-to-date wineries in the world – well, that sure does guarantee consistency. And consistency is what the Victorian end of Lindemans is all about.

MAIN RIDGE

Mornington Peninsula
🍇 *Pinot Noir*
🍇 *Chardonnay*
When they established their tiny, 1000-case winery in one of the coolest spots in the Mornington Peninsula in 1975, Nat and Rosalie White were among the pioneers of the region. Fastidious attention to detail has been a hallmark of White's approach to winemaking from the beginning. A civil engineer in a previous life, Nat studied viticulture and enology at Charles Sturt University. Unlike most Australian vignerons,

Main Ridge
The flagship Half Acre Pinot Noir is outstanding – warm natural yeast fermentations are carried out in small batches using part whole bunches and aging takes place in new French oak for 17 months.

he restricted the vineyard to two varieties (including six clones of Pinot Noir) and has resisted the temptation to irrigate the vines. He has worked hard to restrict yields and to maximize exposure by thoughtful site selection, trellising, shoot and bunch thinning and leaf plucking. The small scale of everything is exemplified by the names of their two Pinots: the excellent 'The Acre' Pinot Noir and the even better 'Half Acre'. And they're not joking. The wines are made by traditional Burgundian methods and it shows in their complexity and restrained, savoury characters. Chardonnay is balanced and fine with impressive weight and the capacity to age well while the Pinot Noir shows dark cherry flavours with spicy, gamy notes.
Best years: (Pinot Noir) 2002, '01, '00, '99, '97.

Mitchelton
Goulburn Valley is thought to produce the best Riesling in the whole of Victoria and Mitchelton's Blackwood Park Riesling is always an extremely classy, citrus-scented wine.

MITCHELTON

Goulburn Valley
🍇 *Shiraz, Grenache, Mourvedre, Cabernet Sauvignon, Merlot*
🍇 *Riesling, Marsanne, Viognier, Roussanne, Chardonnay*
Mitchelton was a real pioneer in Central Victoria. Well, a modern pioneer, anyway. Neighbour TAHBILK has been nestling on the banks of the Goulburn River since the 1860s. Mitchelton, with futuristic architecture and grand designs, arrived in 1973 and is now the largest producer in the region. For 20 years it struggled to balance splendid wines with a business that never gelled and in 1994 it became part of the PETALUMA group from South Australia. High-quality wines sit successfully alongside a tasty bargain-priced selection. Rhône varieties are specialities (Marsanne is perhaps the best-known wine), but there have been some classic Rieslings – look for the Blackwood Park label – and Semillon and Chardonnay are nicely crafted. Reds are best in the juicy easy-drinking style, but Print Label Shiraz can be serious stuff.
Best years: (Print Label Shiraz) 1998, '96, '95, '92, '91, '90.

MOOROODUC ESTATE

Mornington Peninsula
🍇 *Pinot Noir, Shiraz, Cabernet Sauvignon, Merlot, Cabernet Franc*
🍇 *Chardonnay*
The Moorooduc area is in the northern extreme of Mornington and tends to be warmer and drier than other parts of the Peninsula. This tiny family winery was started by surgeon, Richard McIntyre, in 1982 when 2ha were planted. Further plantings have brought the total under vine to 10ha. With some fruit from local growers, this is enough for an 1800-case annual production.

The focus of attention is Chardonnay and Pinot Noir, both of which are produced as regional blends (labelled Devil Bend Creek), estate wines, and single-vineyard varietals (labelled The Moorooduc and sourced from the original Derril Road site). The wild yeast-fermented Chardonnays have gained a deserved reputation. This is a great place to visit, especially to enjoy Jill McIntyre's food in the winery restaurant.
Best years: (The Moorooduc Chardonnay) 2002, '01, '98.

Moorooduc Estate
Chardonnay is the leading variety here – this is the Reserve version and shows a rich, complex citrus fruit nose with buttery hints.

MORRIS

Rutherglen
🍇 *Shiraz, Durif, Cabernet Sauvignon, Cinsaut, Touriga Nacional*
🍇 *Muscat, Muscadelle (Tokay), Chardonnay, Palomino*
Until his retirement in 1992 when he handed over the reins to his son David, Mick Morris was the most important producer of fortified wine in the region. The legacy he's left is so powerful that Morris stickies are still unique and some of the greatest in the region. He made his raisiny, fortified Muscat and aromatic Tokay much as he always had in a winery as antiquated as any in the hemisphere. The Old Premium range sits at the top of the quality tree and despite price rises they are still absolute bargains, given the age and quality of these wines, as are the Mick Morris range at the bottom, the latter selling for a song in Australia and for not that much more abroad. Why is it that the Muscat

Morris
This historic Rutherglen winery makes some of the most magnificent Australian fortifieds, including Liqueur Tokay which is intense, powerful and toffeeish on the finish.

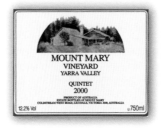

Mount Mary
This classic Yarra estate takes Bordeaux as its role model. Quintet is based on all five of the classic red Bordeaux varieties.

Paringa Estate
Paringa turns out tiny quantities of superb Pinot Noir, Chardonnay and Shiraz which are snapped up by an adoring public.

is always blamed for the hangover? Is it because it's so rich and scented and delicious you can never resist another glass, and another, until the bottle's drained. There are also robust table wines from Shiraz, Cabernet and Durif and Blue Imperial (Cinsaut). Morris has been part of the ORLANDO group since 1970.

MOUNT LANGI GHIRAN

Grampians

❋ *Shiraz, Cabernet Sauvignon, Cabernet Franc, Merlot*
❋ *Riesling, Pinot Gris*

If ever you wish to discover the taste of pepper and spice and sweet black damsons in Shiraz – and a top Rhône Valley wine is not to hand – take a bottle of Mount Langi Ghiran and drink it with a thick piece of rare, char-grilled rump steak. These red wines (the Cabernet Sauvignon is structurally similar but less reliably impressive) are the vinous equivalent of that steak: layers of velvety flavour and great complexity, yet broodingly, impressively dry. The Riesling is refreshingly good, perfumed, yet dry and touched with petrol and lime. And the Pinot Gris is honeyed and delightful. Recently bought by the Rathbone family from Yarra Valley, but winemaker Trevor Mast still remains.
Best years: (Shiraz) 2002, '01, '99, '98, '97, '96, '95, '94, '93, '90, '89, '86.

Mount Langi Ghiran
The exemplary, powerful, peppery Shiraz is utterly distinctive and among Australia's best – its unique flavour makes you wish there were more vineyards planted in the Grampians region.

MOUNT MARY

Yarra Valley

❋ *Cabernet Sauvignon, Pinot Noir, Cabernet Franc and others*
❋ *Chardonnay, Sauvignon Blanc, Semillon, Muscadelle*

I'm gradually coming around to Mount Mary, but it's taken me a very long time. For some wine lovers this is the leading Yarra Valley winery, its tiny production eagerly sought by a fanatically loyal band of followers, but I've always found the ballyhoo about how wonderfully European the wines were a bit irritating.

Of course this was partly because on my many trips to Australia over the years I didn't come to seek out European flavours, conveniently forgetting that for Mount Mary's founder Dr Middleton and a fair number of Melbourne wine fans, the European style of restraint and reserve shown in the wines was exactly what they craved. I think it's texture above all that marks Mount Mary out and of all the Yarra wineries, only YERINGBERG seems to have quite the same touch.

So are we saying that Mount Mary is European in style, or that Mount Mary is the quintessence of Yarra style, as evinced by Yeringberg, one of the very first wineries, started in 1863, and the epitome of restrained elegance ever since? Cabernets Quintet is the most famous wine and it is very sensitive to vintage variations. In good years when the grapes are ripe it has a lovely flavour of blackcurrant and leaf and fresh earth but above all a texture almost syrupy and more red fruit than black that is soothing and mellow and conducive to reflective thought and good conversation. The wines can easily age a decade in this vein. The Pinot Noir also shows some of this seemless texture while the Triolet white, based on white Bordeaux varieties, brings an austere succulence to the art of barrel-fermentation.
Best years: (Quintet) 2002, '01, '00, '99, '98, '97, '96, '95, '94, '93, '92, '91, '90, '88, '86, '84.

PARINGA ESTATE

Mornington Peninsula

❋ *Pinot Noir, Shiraz*
❋ *Chardonnay, Pinot Gris*

Paringa's reputation has been built on outstanding show results over the past decade for its Estate Pinot Noir (fabulously complex with mocca, dark cherry liqueur flavours and velvety texture) and Estate Shiraz (a stylish, cool climate red with spicy black pepper and brambly flavours). Situated at Red Hill and established by Lindsay and Margaret McCall in 1985, it has 4.2ha of vines on the steep slopes of its home vineyard. There are the Estate wines and the Peninsula varietals: Chardonnay, Pinot Noir and Shiraz, sourced from local growers who swell the Paringa production to 6500 cases a year. In outstanding years, such as 2000, Paringa releases small quantities of a Reserve Pinot: the best barrels from the vintage.
Best years: (Pinot Noir) 2002, '01, '00, '99, '97.

Rochford
After an initial flirtation with Cabernet Sauvignon, Rochford now concentrates its red wine efforts on scented, soft-textured Pinot Noir.

ROCHFORD

Macedon Ranges

❋ *Pinot Noir, Merlot*
❋ *Chardonnay, Pinot Gris, Riesling*

This 25-ha vineyard at 600 metres up in the

rugged Macedon Ranges is sizeable by local standards. Yields are low thanks to the ultra cool climate and the unirrigated vineyards and annual production is only about 2000 cases. This will increase slightly as new plantings of Pinot Noir, Chardonnay and Pinot Gris come on stream, but don't expect that much more – it's still real cool up there, the winds still blow and water's still in very short supply.

SEPPELT

Grampians; also South Australia (Barossa)
🌿 *Shiraz, Pinot Noir, Cabernet Sauvignon*
🌿 *Chardonnay, Riesling, Semillon*
Another member of the Southcorp family, Australia's most all-embracing wine company, Seppelt has led the way in Australia in creating good Champagne-method fizz, made from Pinot Noir and Chardonnay: Drumborg (from very cool vineyards in the far south of Victoria) and Salinger are its leading labels, while Great Western, Queen Adelaide and Fleur de Lys are good value. Seppelt's other fizzy speciality is sparkling Shiraz while the new vintages of the still Chalambard and St Peters Shiraz are deep, perfumed and delicious.

Seppelt
Leading Australian sparkling wine producer, Seppelt also makes a wonderful deep, blackberry-rich sparkling Shiraz.

SHADOWFAX

Geelong
🌿 *Shiraz, Pinot Noir*
The strikingly modern Shadowfax and 7-ha winery block are situated at Werribee, a 30-minute drive from Melbourne. Shiraz is sourced from three 30-year-old vineyards at Heathcote, as well as from McLaren Vale and Tallarook in Central Victoria; Pinot Noir from two vineyards in the Geelong region; Sauvignon Blanc and Chardonnay from the Adelaide Hills. Although there are some attractive, reasonably priced, multi-regional blends (I love the 'K Road' Sangiovese/Merlot from the Adelaide Hills and Geelong), the focus for winemaker, Matt Harrop, is on producing distinctive varietals that speak of their source. Pinot Gris and Chardonnay show promise. There are three single-vineyard Heathcote Shirazes – Pink

Shadowfax
You can taste the mellow softness of Yarra Valley fruit blended here with the more assertive flavours of Geelong.

Cliffs and Argyle (both named after railway stations) and One Eye (after the nearby State Forest). Best are the tightly coiled, deeply flavoured, savoury Pink Cliffs and the opulent, concentrated and velvety One Eye.
Best vintages: (One Eye Shiraz) 2002, '01.

STANTON & KILLEEN

Rutherglen
🌿 *Brown Muscat, Shiraz, Durif, Cabernet Sauvignon, Tinta Roriz, Merlot, Touriga Nacional, Tinto Cao, Tinta Barroca*
🌿 *Muscadelle, Chardonnay*
The business partnership formed between the two families in 1953 resulted from the marriage of the parents of current winemaker, Chris Killeen.

Although the Stantons have been in Rutherglen since 1864, the sale of their vineyard and winery to the Campbells in 1940s has deprived this winery of the aged material for their Muscat solera that is the greatest treasure of the top Rutherglen producers. Stanton & Killeen have found ways to make a virtue of adversity. They have gained a reputation for making one of Australia's best vintage 'ports' – and this has been enhanced since they planted Portuguese varieties. Their oldest and best Muscat – Grand Rutherglen – has an average age of 25 years: quality has been maintained

Stanton & Killeen
A red wine and fortified wine specialist, Stanton & Killeen produces Australia's most famous vintage port, which is more similar to true port than most of Australia's examples.

by rigorous selection of the wine that will be added to the solera. Since 1968, only 10 vintages have found their way into the wine. Their Classic Rutherglen fortifieds (average age 12 years) and their reds are among the region's best.

Stonier
Stonier's Reserve Chardonnay, with peachy, honeyed fruit well-integrated with spicy oak, has considerable finesse as well as great length.

STONIER

Mornington Peninsula
🌿 *Pinot Noir, Cabernet Sauvignon*
🌿 *Chardonnay*
It's not often that you conduct your first tasting of a winery's product lying on your back in the rolling surf trying to keep the salt water out of the glass. But that's how it was with Stonier. On my visit in 1996, I arrived to taste, but Tod Dexter, the talented winemaker at that time, is a surfie too. 'The surf's up,' he said, and I just knew that something as mundane as an Englishman asking him how long he kept his Chardonnay in barrels wasn't going to keep him from the waves. So we both went. I was hopeless. He was elegance personified.

And I don't know if it was the brine still sticking to my lips, but the Chardonnay with its lovely melon and cashew freshness and the Reserve, deeper, lusher but still with a classy Burgundian savouriness, tasted fantastic. The Pinot Noirs depend more on the vintage, and can be a little green in colder years, but are delightful at standard and Reserve level when the sun shines. They also make a rather green-streaked Cabernet and since 1999 a Stonier Cuvée fizz. This may be due to the influence of PETALUMA, who bought the company in 1997. With 20ha of vines and 18,000 cases a year, it's the largest winery on the Peninsula and one of the best.
Best years: (Reserve Chardonnay) 2001, '00, '99, '98, '97.

TAHBILK

Goulburn Valley
🌿 *Shiraz, Cabernet Sauvignon*
🌿 *Marsanne, Viognier, Chardonnay, Riesling*
The Tahbilk winery is one of the gems of Australia's wine industry. Largely unaltered

Tahbilk
Enjoying a distinct honeysuckle aroma, the Marsanne from this wonderfully old-fashioned family company is a regional benchmark.

since its construction in the 1870s, and still possessing a block of Shiraz vines planted in 1860 (whose wine is released under the 1860 Vines label), Tahbilk's reds are reminders of another era in Australian wine, while the white Marsanne – a rarity in itself – was served to the young Queen Elizabeth in 1953. The Reserve Shiraz (1860 Vines) and Cabernet have mouth-ripping tannin but enough flesh and fruit to persuade you that the 20- to 30-year wait will be worthwhile. The Marsanne is perfumed and attractive, as is a floral-scented Viognier. Other whites tend to be a bit more foursquare.
Best years: (1860 Vines) 1998, '96, '95, '94, '92, '91, '90, '87, '86, '82.

TARRAWARRA

Yarra Valley
❊ *Pinot Noir, Shiraz, Merlot*
❊ *Chardonnay*
Local wits call TarraWarra Disneyland; certainly until DOMAINE CHANDON came along it was the Yarra's only answer to the Napa Valley. Multi-millionaire owners Marc and Eva Besen and their son Daniel have spared no

TarraWarra
This winery is dedicated to producing high-quality Burgundian style wines, using a whole range of sophisticated vinification techniques and stuff the expense; the results are impressively mouthfilling.

expense on the winery in their quest to make an Australian Montrachet. Winemaker Clare Halloran fashions a rich, slow-maturing Chardonnay. Her dense, dark plum Pinot Noir is high quality but equally slow to mature. New less pricey Tin Cows label includes the varieties plus Merlot and Shiraz.
Best years: (Pinot Noir) 2002, '01, '00, '99, '98, '97, '96, '94, '92.

Yarra Burn
The name Bastard Hill comes from the terrifyingly steep slopes of Yarra Burn's Hoddles Creek vineyard in the Upper Yarra. This is the coldest patch of the valley and fruit can take up to eight weeks longer to ripen here than down on the valley floor.

YARRA BURN

Yarra Valley
❊ *Pinot Noir, Shiraz, Cabernet Sauvignon*
❊ *Chardonnay, Sauvignon Blanc, Semillon*
Acquired by HARDYS in the mid-1990s, along with two of the largest independent Yarra Valley vineyards, much of the wide range of fruit goes to making Hardys' top-end sparkling wines and (in varying proportions) its Eileen Hardy Chardonnay. Bastard Hill Chardonnay and Pinot Noir are the best two Yarra Burn wines. Best years: 2002, '00, '99, '98, '97, '94.

YARRA RIDGE

Yarra Valley
❊ *Pinot Noir, Cabernet Sauvignon, Merlot*
❊ *Chardonnay, Sauvignon Blanc*

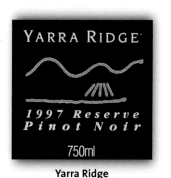

Yarra Ridge
Yarra Ridge is today a pretty large operation owned by Beringer Blass but its Reserve Pinot Noir still exhibits a mellow, rounded Yarra style.

Founded in 1983, Yarra Ridge enjoyed a meteoric rise in production and reputation, then was acquired by Beringer Blass. Yarra Ridge made its reputation with a trail-blazing, tangy, tropical gooseberry Sauvignon Blanc, but as volume grew rapidly, it lost its edge and indeed moved outside the Yarra for its grape sources. Pinot Noir, however, is the main focus, and the Reserve in particular, based on mature vineyards tucked into the Christmas Hills, is a ripe, smooth-textured wine. Chardonnay is also good. Best years: 2002, '00, '99, '98, '97, '96, '95.

YARRA YERING

Yarra Valley
❊ *Cabernet Sauvignon, Shiraz, Pinot Noir and others*
❊ *Chardonnay, Viognier*
Bailey Carrodus makes the richest, deepest, most complex and (for many years) least understood reds in the Yarra Valley, hiding their laurels under the enigmatic labels Dry Red Wine No 1 (a Bordeaux blend) and Dry Red Wine No 2 (a Rhône-style wine based on Shiraz but including some white Viognier). Carrodus believes that great wine is made in the vineyard, and practises benign neglect (except for a generous purchase of new oak barrels each year) in his winemaking, allowing vintage variation full play. The result is red wines crammed full of personality, which make the blood race despite sometimes upsetting the purists. They may not always fit into a mainstream style based solely on varietal flavours – but so what? You don't buy Yarra Yering in a spirit of complacent certainty but rather in a lather of uncertain anticipation.

Carrodus's latest mould-breaking wines are a delicious, idiosyncratic Pinot Noir and

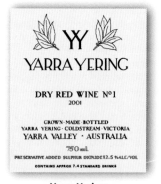

Yarra Yering
Bailey Carrodus creates extraordinary wines. This one is a delicious, perfumed Bordeaux blend with blackcurrant fruit that develops cedar spice with age.

a Chardonnay strongly reminiscent of old-fashioned Puligny-Montrachet from Burgundy. Yarra Yering also releases some peppery Shiraz under the Underhill label and a few cases of frighteningly expensive Merlot.

Best years: (No. 1) 2001, '99, '98, '97, '96, '94, '93, '91, '90, '89, '86.

Yellowglen

The quality at Yellowglen has been improving in recent years, as has all Australian fizz, but it still doesn't quite have the cool climate elegance of style that some of its competition possess.

YELLOWGLEN

Ballarat
❉ *Pinot Noir*
❧ *Chardonnay, Semillon*

Yellowglen just does sparkling wine. Visiting its winery just outside Ballarat in Victoria for the first time, I remember thinking – isn't this a bit hot to be growing grapes for fizz? Well, yes it is, and Yellowglen has never been the subtlest of wines, but it was created as a marketing venture – not a wine venture – and that included having a winemaker from Champagne. It's now a highly successful operation, sourcing its grapes from far and wide yet still playing on its homespun Ballarat roots and its Champenois winemaker.

YERING STATION

Yarra Valley
❉ *Pinot Noir, Cabernet Sauvignon, Shiraz, Merlot, Cabernet Franc and others*
❧ *Chardonnay and others*

Historic Yering Station is now a vibrant, modern winery/restaurant complex whose chief claim to fame is a successful joint venture for fizz with the French Champagne house of Devaux. And beneath all the glitz lie the very first vineyards to be planted in the State of Victoria way back in 1838. The grapes were hardly top drawer – Black Muscat and something called 'Sweet Water', but in the 1850s they obtained cuttings from Ch. Lafite-Rothschild in Bordeaux and by 1861 Yering Station had won the 'best vineyard in Victoria' award. So the pedigree is there, and the modern wines are good – fine toasty Yarrabank fizz, top, scented

Yering Station

Yering Station is now a huge tourist complex in the Yarra Valley but still produces a wide range of wines, including one of the valley's ripest Cabernets.

Shiraz/Viognier, fine Pinot Noir and Chardonnay and – perhaps reflecting those old Ch. Lafite Cabernet vines – one of Yarra Valley's ripest Cabernets.

YERINGBERG

Yarra Valley
❉ *Cabernet Sauvignon, Pinot Noir, Cabernet Franc, Merlot, Malbec*
❧ *Chardonnay, Marsanne, Roussanne*

From Guillaume, Baron de Pury, formerly of Neuchâtel in Switzerland and cousin of the first Governor of Victoria, Charles la Trobe, the ownership of Yeringberg has passed in direct succession to his grandson, Guill de Pury. The once-large vineyards are now reduced to a token 3ha, and de Pury makes a little wine for his health's sake in the well-preserved wooden winery, built in 1885. The wines rival those of YARRA YERING for depth and interest but are quite different in style, and have a silken elegance that makes you wonder – is this what wines were like a century ago?

But with the next generation keen to get involved, we might be in for a little controlled expansion. I'd be all for it, because these are splendid wines. The Marsanne/Roussanne has lush ripe fruit and honeysuckle scent. The red, based on Bordeaux grape varieties, has a remarkable timeless quality, beguilingly easy to drink, silken in texture yet unobtrusively impressive.

Best years: 2001, '00, '99, '98, '97, '96, '94, '92, '91, '90, '88, '86, '85.

Yeringberg

The dry red wine at this small but historically important winery is simply called Yeringberg. It is a Cabernet Sauvignon blend with deep fruit, fine balance and great aging potential.

WESTERN AUSTRALIA

IT'S THE SHEER VASTNESS of Western Australia that hits you first. That and the emptiness. If you approach Perth, the one centre of population, from the north or the east, you can gaze from the plane window in vain for any signs of life. Any township, any road or railway, any river even, or lake – and the searing orange soils glare back at you, offering nothing and no-one. Since the state covers well over a third of Australia's landmass, yet boasts a population of a mere 1.9 million, you begin to understand how isolated the few inhabitants must feel. The export markets of Asia are closer to Perth than the domestic markets of the rest of Australia to the east.

Yet Western Australia can lay fair claim to being one of the originators of vineyards in Australia. Though New South Wales, where the first fleet arrived in 1788, was the first to plant vines, Western Australia wasn't far behind – and was way ahead of South Australia and Victoria. Olive Farm had vines planted in 1829 on the banks of the Swan River just outside Perth, and since it is still going today, counts as the oldest operating winery in Australia. And it must have been reasonably decent stuff, because towards the end of the nineteenth century the Swan Valley had more wineries than any other Australian region. And until the 1970s most of the wine was drunk locally.

Despite the continual success of large companies based in the Swan, like Houghton and Sandalford – who both, by the way, source much of their fruit from elsewhere – the winds of fashion are blowing most of our attention way to the south – to the Margaret River and Great Southern regions. The conditions couldn't be more different from the Swan District – cool and temperate rather than baking hot. And the wines are totally different too.

The Porongurups overlooking the Mount Barker vineyards in Great Southern are said to be the oldest hills in the world. The vineyards are high and the conditions are cool, favouring lean but fragrant Riesling. As for the views, they're fantastic.

SPOTLIGHT ON
Western Australia

The Swan Valley is an incredibly hot vineyard region but in the north of the valley the vineyards around Gingin, at a slightly higher altitude and enjoying a slightly cooler climate, have a reputation for good whites. Even so, to get the best out of the grapes they are harvested at night when temperatures are lower. These Chardonnay grapes at Houghton's Moondah Brook Estate at Gin Gin are also benefiting from a mobile crushing and refrigeration plant.

To understand Western Australia's future, perhaps you should approach Perth from the north-west, having stopped off at Bangkok or Kuala Lumpur or Singapore. Then you'll realize how close to Indonesia and Asia this sliver of cultivable land on the far western edge of Australia is. It would be normal to think of the Asian countries as perhaps even more natural trading partners than the big populous Australian states to the east. And perhaps they will be.

So to understand Australia's present and past, it's best to approach Perth from the east. Take the plane from, say, Sydney or Brisbane, on the east coast. Make sure you've got a window seat – left or right, it really won't matter. Gaze contentedly as the plane rises up above the Great Dividing Range. This won't take more then half an hour, as the mountains and forests recede, the fertile plateau land drops away and you enter the hot heart of Australia. For a while the landscape is merely dun-coloured, exhausted, bleached by drought and sun, but you can run a few hardy sheep or cattle on some of this unforgiving land, and a handful of ferocious outback farmers do. You can tell someone's there by the occasional track through the barren scrub visible from on high. But this is the easy part. After another hour or so, even the infrequent tracks are all but gone, and the earth has assumed a glowering orange-red quality that defies the best efforts of European man to settle or to survive. But you can see whorls and swirls in the arid soils as the marks of ancient rivers and lakes which were formed millions of years ago still stain the landscape and give it an illusive sense of life and activity it doesn't deserve. And this goes on for hours.

It's 4400 kilometres from Brisbane to Perth, and about 4000 kilometres from Sydney, and during almost all of the journey – a brilliant, awesome, humbling nothingness sprawls beneath the wings of the plane. It almost seems to get worse towards the end of the flight as even the colour orange is drained from the earth and enormous bright white salt pans start to scar the land like leprosy. Then suddenly – tracks, roads, forest, reservoirs, a golf course, tree-filled suburbs – and the sea. From nothing to Western Australia's metropolis in 15 minutes.

And now imagine what it was like before airplanes. What it was like before the Transcontinental Railway took on the Nullarbor Plain – Nullarbor, that means 'not a tree' – and like the desperate lunge of a javelin thrower with one last chance to win – speared the steel rails straight as a die to connect east and west. But imagine, in the days before refrigeration, did this really help trade in grapes and wine? And in recent times, as the states of South Australia, Victoria and New South Wales have ramped up their

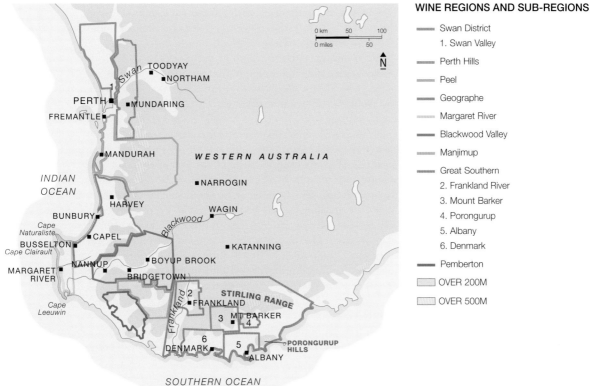

WINE REGIONS AND SUB-REGIONS

▬ Swan District
 1. Swan Valley

▬ Perth Hills

▬ Peel

▬ Geographe

▬ Margaret River

▬ Blackwood Valley

▬ Manjimup

▬ Great Southern
 2. Frankland River
 3. Mount Barker
 4. Porongurup
 5. Albany
 6. Denmark

▬ Pemberton

▢ OVER 200M

▢ OVER 500M

production and their quality – has it been easy for Western Australia to make an impact upon anyone but themselves?

No, it hasn't. And the lack of population in the West, allied to the vast distance to unwilling markets in the East has meant they've had to do it on their own, and largely for themselves. Typically, their wine industry began, as elsewhere in Australia, on the first suitable patches of land settlers found within hailing distance of the new metropolis, Perth. These were in the Swan Valley. And the Swan wine industry did a good job of providing for the needs of Perth and the handful of other settlements on the west coast. It even managed to create a wine – Houghton's White Burgundy – which became Western Australia's only big seller in the eastern states – and as HWB it's still a success today. But although efforts, both by individuals and governments, to expand the wine industry into

Climate The further south you go in Western Australia, the cooler it is. The coastal regions enjoy a maritime climate and regions further inland and to the north are hotter, drier and more continental.

Soil The soils are mainly brown or grey-brown alluvial topsoil, frequently fairly sandy with some gravel.

Aspect Vineyards are concentrated on the valley floors or gentle slopes along the coast, although there are some vines in more hilly areas along the Darling Ranges.

Do regions or vintages matter? Margaret River, Great Southern and neighbouring Pemberton have cool climates and definite vintage variation. Swan District is hot and more consistent.

Organization Houghton, based in the Swan Valley and now owned by the multinational Constellation group, is the dominant wine company and was until relatively recently the only Western Australian company to have much of a profile outside the state let alone on the export market. With so many isolated wine regions, the rest of the wine

industry in the state is largely made up of boutique wine producers and contract growers.

A few facts 11,736ha of vineyards, 7 per cent of Australia's total plantings; 4 per cent of total production; plantings increased by 140% between 1998 and 2001, and volume went from 19,000 tonnes in 1996 to 60,000 tonnes in 2003. Yet half of Western Australia's vines are only about to produce their first crop. Exports are currently 10% of sales. This will have to increase substantially if a crisis is to be avoided.

the vast and eminently suitable acres of the state's south were made intermittently during the twentieth century, since there was little population and almost no passing or tourist trade, not much was achieved.

But following upon two reports by scientists as to the suitability of the south for high quality grapes, and with the rest of Australia just beginning to indulge in the birth pangs of the great modern Australian wine era, echoes were felt in the distant west, and during the 1960s and 1970s a strange but potent collection of doctors, farmers and businessmen began to plant vines. But still it was just for themselves. Luckily Western Australia was going to experience a remarkable mineral wealth-led boom over the next decades, so there were people with money prepared to pay for decent local wines. Decent became good. Good became superb, some of the best in the land, so that by the twenty-first century such areas as Margaret River, Mount Barker and Frankland River, with such diverse offerings as Chardonnay, Riesling, Semillon/Sauvignon, Cabernet/Merlot and Shiraz, are equalling the very best in the rest of Australia. But that doesn't mean they'll be easy to find in Melbourne or Sydney or Brisbane. There's a glut of wine in the east, much of it very good. The West, as always, has to look after itself, and as it too starts to produce more wine than it can drink or sell, the West looks further west – to Asia and Europe – in the hope that they'll realize the startling quality of the wines now being produced, but also be prepared to pay the higher than average price.

SWAN VALLEY

But it all began in the Swan Valley. The *Parmelia* landed in 1829 to establish the colony, The first landfall to 'claim' Western Australia for Britain had been way south at Albany on Christmas Day 1826, but Perth is where the settlers for the new colony centred themselves.

Vineyards of Goundrey Wines, Mount Barker. This is the original vineyard of the exciting Great Southern region, but to begin with progress was slow and even now lack of water holds up further expansion. Even so, quality is high and superb whites and Shiraz reds have been produced.

Between then and the late 1970s when the Margaret River medical pioneers began to make waves, Perth's Swan Valley was about it for wines. Indeed at the end of the nineteenth century the Swan had more wineries than any other viticultural area of Australia. Add to that a boom during the 1890s when Victoria's vineyards were destroyed by the phylloxera aphid, and a Western Gold Rush, which like elsewhere in Australia created throngs of spendthrift thirst-crazed prospectors. Things were good in the Swan. Then after the First and Second World Wars there were big influxes of Yugoslav refugees and they enthusiastically developed the Swan wine culture, both in terms of large amounts of jug wines for themselves and their friends, and fortifieds for the market in general. For perhaps two-thirds of the twentieth century, the domestic market wanted strong, sweet 'ports' and 'sherries'. The Swan was and is the perfect place to make them. It's the hottest of any of Australia's major wine regions, with the most sunshine hours, January and February temperatures that can soar to 45°C, and the lowest summer rainfall (with the odd exception when there's a deluge in February). Cool sea breezes do get sucked up the valley each day, and that tempers things a bit. But, frankly, in the Swan people bake and grapes bake. Fortifieds are out of fashion now, yet this is a marvellous place to make them.

But largely thanks to one man, the story isn't just fortifieds and jug wine. Jack Mann was winemaker at Houghton – the Swan's major producer – from 1922 to 1972, and chief winemaker since 1930. He made famous fortifieds, but he also created a famous white – Houghton's White Burgundy. We might hardly recognize it as a table wine at all today, because he never picked his grapes until the sun-baked vine had simply nothing left to offer them. And then he'd always follow his philosophy, 'Wines should be resplendent with generosity: unless a wine can be diluted with an equal volume of water, it wasn't worth making in the first place'. I've tasted some of those old Houghton White Burgundies – deep, thick, viscous, golden wines, oozing with overripeness but aging with all the sequinned majesty of a dowager in love with a chorus boy.

For a long time Houghton was really the only winery that had more than a local trade. I was always most impressed by the way they could produce delicious, full-bodied but crisp whites, especially from Chenin and Verdelho. Partly this is because Chenin can hold its acid in torrid conditions and Verdelho comes from the sub-tropical island of Madeira off West Africa. But it's also because further up the Swan at Gingin in the bizarre way of these things, it cools down and Houghton's Moondah Brook vineyard in particular, takes full advantage. Yet Houghton also makes excellent Chardonnays and Rieslings, as well as top quality reds. For these, we have to head way south – to the large expanse of the Great Southern.

GREAT SOUTHERN

A visiting professor – Harold Olmo from California – had written a report for the government in 1955, telling them how to deal with vine problems in the Swan, but remarking that Frankland River and Mount Barker – north of Albany and now the heart of Great Southern – were far better suited for vines. Dr John Gladstones repeated this view in 1963. People had been saying this on and off for most of the twentieth century – but Great Southern was a wild landscape of mighty jarrah and red gum trees, barely tameable scrub, sudden great outcrops of granite, weather patterns that might look good on paper but which no-one had tested – and very few inhabitants.

Even so, the 1960s and '70s threw up enough individualists prepared to give it a go – graziers, businessmen and, luckily, the State viticulturalist. Probably the crucial thing was that Houghton liked the fruit and offered contracts which led to the establishment of the 100-hectare Westfield vineyard at Frankland to provide them with grapes. Alkoomi vineyard was established nearby in 1971. Plantagenet Winery was founded at Mount Barker in 1974, Goundrey in 1975. All of these are now formidable players in the area. Further important producers like Howard Park (1986) and Frankland River (1988) followed in the 1980s and in the 1990s there was another surge of plantings encouraged by favourable tax deals being offered for vineyard plantations, and Ferngrove (1997) is the most important of these. The thing I like about this bunch is the quality of their wine is

Quick guide ◆
The problems of distance

In South Australia the vine barely manages to sidle further west than Adelaide. It's about a four-hour flight westward before you hit the next vineyards, and they're on the far side of Western Australia. There's not much in between, either; no big centres of population, not much in the way of mountain ranges. Just a lot of desert and a lot of sea.

This meant that if the early settlers in Western Australia wanted wine, they had to grow it themselves and since the spot chosen for the early settlements was the mouth of the Swan river where it opens to form a natural harbour, it made sense to plant the vines a little way upriver, hence the Swan District.

This was the pattern of wine development all over Australia – and, frankly, all over the world. Before the days of railways and tarmac roads, transport of anything heavy for any distance was difficult, so you established your vineyards as close as possible to your customers – preferably just outside the town. The one way you could transport heavy materials like barrels of wine was by water. So river valleys can support vineyards some way from towns. Indeed, many of Europe's most famous vineyard regions – in France, Germany, Spain, Portugal and elsewhere – are established in river valleys – often at some distance from their main markets. Rivers with their steep slopes and their twists and turns also provide many superb vineyard sites . That's especially important in cool marginal conditions, but only Tasmania in Australia generally needs to warm up its conditions.

No, in Australia, each state developed its own local wine industry, and until the relatively recent development of national brands, people mostly drank the local stuff. Since each state can make good wine – with the exception of the Northern Territory, there was little incentive to buy another state's wine. South Australia, by its development of vast irrigated vineyards in the Murray River Valley, could send their wine further afield because they were producing wine cheaper than anyone else. Western Australia is thousands of kilometres from the next settled area of Australia. No-one was going to ask for the wines until places like Margaret River produced such different and such high quality wines, the rest of Australia had to take notice.

These are the kind of fantastic forests you'll discover in Western Australia's Great Southern region, especially if you take any of the little roads off the South Coast Highway between Albany, Denmark and Walpole. Giant karri trees, shade – and silence.

never worse than good, and can be some of the best in Australia, even where vineyards are less than a decade old. So let's take a close look at this 'Great Southern'.

First, it's big – 150 kilometres deep and 100 kilometres wide. The two most important regions are Frankland River and Mount Barker. But there are several others. Denmark, west of Albany on the coast, is cool and mostly a little damp, but it does produce some excellent Chardonnay, Pinot Noir and Riesling, and alongside and just to the south of the Scottsdale Road north-west of Denmark, the mix of attractive wines, wineries and outstanding karri forest scenery makes this the most tourist friendly part of Great Southern. Forest Hill, the original Great Southern vineyard inland at Mount Barker, has just established its new winery and cellar door right among the tourists just west of Denmark. Albany is the main southern city and is chiefly famous for Wignalls who have produced a string of award-winning Pinot Noirs, but Albany Chardonnay and Shiraz are also good. Well inland, north of Albany, is Porongurups. Planted on slopes at heights up to 350 metres these are cool conditions in a cool region and seem best suited to Riesling. And to sightseeing. The Porongurups Range is an unexpected bulging mass of granite boulders and outcrops that is memorable by daylight, and magical at dawn and dusk.

Mount Barker is the home of Forest Hill, the region's original vineyard, but also of Plantagenet, the first local winery which was founded in an old apple-packing shed in 1974 – a reminder that this region used to be one of Australia's top apple districts. Their original refrigeration equipment was bought from an old whaling station in Albany – another reminder of the past. With no wine infrastructure and little local knowledge, the establishment of vines around Mount Barker was slow and difficult, but led by Plantagenet, the region has proved to be excellent for cool climate fruit. It actually harvests later than the coastal vineyards to the south, can produce thrilling Rieslings and fabulous spicy Shiraz. However, if there's any cyclonic activity in Western Australia it's more than likely to affect Mount Barker. In 2000 160mm of rain fell in one day right at vintage.

The other problem here is water – and this affects Frankland River too. These areas were covered with vast forests before bulldozers left over from the Second World War managed to rip out the giant trees and tame the land. But loss of forest has meant a very saline water table. This means water has to be collected in dams from winter rainfall – there's rarely enough in the summer – and many south-facing slopes are covered in a zig-zag of channels to catch irrigation water. But the effort is worth it. Frankland River is probably producing more top quality white grapes than any other region of Western Australia, and its Shiraz is deep, soft-textured and thrillingly fresh, helped by consistently sunny days and ice cold nights. Led by large projects like Ferngrove and Houghton's Frankland River Vineyards, there are now about 1300 hectares of vines in Frankland. If water problems can be solved, there is room for thousands more hectares of vines and the establishment of a reputation as one of the New World's great cool-climate regions.

OTHER WINE REGIONS

Directly to the west of Great Southern are Pemberton and Manjimup. These used to be considered as one entity, but they are different – Pemberton is closer to the coast with different soil types, so the division is fair enough. Pemberton is better known, perhaps because it has higher profile producers like Picardy, Salitage and the Petaluma-owned Smithbrook. However, I've always found the wine style a bit erratic, occasionally loving a Chardonnay, a Pinot Noir or a Shiraz, but just as often finding them diluted and not fully ripe. Certainly cool climate is one reason, but Pemberton also has a lot of extremely fertile loamy soil and a minority of well-drained gravelly soil. Vineyards have been planted on both, but cool climate and fertile loam makes ripening a hard task. Manjimup, further inland but adjoining, has more gravelly soil, is slightly warmer, and the scientist Dr Gladstones thought its conditions were pretty similar to those of Bordeaux in France. And so far cool but spicy reds from Shiraz and the Bordeaux grape varieties seem to be giving the best results.

The main quality action in the state is taking place in Margaret River and the areas to the south. However, between Margaret River and Perth there are a couple of regions

The classic Bordeaux and Burgundy grape varieties thrive at Salitage, one of the leading wineries in the recently established Pemberton region. Salitage enjoys an excellent hilltop site with gravelly soils and cool, even temperatures during the ripening season. These gravelly soils are important. Pemberton can get wet, and the commonly found heavy loam soils struggle to ripen their crops.

making good use of the warmer conditions – Geographe and Peel. The Geographe Bay is curved like a giant J and runs across the top of Margaret River before turning north towards Perth. Initially the Geographe wine region merely referred to a few vineyards down by the coast, but nowadays the boundaries extend inland past Donnybrook and up the Ferguson River. The coastal area is characterized by very pale 'Tuart' sandy soils, but major wineries like Capel Vale make use of fertile loams on the river banks. These are fairly warm conditions. There are cooler sites up the Ferguson Valley where vines are planted at up to 300 metres. The whole gamut of grape varieties is planted, from Riesling, Sauvignon and Chardonnay, to Merlot, Cabernet and even Nebbiolo. The recently established Willow Bridge Estate is the leading producer. Donnybrook is pretty warm and grows varieties like Shiraz, Cabernet, Grenache and a little Zinfandel.

Peel runs up almost to the southern suburbs of Perth. It isn't that well known but vineyards were established here as early as 1857 and Peel Estate has been going since 1976, growing a famous Chenin Blanc and a variety of reds headed by Shiraz, but including such delights as Zinfandel and the Portuguese Port varieties. The Peel vineyards are worth a visit if only to walk barefoot in the pale grey, powdery Tuart sands. One further area is the Blackwood Valley inland from Margaret River towards Nannup where Hardys have recently established a large winery to service their vineyards and growers all over the south-west.

PERTH HILLS

The other small region is the Perth Hills which are, in effect, the Darling Range. These overlook Perth from 20–30 kilometres inland, and the wooded valleys have vineyards established at between 150 and 400 metres above sea level. Sea breezes blowing in across the range's western escarpment reduce daytime temperatures; by contrast, warm sea air stops the temperature dropping too much at night. The hilly, irregular nature of the valleys creates widely differing mesoclimates that, at their coolest, ripen grapes two to three weeks later than those in vineyards in the nearby Swan Valley flats. Soils are good, with a fair amount of gravelly loam, and rainfall is high – but almost all of it is in the winter. If you've got storage dams for spring and summer irrigation, that's no problem; but if you haven't, those gravelly soils will be too free-draining to raise a crop.

Quick guide ◆
Wine Doctors

Wineries have been founded by people of all walks of life but doctors seem to have done more than their fair share, and especially those of Western Australia. It was lupin expert Dr John Gladstones who in 1965 recommended planting vines in Margaret River; Dr Tom Cullity founded Vasse Felix there two years later, and was followed by Dr Bill Pannell of Moss Wood and Dr Kevin Cullen of Cullens.

The medical role in Australian wine started early, from the moment the First Fleet set sail in 1787 when the doctor in charge made sure that there was enough wine on board to be used as a medicine and also to help prevent malnutrition. The famous Penfold and Lindeman brands were founded by doctors in the nineteenth century. These doctors clearly knew wine was good for you long ago.

MARGARET RIVER

The Cape Mentelle barrel room. This may make it look as though there is a vast amount of oak being used in Margaret River. Well, there is, but a lot of these barrels will already have been used and so won't give off powerful vanilla flavours. The character of Margaret River Cabernet in particular is so strong, it doesn't need lashings of new wood. Cape Mentelle is famous for reds of a restrained yet intense beauty.

IN MY EARLY VISITS TO AUSTRALIA, I didn't get to Western Australia. In my early wine-tasting days, I hardly ever tasted a bottle from the West. Especially a bottle from Margaret River. The people in Europe who did see the odd bottle were old timers, the Bordeaux and Burgundy brigade, the chaps – and they were almost universally male – who might be prepared to let the New World raise their blood pressure just a point or two if it could prove capable of aping the reds of Bordeaux and the whites of Burgundy. But they largely kept the bottles to themselves, perhaps unable to fully come to terms with the disturbing fact that Margaret River could indeed emulate and even improve upon the Bordeaux and Burgundy styles. In any case, I was infatuated by the warmer, richer styles of further east in Australia, so it took me a while to start appreciating the undoubted brilliance of Margaret River's wines.

But then, it took Margaret River a fair while to get going itself, and it might never have been discovered as a fine wine vineyard area had it not been for a clutch of beady-eyed local doctors. They saw a couple of reports in the mid-1960s produced by a Western Australian scientist, Dr John Gladstones, that the Margaret River had unusually close climatic analogies with Bordeaux, but with less spring frost, more reliable summer sunshine, and less risk of hail or excessive rain during ripening. For

WHERE THE VINEYARDS ARE You shouldn't have too much trouble getting casual labour around vintage time in Margaret River. But be warned – it may be very casual, depending on the size of the waves, rather than the ripeness of the grapes, because that long, inviting coastline that you see on the left of the map is one of the greatest surfing beaches in the world. So don't expect the pickers to stay bent over the vines when the waves get up.

The sea's influence, though, is one of the crucial aspects of Margaret River. That's the Indian Ocean there. It's a warm sea, and the difference between summer and winter temperatures is smaller here than anywhere else in the whole of Australia. But this isn't always a bonus: early-flowering varieties, like Chardonnay, often get lashed by westerly gales just when they are trying to set a crop, and the winds can carry salt miles inland; grapes and salt don't get on. On the other hand, Margaret River's long, baking, sun-soaked autumns will ripen most varieties of grape to perfection.

The first group of vineyards, those that were established by those doctors in the 1960s, are the ones you can see in the middle of the map. They are still the most important group. It becomes cooler as you head south to below the Margaret River itself, but some of the most famous vineyards (for example, Leeuwin's) are those shown right at the bottom of the map.

Well inland from Cape Clairault, at the top of the map, are the large and somewhat controversial flatland plantings of Jindong. South of the map there are increasing plantings in cool conditions towards Karridale.

CAPE CLAIRAULT

GRACETOWN ■

PREVELLY ■

SELECTED WINERIES

1. Amberley Estate
2. Clairault
3. Moss Wood
4. Evans & Tate
5. Brookland Valley
6. Pierro
7. Gralyn
8. Cullen Wines
9. Vasse Felix
10. Howard Park
11. Ashbrook Estate
12. Sandalford
13. Willespie
14. Hay Shed Hill
15. Woody Nook
16. Cape Mentelle
17. Xanadu Wines
18. Redgate
19. Voyager Estate
20. Stella Bella
21. Leeuwin Estate
22. Devil's Lair
23. Suckfizzle

NORTHERN MARGARET RIVER

TOTAL DISTANCE NORTH
TO SOUTH 39.5KM

VINEYARDS

0 km   1   2
0 miles   1

some reason, Australian doctors right across the nation have never been able to resist such pronouncements. First Dr Tom Cullity at Vasse Felix, then fellow doctors Bill Pannell at Moss Wood and Kevin Cullen of Cullen Wines, planted vineyards that were to form the heart of the Margaret River region right from the start. Indeed, Margaret River went on to establish itself as a remarkably versatile, if somewhat capricious, cool-climate region which was as good as any in Australia. But was it Bordeaux? Well, yes and no.

In fact Dr Gladstones was supposed to be doing research on lupins – rather the same as Cullity and Co. were supposed to be keeping the locals hale and hearty – but his good luck was that the legendary winemaker, Jack Mann, at Houghton vineyard in the Swan Valley let him use a spare couple of acres of land next to the winery cellars for his lupin experiments. Lupins are all very well, but the ever-open cellar door at his neighbour's winery began to weave its magic on the doctor and distract him from his original research. The possibilities in Western Australia for fine wine, as yet barely touched upon by winemakers in the torrid Swan Valley, began to take up more and more of Dr Gladstones' time.

A visiting Californian viticulturalist, Professor Harold Olmo, commissioned by the state government to prepare a report on Western Australia's wine industry, had already suggested in 1956 that the far south of the state, near Mount Barker and Rocky Gully, would make a high-

Red grapes The main varieties are Cabernet Sauvignon, Shiraz and Merlot.

White grapes Chardonnay leads the way and there are substantial amounts of Semillon and Sauvignon Blanc, often blended together, and also some Chenin Blanc and Verdelho.

Climate The maritime climate has a coolish growing season and a mild, wet winter. Cold Antarctic currents flowing south of the land mass, and westerly winds from the Indian Ocean make it more temperate than Perth to the north. Sea breezes are good for preventing overheating, but bad for drying out the soil, sometimes making irrigation necessary.

Soil The topsoil tends to be sand or gravel, the subsoil is often clay loam which has the capacity to retain water, but irrigation is still often necessary.

Aspect Vines are planted on low, gentle slopes, at around 40m above sea level.

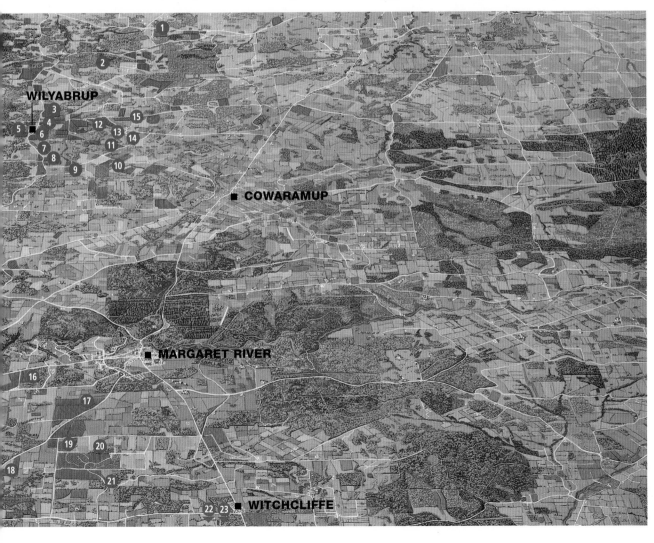

Magnificent marri trees, also known as red gums, skirt the vineyards at Pierro, home to one of Australia's top Chardonnays, and protect the vines from the strong prevailing winds in spring and early summer. The trees come into blossom in February and March and provide plenty of nectar for the silvereye birds who otherwise would devour the grapes in the run-up to harvest.

quality vineyard site. Gladstones thought the area on the south-west coast, about 130 kilometres further north, between Cape Leeuwin and Cape Naturaliste, would be warmer and more predictable in weather and more flexible in the varieties of grapes that could be grown. He felt the Great Southern region, with its cool, southerly maritime influence could indeed match Bordeaux's cooler regions, but that the Margaret River, influenced by the Indian Ocean along its western edge, could match the warmer Bordeaux regions of Pomerol and St-Émilion. The added advantage for Margaret River was that it was an area free of the risk of frost and rain at vintage that so often spoiled things in Bordeaux. It was these thoughts that galvanized the local winemaking doctors into action.

Yet there are problems, and the most intractable is wind. Sea breezes are crucial for cooling down vines in many areas of Australia, but these are gales we're talking about – especially in spring – when salt-laden winds power in off the Indian Ocean and can crucially affect the vine as it attempts to flower and set a crop. Given the fact that the winters are some of the mildest in Australia, vines are likely to wake up early here and so the early-budding Chardonnay and Merlot often get into trouble.

And then there's the wildlife. Those lovely mysterious stands of tall karri gums found throughout the region are home to legions of kangaroos. Delightful, shy little roos; how we Europeans wish they were less timid so that we could feed them lettuce leaves from the palms of our hands. Try giving that sentimental tosh to a grape-grower in springtime when the little fellas have nipped out overnight and chewed all the emerging buds off his vines.

And don't talk to him about how divine those lime green parrots are fluttering and cawing among the vines. They are rapacious pests that munch away at the grapes for nourishment and then, replete with his best Cabernet Sauvignon, chew through the vine branches just for recreation. And don't mention silvereyes either, those sweet little migratory birds that find the netting protecting the vines rather good for nesting in – and anyway they're tiny enough to wriggle through and devour the crop under the nets.

Such problems rarely occur in Europe – or in traditional Australian wine districts. But where new vineyards are carved from virgin land there are bound to be upsets. In such thinly populated regions as Margaret River, the relatively small areas of vines and grapes make easy targets for hungry wildlife. Interestingly, the only effective defence against the yearly silvereye invasion is a natural one: their favourite refuelling food is the nectar of red gum blossom. When the gums flower on time, the silvereyes relish this feast, but if the flowering is late, they turn to the sugar-sweet grapes.

But it does all seem to be worth it. Today, across a remarkable spectrum of wines, the quality of the Margaret River fruit sings out loud and clear. These range from mighty, gum-scented Pinot Noirs to classic structured Cabernet Sauvignons and Chardonnays, from unnervingly French, yet tantalizingly individual Semillons and Sauvignon Blancs to positively un-Australian Shiraz and Zinfandel, and even to vintage 'port'.

VINEYARD AREAS

There were intermittent attempts in the nineteenth century to plant the area, but Doctors Cullity, Pannell and Cullen really showed the way in the late 1960s and early '70s, when they planted small vineyards in the locality of Wilyabrup around Cowaramup, about 15 kilometres north of the township of Margaret River, an area which still boasts the most flagship estates in the region.

However, some of the highest profile estates – Cape Mentelle, Leeuwin Estate, Voyager and Xanadu – are actually located south of the Margaret River. There has also been a lot of vineyard development around Karridale in the extreme south of the region. Here summers are cooler than in the northern plots, although it also benefits from prolonged mild sunny weather into late autumn. And in the far north-west, around Yallingup, between Cape Clairault and Cape Naturaliste, are wineries such as Abbey Vale, Amberley, Clairault and Happs. In general average temperatures rise as you move north through Margaret River, and leading estates south of the Margaret River definitely produce wines of a cooler fruit flavour than those to the north.

On the other side of the Bussell Highway, in the north-east, is the former potato-growing area of Jindong. Ex-potato fields are not famous for producing high-quality grapes and the jury is still out as to whether these ones will prove an exception. But its flat land, fertile soil, plentiful water supply and moderate climate have encouraged Evans & Tate, Vasse Felix and Selwyn wineries to establish large vineyards here, and the wines are mostly pretty good if a little soft. And they're cheaper too.

CLIMATE AND SOIL

Soils do differ, but most good vineyard sites in Margaret River are either located on gravels or sands over clay. These tend to drain well – which is fine as long as you've built plenty of dams to store your irrigation water – while the clay subsoil holds th winter moisture effectively. Of the area's annual 1160mm rainfall, just 200mm falls in the all-important growing season – between October and April – when the vines need it most. Efficient irrigation is vital.

The intensity of the fruit, and the acid and tannin structure in the wines are the best rebuttal I can think of when people suggest that you can't make great wines using irrigation. With a few outstanding exceptions, such as the excellent Moss Wood, Cullen and Leeuwin estates, in the Margaret River region you can't make great wines without it.

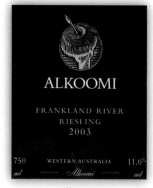

Alkoomi

Riesling was among the first varieties planted at Alkoomi, the pioneer winery in Frankland back in 1971, and the wine helped forge the region's reputation for the variety.

ALKOOMI

Great Southern

✣ *Cabernet Sauvignon, Shiraz, Malbec, Merlot and others*

✣ *Riesling, Chardonnay, Sauvignon Blanc and others*

If you had stood on the porch of Merv and Judy Lange's Alkoomi property in the 1970s, you would have seen the vast expanse of gently undulating, dun-coloured land that marks out a sheep station and a grain farm. That's what the Langes and everybody in the far south of Western Australia did then. But if you'd looked left, you'd have seen something totally new – a patch of leafy green vines just about to give their first fruit. The Langes were alone in seeing the potential of Frankland back in 1971 – perhaps they just wanted a bit more colour in the view from their porch – but they were truly prescient. They now have 70ha of vines and devote themselves full time to wine. It was their Riesling that first got my attention – lean, but beautifully scented with lime. Alkoomi were one of the first producers to insist on keeping the alcohol low in Australian Rieslings, and it really shows in the wine. Their reds are also cool in flavour, with good dry Shiraz and Cabernet and dark Bordeaux blend Blackbutt. And now, if you stand on the porch, you can see hardly a patch of the old dun colour as Frankland proves itself to be one of the best new vineyard sites in Australia.
Best years: (Blackbutt) 2002, '01, '99, '98, '97, '96, '95, '94.

BROOKLAND VALLEY

Margaret River

✣ *Cabernet Sauvignon, Shiraz, Cabernet Franc, Merlot*

✣ *Chardonnay, Sauvignon Blanc*

Established 20 years ago by Malcolm and Dee Jones on the banks of the Wilyabrup Brook, this Caves Road property boasts one of the region's picture postcard vineyards. The HARDY WINE COMPANY bought 50% of Brookland Valley in 1997 and are involved in contract winemaking and distribution while the Joneses handle the day-to-day running of the vineyard. A major development since then has been the introduction of the Verse 1 range (most notably Semillon/Sauvignon Blanc and Cabernet/Merlot). These are sourced from 150ha of vineyards run by long-term growers in different parts of the Margaret River region and have allowed the Brookland Valley brand to grow to 80,000 cases. The estate wines (especially the sublime Reserve Chardonnay, consistently good Sauvignon Blanc and both Cabernets) still drive the vineyard's image and have never been better than in the last few years under HOUGHTON's Larry Cherubino (now sadly departed but I expect the quality level he established to be maintained).
Best years: (Reserve Chardonnay) 2002.

Brookland Valley

Sauvignon Blanc thrives in Margaret River and this example shows plenty of varietal character, with hints of passionfruit and gooseberry, refreshing acidity and excellent length.

CAPE MENTELLE

Margaret River

✣ *Cabernet Sauvignon, Shiraz, Zinfandel*

✣ *Semillon, Sauvignon Blanc, Chardonnay*

The rammed-earth walls and local timber of one of Margaret River's leading wineries blend perfectly into the landscape, with its exotic native plants and a tiny rivulet meandering by.

Now owned by French luxury goods brand LVMH, along with New Zealand's Cloudy Bay, the question of the moment is how it will fare without its founder David Hohnen who crafted the wines with intense care and sensitivity. He worked hard to

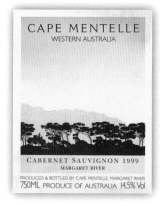

Cape Mentelle

This leading Margaret River winery makes superb, cedary Cabernet Sauvignon that benefits from up to ten years' aging after bottle.

invest his Cabernet Sauvignon with the right amount of tannin to balance its full, dark fruit, and did so to such effect that I often included the wine or the equally tasty Cabernet/Merlot in Bordeaux line-ups – always with great success. It was never out-classed. Not once. It usually won.

I also love the peppery brilliance of the Shiraz and the inspired 'almost over the top' richness of the Zinfandel. Put these with top Chardonnay and excellent tangy Semillon/Sauvignon and you have one of Australia's most consistently fine wineries. But it wasn't just winemaking that made David special. He managed to mix passion with famously dry wit, and his inspiration created teams at both Cape Mentelle and Cloudy Bay of unswerving loyalty. And wit. Rugged independence – hey, don't forget the wit – has always been the Cape Mentelle way, so let's hope the winemaker John Durham and his team continue the good work and don't let LVMH interfere too much.
Best years: (Cabernet Sauvignon) 2002, '01, '00, '99, '98, '96, '95, '94, '92, '91, '90.

CAPEL VALE

Geographe

✣ *Shiraz, Cabernet Sauvignon, Merlot, Malbec, Pinot Noir, Nebbiolo*

✣ *Chardonnay, Sauvignon Blanc, Riesling, Verdelho, Semillon, Viognier, Chenin Blanc*

Dr Peter Pratten's winery sources fruit from Geographe, Mount Barker, Pemberton and Margaret River. Rieslings have consistently been the top wines, especially the classy Whispering Hill, which is basically Mount Barker wine, while others in the top Black Label range have been variable. However, recent winemaking changes promise much more emphasis on the high-quality vineyard origins of the fruit and

Capel Vale
Classy Whispering Hill Riesling, with bright citrus fruit, is one of the best wines at Capel Vale, by far the largest and oldest winery in the Geographe region.

The late Di Cullen and her husband Kevin were the original wine pioneers in Margaret River. Di is seen here with her daughter Vanya who is now one of Australia's top winemakers.

consequently finer, more focused wines. I'm particularly looking forward to future releases of top Shiraz and Cabernet/Merlot vintages, hopefully with regional differences evident in the glass.
Best years: (Whispering Hill Riesling) 2003, '02, '01, '00, '98, '97.

CULLEN WINES

Margaret River
❦ *Cabernet Sauvignon, Merlot, Pinot Noir and others*
❦ *Chardonnay, Sauvignon Blanc, Semillon*
Cullens was one of the original pioneer wineries in Margaret River, and is still one of the quality leaders, now run by the highly talented and refreshingly opinionated Vanya Cullen, and making marvellously self-confident wines. Its complex, structured Cabernet/Merlot is generally one of Australia's best, and time after time it is put into tastings of top Cabernet/Merlots from all around the world – including Bordeaux – and the sheer pristine beauty of its fruit and balance make you want to taste the others, and drink this one. New release Mangan from Malbec, Petit Verdot and Merlot is richly idiosyncratic with an irresistible lush texture from Malbec, and violet scent from the Petit Verdot. The Chardonnay is oaky but long-lived and now that it is 100% wild yeast-fermented it has a memorable oatmealy weight. Partially barrel-fermented Semillon/Sauvignon is

bright and leafy and scented with nectarines, but also capable of long aging. That's the wines.
Now the woman Vanya Cullen is a vocal opinion-former who cares passionately about the uniqueness of Margaret River. As vineyards expand into previously untried areas, her voice needs to be heard.
Best years: (reds) 2002, '01, '00, '99, '98, '97, '96, '95, '94, '92, '91, '90, '86, '84, '82.

DEVIL'S LAIR

Margaret River
❦ *Cabernet Sauvignon, Merlot, Cabernet Franc, Petit Verdot, Shiraz*
❦ *Chardonnay, Sauvignon Blanc, Semillon*
Established by entrepreneur, Phil Sexton, in 1981, Devil's Lair was then one of the most southerly of the Margaret River vineyards. It became one of the region's most fashionable labels and was purchased by Southcorp in 1997. Their plan was to capitalize on its stylish packaging and cult following to grow the brand – I hate that phrase – largely through expansion of the second label (Fifth Leg). Since then, the home vineyard has more than trebled in size (35 to 124ha) and production is up from

15,000 to 40,000 cases. Winemaker, Stuart Pym, has continued the good work of his partner, Janice McDonald, from whom he took over in 1999. Tweaking in the vineyard and winery combined with increased vine age has resulted in substantial improvement especially with the intense, fine, racy Chardonnay, while the Cabernet blend defies conventional wisdom about the location of the region's best reds by being grown in the cool south and yet being dark and delicious. The Fifth Leg White and Red are excellent value regional wines.
Best years: (Chardonnay) 2002, '01, '00, '99, '97.

Cullen
This is one of the original and best Margaret River wineries. The Cabernet/Merlot blend is deep, well-structured and scented, and even better now that the Reserve version is no longer being made.

Devil's Lair
Powerful Chardonnay with intense grapefruit, honey and toast flavours has been a winning style here since the winery's early days.

Evans & Tate
This winery is on a roll at the moment and each vintage seems to be better than the last. The concentrated yet drinkable Shiraz has nicely integrated, subtle, smoky vanilla oak.

EVANS & TATE

Margaret River
❧ *Cabernet Sauvignon, Shiraz, Merlot*
❧ *Chardonnay, Semillon, Sauvignon Blanc*
Having started life in the Swan Valley with its Gnangara Shiraz/Cabernet, transforming the then-prevalent disdain for the Swan Valley, Evans & Tate has now moved its operations to the Margaret River, where it has grown at an exponential rate and is the winery most involved in developing the controversial Jindong region of Margaret River, a high-yielding area not approved of by traditionalists. The thing is, if Jindong wasn't challenging the traditional Margaret River exclusivity and reserved, ageworthy wine style with its large vineyards, high crops and keenly-priced, easy-going wine styles, it would be regarded as a fine vineyard area.

In fact, Evans & Tate take fruit from all over the region, and each vintage do a better job with it. New millennium vintages of Semillon and Chardonnay are high quality, and the Sauvignon/Semillon is leafy and good. The Shiraz, Merlot and Cabernet are richer and riper than they used to be. Classic is either red or white, and relies on amiable Jindong fruit. Gnangara is a reliable red or white volume brand.
Best years: (Cabernet Sauvignon) 2002, '01, '00, '99, '98, '96, '94.

FERNGROVE

Great Southern
❧ *Cabernet Sauvignon, Merlot, Shiraz, Malbec*
❧ *Riesling, Semillon, Sauvignon Blanc, Chardonnay*
This is arguably the most successful of the new breed of Western Australian wineries which have been financed by a large investor base attracted to the project by taxation incentives. It shows the fantastic potential of the Great Southern region – and in particular the Frankland River region,

which, if sensitively developed, has the potential to be one of the best wine regions in the whole of Australia.

In fact, quite a lot of the new 'investor' schemes are in potentially top areas. Some of them will come a cropper as the market requirements of supply and demand fluctuate. But once a vineyard is planted and bearing fruit, it's unlikely to simply get ripped out again. In the long term, these investor schemes should greatly enhance the general quality level of wines in Australia.

Ferngrove has four major vineyards (three in Frankland River and one in Mount Barker), with a total of nearly 300ha. Their cheapest wines (Semillon/Sauvignon Blanc and Cabernet/Merlot) are extremely good quaffing wines, the modestly priced range of varietals have loads of fruit and character, and a slightly more expensive Premium Range is full of seriously delicious wines. The best of these are the Cossack Riesling (2002 was top wine at the Sydney Show), Butterfly Chardonnay, and the red Shiraz and Bordeaux blends. The wines are surprisingly good given the relatively young age of the vines.
Best years: (Cossack Riesling) 2003, '02.

Ferngrove
This is the wine that rocketed Ferngrove to fame when it won the top award at the Sydney Show. It's a very delicate, citrus white and deliciously refreshing.

FRANKLAND ESTATE

Great Southern
❧ *Shiraz, Cabernet Franc, Merlot, Cabernet Sauvignon, Petit Verdot*
❧ *Riesling, Chardonnay, Sauvignon Blanc*
Sheep and grain farmers Barrie Smith and Judi Cullam were attracted to the wine industry following a tour of France's wine regions in 1985 and established the vineyard three years later. What could have been described as an attempt to diversify and make the farm more profitable has become an obsession. Working two

Frankland Estate
Olmo's Reward is a Bordeaux-style red blend, mainly Cabernet Franc and Merlot, and named after Dr Olmo, the renowned US viticulturalist who first identified the Frankland region's potential for wine.

vintages in Bordeaux and employing Jenny Dobson (formerly of Chateau Senejac) as winemaker and then consultant helped to establish the winery. The entire family is now working full-time in the winery (though they do run 10,000 merinos on the side) and Judi Cullam is proving to be one of the industry's most engaging marketers.

Frankland Estate sponsors a bi-annual International Riesling Tasting on the eastern seaboard which has attracted many German and Austrian Riesling-makers to Australia. They make three distinctive single-vineyard Rieslings (Isolation Ridge, Cooladerra and Poison Hill). A comparison of the three is fascinating though Isolation Ridge is usually best: tight, lean, minerally and fine. Isolation Ridge Chardonnay is also a top, oatmealy wine.

They're very proud of their Merlot and Cabernet Franc-dominated Olmo's Reward, but I find it rather overdoes the French restraint – I'd like them to increase the currently small percentages of Cabernet Sauvignon, Malbec and Petit Verdot. The Shiraz is in a good, peppery style. The whites should generally be drunk on release but the reds, like the Riesling, will peak at five to six years.
Best years: (Isolation Ridge Riesling) 2003, '02, '01, '98, '96.

GOUNDREY WINES

Great Southern
❧ *Cabernet Sauvignon, Shiraz, Merlot, Pinot Noir*
❧ *Chardonnay, Sauvignon Blanc, Semillon, Riesling*
Important winery in the Mount Barker region that has led a rather topsy-turvy existence since its establishment by Michael Goundrey in 1976. Perth millionaire Jack Bendat acquired it in 1995 and sales then exploded from a mere 17,000 cases to 260,000 in 2002. Some of the fruit is from their own vines but much of it from further afield. The Canadian giant Vincor bought

Goundrey
Riesling was one of the first varieties planted at Goundrey's original Windy Hill property in Mount Barker. Current releases are tangy and citrus.

the operation in 2003 and intends to increase sales even more. Overall quality has actually held up reasonably well, given the expansion, and while no current wines really shine, all are enjoyable. Riesling and unoaked Chardonnay are important here but peppery Shiraz can be good too. Fox River is a second label.

Best years: (Riesling) 2001, '99, '98, '97, '96, '94, '93, '92, '91.

HOUGHTON
Swan District and Great Southern
❧ *Cabernet Sauvignon, Shiraz, Merlot and others*
❧ *Chardonnay, Chenin Blanc, Sauvignon Blanc, Semillon, Verdelho, Riesling and others*
HWB, sold outside the EU as Houghton 'White Burgundy', is one of Australia's most successful white wines. It is a modestly priced blend of Chenin Blanc, Chardonnay, Verdelho, Semillon, Sauvignon Blanc and Muscadelle and made in huge quantities. Older vintages can be remarkable, and small quantities are held back for release under the Show Reserve label, which is well worth the search and the money.

Houghton, now part of the giant HARDY group, is based in Swan District near Perth but has large vineyard holdings in the

Frankland River sub-region of the Great Southern, and takes significant quantities of grapes from the Pemberton region and from Margaret River. Supplemented by its Moondah Brook vineyard (and brand) it produces a kaleidoscopic array of wines, ranging from the monumental Jack Mann Cabernet Sauvignon (in memory of the great winemaker and one of Australia's most innovative, who did over 50 consecutive vintages with the company, beginning in 1920) and Gladstones Shiraz through to fine, subtly oaked Semillon/ Sauvignon Blanc and Chardonnay, together with some startling grapefruit- and passionfruit-accented Riesling.

Houghton has always been a good producer but recent focus on particular regions and their individual strengths as well as inspired winemaking is creating their best ever range of wines. Top winemaker Larry Cherubino has now left, but I can' see standards dropping.

Best years: (Jack Mann) 2002, '01, '00, '99, '98, '96, '95, '94.

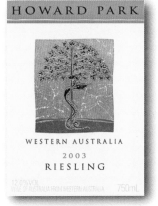

Howard Park
Back in the 1980s Howard Park's first release from its Denmark winery was Riesling, a lovely floral, aromatic wine with crisp acidity and intense fruit depth.

HOWARD PARK
Margaret River and Great Southern
❧ *Cabernet Sauvignon, Shiraz, Merlot, Cabernet Franc*
❧ *Riesling, Chardonnay*
After leaving an indelible mark as the maker of WYNNS' first John Riddoch Cabernet Sauvignon (in 1982), John Wade moved to the Great Southern region in the far south of Western Australia, setting up an immensely successful career as a contract winemaker and consultant while simultaneously establishing his Howard Park label, and ultimately the second label, Madfish. He has now moved on and

Howard Park has expanded to a second winery in Margaret River, but his signature style remains – rapier-like Riesling and Cabernet/Merlot built for long cellaring, which in top years is sublime. The supremely classy Chardonnay is very nearly as impressive, and Madfish whites and reds are darlings of the smart brasserie set. The Scotsdale Shiraz and Cabernet from Great Southern and Leston Cabernet and Shiraz from Margaret River are part of an impressive range of regional reds that really do show powerful local flavours.

Best years: (Cabernet/Merlot) 2002, '01, '99, '98, '96, '94, '93, '92, '90, '89, '88, '86; (Riesling) 2003, '02, '01, '00, '98, '97, '96, '95, '94, '93, '92, '91, '90, '88, '86.

LAMONT
Swan District
❧ *Shiraz, Cabernet Sauvignon, Brown Muscat*
❧ *Verdelho*
Through his daughter, Corin, and granddaughters, Kate and Fiona, who now run it, this small family winery continues the legacy of Jack Mann, HOUGHTON's legendary winemaker for more than 50 years (1920–74). Started by Corin and Neil Lamont in 1978 and, following an upgrading of equipment, Lamont has been revitalized by skillful winemaking over the past five years or so.

Lamont makes some excellent Swan Valley wines: most notably Verdelho, Shiraz, Family Reserve Cabernet Sauvignon and Vintage Port. They have expanded the range by producing an outstanding Frankland River Riesling and Semillon/Sauvignon Blanc, Chardonnay and Cabernet from Margaret River. Kate Lamont has proved herself to be an astute business woman and a talented chef and runs successful restaurants at the winery, in East Perth and Margaret River through which much of the wine is sold.

Best years: (Frankland Riesling) 2003, '02, '99.

Houghton
Houghton's flagship wine was created in honour of Jack Mann, one of Australia's greatest winemakers. First released in 1997, when there's lots of Malbec in the blend it has an almost amarone-like, date and black chocolate richness. When Cabernet dominates, it has a wonderful rich perfume and a deep, lush texture.

Lamont
Shiraz thrives in the hot dry climate of the Swan Valley, producing full-flavoured wines such as this example from Lamont.

Leeuwin Estate
Leeuwin may be better known for its Chardonnay but this delicate lemon-scented Riesling is one of Western Australia's top examples.

LEEUWIN ESTATE

Margaret River
❋ *Cabernet Sauvignon, Shiraz*
❖ *Chardonnay, Riesling, Sauvignon Blanc*

In 1972 the famous Californian wine producer Robert Mondavi was delighted when he finally found the plot of land he thought would make Australia's finest Cabernet and Chardonnay wines. The trouble is, owner Denis Horgan wasn't selling. But he was very interested in hearing what Mondavi had to say, so the two men went into partnership (until 1979), and Horgan, who had intended that his 600-ha property in the Margaret River would be used to raise champion cattle instead found himself at the helm of an ambitious project to produce the best wines in Australia. And to many people that's what he's done.

Certainly his Chardonnay is frequently rated as Australia's finest, his Riesling too is right up there, and, after a period in the 1980s and 1990s when the attempt to reproduce a lean, reserved, Bordeaux style of red went a little too far in the underripe direction, he is now producing a Cabernet that in years like 2001, is indeed one of the greatest reds in Australia.

And he's shown he's no slouch in promoting his wines either. He took the idea from Bordeaux's Château Mouton-Rothschild of getting top artists to design his labels. It didn't start out so well. Sir Sidney Nolan, when asked if he would kick things off, replied rather grandly that he didn't paint for wine labels. So Horgan sent him a couple of bottles of the 1982 Cabernet Sauvignon, unlabelled. They had a Nolan label on the way almost as soon as he'd swallowed the first glass. And there's more. In 1985 Horgan was asked to underwrite a visit to Perth by the London Philharmonic Orchestra. Sure he would. So long as the orchestra decamped 300km south from Perth to perform an extra concert in a forest glade in front of his winery. Which they did. And top performers like Kiri Te Kanawa, Ray Charles and Tom Jones have come every year since. I've sat out under the stars listening to Julio Iglesias. I can tell you, it's magic.

Luckily the wines are magic too. The Art Series is the top label, based very precisely on particular plots of vineyard that have been quietly maturing since the 1970s. The Riesling is a classic lemon blossom-scented delight. The later Cabernets have superb black cherry and blackcurrant fruit fine-tuned with cedar. And the Chardonnay starts full of nectarine and pineapple fruit and ages to a sublime oatmeal and roasted nuts maturity sometimes rounded out with a cedar savouriness that is remarkable. The Prelude label provides excellent varietals at a lower price level and lesser levels of intensity. Siblings is a new venture based on a mixture of estate and bought-in fruit, which is also extremely good. And just think. He could have sold the lot to a Californian.
Best years: (Art Series Chardonnay) 2002, '01, '00, '99, '98, '97, '96, '95, '94, '92, '90, '87, '86, '85, '83, '82, '81, '80.

Moss Wood
This consistently fine, powerful, full-bodied red, with tiny additions of Cabernet Franc and Petit Verdot, is made for long aging and is in high demand on the Australian wine market.

MOSS WOOD

Margaret River
❋ *Cabernet Sauvignon, Pinot Noir*
❖ *Semillon, Chardonnay*

Moss Wood is the second of the famous medico-owned wineries that spawned the great Margaret River region of today. It was Dr Bill Pannell who founded Moss Wood and sold it in 1985 to current boss Keith Mugford while he moved south to found PICARDY ESTATE in Pemberton. Moss Wood has always made restrained but impressive reds and whites. Texture seems to be of prime importance to Mugford. The Semillons, one oak-matured, the other not, are no less delicious, honeyed rather than grassy, with a long finish and capable of considerable aging. The Chardonnay can be dazzling in its peachy, butterscotch opulence, and one or two lovely, gentle Pinot Noirs have emerged. In 2000 Moss Wood bought neighbouring Ribbon Vale and so far has released very good Semillon/Sauvignon, Merlot and a Cabernet/Merlot blend. The style is quite different, but the quality is very good.
Best years: (Cabernet) 2002, '01, '00, '99, '98, '96, '95, '94, '91, '90, '85.

Picardy
The Pannells' passion for Burgundy means that their Chardonnay is produced in a delicate, refined Burgundian style. It is barrel fermented and aged on its lees in French oak for 10 months.

PICARDY

Pemberton
❋ *Pinot Noir, Shiraz, Merlot, Cabernet Franc, Cabernet Sauvignon*
❖ *Chardonnay*

Having established and ran MOSS WOOD for 15 years, Bill and Sandra Pannell are pioneers of a new wine region for the second time. With son, Daniel, and his wife Jodie they run one of Pemberton's most meticulously worked vineyards – and the results show in the winery. The Pannells are unashamedly admirers of Burgundy – they owned a bit of Volnay's famous Domaine de la Pousse d'Or for a time – and believe that Pemberton offers ideal conditions for growing Chardonnay and Pinot Noir, the two classic Burgundian grapes. They were among the first to import new Burgundian clones of both varieties and this appears to be a key ingredient in their success. The Chardonnay is tight, taut and minerally with refreshing racy acidity while both Pinots are complex, silkily textured yet with savoury, gamey characters to liven things up.
Best years: (Chardonnay) 2002, '01, '00, '99.

PIERRO

Margaret River
❋ *Cabernet Sauvignon, Cabernet Franc, Merlot, Pinot Noir and others*
❖ *Chardonnay, Semillon, Sauvignon Blanc*

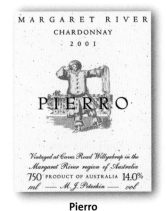

Pierro

Classically made and multi-layered with exquisite fruit aromas and complexity, this consistently classy wine is one of the finest and most exciting Chardonnays made in Australia.

Pierro is not a wine I taste very often, but then, it makes such an impression I'm not sure I need to! The owner, Dr Michael Peterkin, has an iconoclastic attitude to winemaking, and dislikes pigeon-hole descriptions of his winemaking practices and philosophy. His Chardonnay is frequently so rich it almost tastes like chocolate, and with its generally high alcohol, you wonder if it can age – but it does, to a deep and eminently satisfying toasty maturity; his potent Cabernets (an impressive, five-varietal Bordeaux-style blend) is equally powerful and long-lived. The Semillon/Sauvignon Blanc LTC (Les Trois Cuvées or a Little Touch of Chardonnay – take your pick) is a fruity, crisp style for early drinking. The Fire Gully range is sourced from a separate vineyard, owned and managed by Peterkin.

Best years: (Chardonnay) 2002, '01, '00, '99, '97, '96, '94, '93.

PLANTAGENET

Great Southern
❋ Shiraz, Cabernet Sauvignon, Pinot Noir
❋ Riesling, Chardonnay, Sauvignon Blanc

Founded in 1974, Plantagenet is the largest winery in the Mount Barker sub-region of the Great Southern region, making around 35,000 cases a year on its own account but also providing a foster home for many other producers in the region by supplying winemaking facilities.

The quality of the wine is usually very good and sometimes outstanding: an intense, lime-and-passionfruit Riesling, a stylish, spicy oak, melon-fresh Chardonnay, an indulgently, riotously spicy, peppery Shiraz that is frequently one of Western Australia's best and a wonderfully supple and complex, cherried Cabernet Sauvignon lead the way – and

Plantagenet

Plantagenet, a leading winery in the Great Southern region, produces consistently flavourful wines including a positively succulent damson and pepper-flavoured Shiraz.

all made in an unglamorous apple-packing shed. The reds in general benefit from a little aging. Omrah is the second label, made from bought-in grapes, with good Sauvignon Blanc, Chardonnay and Shiraz.

Best years: (Cabernet Sauvignon) 2002, '01, '98, '97, '96, '95, '94, '93, '91, '90, '86, '85.

Salitage

Chardonnay is the most widely planted and successful grape variety so far in Pemberton, one of Western Australia's newest wine regions.

SALITAGE

Pemberton
❋ Pinot Noir, Cabernet Sauvignon and others
❋ Chardonnay, Sauvignon Blanc

John Horgan established Pemberton's first and largest winery in 1989 and until the emergence of PICARDY was unquestionably Pemberton's quality leader. There are now several challengers, but Salitage still holds its own. The wines are always good, sometimes excellent: no-holds-barred barrel-fermented Chardonnay, Unwooded Chardonnay, Pinot Noir and Cabernet Blend (from both Cabernet Sauvignon and Franc plus Merlot and Petit Verdot).

The second label Treehouse, mainly using fruit from the nearby Omodei vineyard, produces good Chardonnay/Verdelho. Top reds will age for 3–7 years. Production is about 12,000 cases a year for the Salitage label and 10,000 cases for Treehouse.

SANDALFORD

Swan District and Margaret River
❋ Cabernet Sauvignon, Shiraz, Merlot
❋ Riesling, Chardonnay, Sauvignon Blanc, Verdelho, Chenin Blanc

Although based in the Swan District, Sandalford, one of Western Australia's oldest wineries (established in 1840), was among the pioneers of the Margaret River as they planted the region's largest vineyard (105ha) in 1972. Although there has been a gradual improvement since the current owners Peter and Debra Prendiville took it over in 1992, Sandalford under-performed until the arrival of winemaker, Paul Boulden, in 2001.

The Element range are well-made, tasty quaffing wines. The focus with the premium range, under Boulden, has moved from multi-regional to wines with much more focus on their origins. In particular, they have a marvellous source of Cabernet Sauvignon opposite Moss Wood in Margaret River that all used to get blended away. And they traditionally used fruit from the excellent Frankland River Vineyard in the far south. Yet only now can you taste it in the wine. The Semillon/Sauvignon is intense and leafy, the Riesling one of the leaders of the low alcohol, citrus and blossom-scented modern style. Old-vine Chardonnay is also beautifully balanced. The Shiraz is packed with blackberry fruit and pepper scent. And that Margaret River Cabernet is outstanding – ripe, dark yet seductively scented for drinking now or in 10 years' time. The 2002 was top wine at the Margaret River Show. I can see why.

Best years: (Cabernet Sauvignon) 2002, '01, '00, '99.

Sandalford

Verdelho is one of the noble grape varieties for Madeira but is currently proving very successful in Australia, as shown in this wine full of ripe tropical fruit flavours, yet with a green streak from a proportion of fruit being picked very early.

Suckfizzle

Suckfizzle's cult white is an oaked Bordeaux-style blend of two varieties that have now become classics in Margaret River too.

SUCKFIZZLE

Margaret River
☆ *Cabernet Sauvignon, Merlot, Sangiovese*
☆ *Semillon, Sauvignon Blanc, Chardonnay*

The former and the incumbent DEVIL'S LAIR winemaker, Janice McDonald and Stuart Pym, took advantage of the long-term lease of a vineyard at Augusta in the extreme south of the Margaret River region to start their own label. The plan was to make two premium single-vineyard wines: an oaked Sauvignon Blanc/Semillon and a Cabernet. Both wines have impressed, with the white showing subtle oak, powerful leafy characters, creamy texture and a tangy, dry finish while the red has bold cassis and cedary oak flavours and a very cool tight structure as you'd expect from far southern grapes. The catchy name came from a character in Rabelais' *Gargantua*.

A second label, Stella Bella, has quickly expanded as they formed a partnership with local businessman, John Britton, who owns a 20-ha vineyard close to VOYAGER. Best of this range is the vibrant Sauvignon Blanc and the Sangiovese/Cabernet blend.
Best years: (Sauvignon Blanc/Semillon) 2002, '01, '00, '99, '98.

UPPER REACH

Swan District
☆ *Shiraz, Cabernet Sauvignon, Merlot*
☆ *Chardonnay, Verdelho*

This is the very model of a modern, family-run Swan Valley winery. It was established when Derek and Laura Pearse, in partnership with Derek's wheat-farming parents, purchased an established 10-ha vineyard in the upper reaches of the Swan River. The vineyard is picture perfect and all the buildings which have been added – winery, open air cellar door, cafe – have a casual elegance. The wines, all from the estate vineyard, are made by Pearse and consultant, John Griffiths, and reflect what the warm Swan Valley does best: delicate, passionfruit-flavoured Verdelho and big, ripe, plummy, approachable Shiraz. The Unwooded Chardonnay has pristine tropical fruits while, in the best years, the Chardonnay can show cool climate grapefruit and melon characters.
Best years: (Shiraz) 2002, '01, '00.

Upper Reach

Chardonnay is the main variety grown at this small property in the upper reaches of the Swan River. The fish on the label is the black bream which can be found in the pools of the river in the summer.

VASSE FELIX

Margaret River
☆ *Cabernet Sauvignon, Shiraz, Merlot and others*
☆ *Semillon, Chardonnay, Sauvignon Blanc and others*

One of the original wineries responsible for

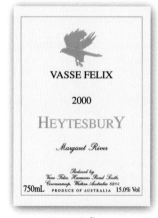

Vasse Felix

This elegant Bordeaux blend is Vasse Felix's flagship wine and shows typical Margaret River ripe and rich cassis fruit with supple, well-extracted tannins.

Margaret River rocketing to fame in the 1970s, with decadently rich Cabernet Sauvignon and Shiraz and owned since 1987 by the wealthy Holmes à Court family.

The winemaking style has continued along the lines of lush fruit and generous use of oak, and the flagship red and white Heytesbury take this style even further. While such a swamping blast of fruit works pretty well in the red Heytesbury, I think it makes the Chardonnay seem rather fat and old-fashioned.
Best years: (Heytesbury) 2002, '01, '99, '98, '97, '96, '95.

VOYAGER ESTATE

Margaret River
☆ *Cabernet Sauvignon, Shiraz, Merlot, Petit Verdot, Malbec*
☆ *Chardonnay, Sauvignon Blanc, Semillon, Chenin Blanc*

The original 20-ha vineyard, planted in 1978, has been expanded to 100ha since the takeover by minerals millionaire Michael Wright in 1992. While the public focus may have been on Voyager as a showcase Margaret River property (with striking Cape Dutch architecture, lavish rose gardens, Australia's second largest flag), the wines have always been good and steadily improving from vintage to vintage. Whites are best which is not surprising given its cool location to the south of the Margaret River township (next to LEEUWIN).

Since 1997, the Chardonnay has been considered to be among the region's best half dozen and you can see why with its buttery-nutty texture and Burgundian flavour of oatmeal. Semillon/Sauvignon under the top Tom Price label is an excellent blend of cream and green leaf. Despite being in the cooler southern part of Margaret River, Shiraz and Cabernet/Merlot

Voyager Estate

In a little over a decade Voyager Estate has become one of Margaret River's showcase wineries, producing rich-textured, barrel-fermented Chardonnay.

reds have tons of flavour and fruit, while Tom Price is an outstanding Bordeaux blend.
Best years: (Chardonnay) 2002, '01, '00, '99, '97.

WEST CAPE HOWE

Great Southern
❋ *Shiraz*
❋ *Chardonnay, Sauvignon Blanc*

Local boy, Brenden Smith, made good during his four years as Chief Winemaker at GOUNDREY and so he left in 1997 to set up a contract winemaking facility at Denmark. While contract work still makes up half of the business, the West Cape Howe has mushroomed to a 40,000-case brand. Access to quality fruit from the large, long-established Landsdale vineyard at Mount Barker and from those whose fruit is processed by the winery has been crucial to the growth of the brand.

There is a budget priced Core Range: best are the lively Semillon/Sauvignon Blanc and robust Shiraz. The Premium Range is also reasonably priced: delicious tropical-fruited Sauvignon Blanc, full-flavoured, scented Riesling and rich, velvety Cabernet Sauvignon are best. Smith left in 2004 saying he was spending all his time organizing and what he wanted to do was make wine again.
Best years: (Cabernet Sauvignon) 2002, '01.

West Cape Howe
This Semillon/Sauvignon Blanc blend shows what the Great Southern region can do so well: lively, tasty wines for everyday quaffing.

WILLOW BRIDGE

Geographe
❋ *Shiraz, Cabernet Sauvignon, Merlot*
❋ *Semillon, Chardonnay, Sauvignon Blanc, Chenin Blanc*

With 60ha under vines, this is the largest producer in the rapidly expanding Ferguson Valley area in the Bunbury hinterland. Willow Bridge got off to an excellent start because it had the region's most experi-

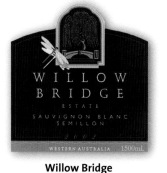

Willow Bridge
Crisp, tangy Sauvignon Blanc/Semillon for early drinking is one of the most successful wines from this relative newcomer.

enced winemaker, Rob Bowen, at the helm before he moved on to the plum job of Chief Winemaker at HOUGHTON.

Willow Bridge is making some excellent Sauvignon Blanc and a Sauvignon Blanc/Semillon blend. Their reds – Cabernet Sauvignon, Shiraz and Merlot – show promise but, at present, suffer from being made from young vines. The Black Dog Shiraz, a highly alcoholic, oaky monster, has a cult following and so commands high prices: however, it is strictly for lovers of the style.
Best years: (Sauvignon Blanc) 2003, '02, '01, '00.

XANADU

Margaret River
❋ *Cabernet Sauvignon, Cabernet Franc, Merlot*
❋ *Semillon, Chardonnay, Sauvignon Blanc*

Xanadu was established (in 1977) as a family winery in Margaret River. Substantial investment followed a 1999 takeover. Another 68ha has been added to the home vineyard along with 45ha of vines at Karridale further south. Xanadu also source a significant amount of fruit from the Frankland River region.

Expansion has been dramatic. From 1998 to 2001, sales increased from 10,000 to 90,000 cases. Takeovers of South Australian firms, Normans and NXG, have expanded the group's production fourfold. Whites are best at present with the complex, vibrant Chardonnay and tightly-structured, oaked Semillon, both winning gold at the Margaret River Show. Merlot can be good in the best years and the flagship Lagan Reserve Cabernet is robust, powerful and oaky yet with deep cassis flavours. The quaffing Secession label represents good value, especially the whites.

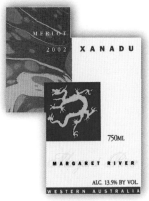

Xanadu
From the original estate vineyard and aged in new French oak, this Merlot is one of several stylish wines from Xanadu.

Quick guide ◆ Best producers

Geographe
Capel Vale, Ferguson Falls, Willow Bridge.

Great Southern
Alkoomi, Ferngrove, Frankland Estate, Gilberts, Goundrey, Houghton, Howard Park, Jingalla, Plantagenet, West Cape Howe, Wignalls King River.

Manjimup
Chestnut Grove.

Margaret River
Amberley Estate, Arlewood, Brookland Valley, Cape Mentelle, Cullen, Devil's Lair, Evans & Tate, Gralyn, Howard Park, Leeuwin Estate, Moss Wood, Pierro, Sandalford, Suckfizzle, Vasse Felix, Voyager Estate, Xanadu.

Peel
Peel Estate.

Pemberton
Mountford, Phillips, Picardy, Salitage, Smithbrook.

Perth Hills
Darlington, Hainault, Francois Jacquard, Piesse Brook, Scarp Valley.

Swan District
Paul Conti, Houghton, Lamont, Sandalford, Upper Reach, Westfield.

TASMANIA

Outside the main wine regions, Australia can offer extremes of heat and cold – and winemakers being what they are, if a spot is really difficult you can bet somebody will start planting vines on it. Tasmania is a case in point. Logically, it could be the best spot in Australia to grow vines, if cool climate sites are what you seek. The trouble is that most of Tasmania is just too cool. Even when the temperature looks about right (about the same as Burgundy, that is) the wind can make life impossible. Tasmania supplied the grape vines which established the original wine industries in both Victoria and South Australia; wine was sold on a commercial scale in Tasmania before those states' vines were even planted, but vine-growing faded away on the island by 1860 and wasn't revived until 1956.

When Tasmania has a good vintage it can be very good indeed; it can produce superb, perfumed Pinot Noir, Tasmania's finest red, and elegant, lean Chardonnay; but vintages can be wildly irregular here – just as they are, of course, in Burgundy. Some Cabernet is grown for lighter reds but in less good years these can have a distinct green pepper flavour. Riesling, Pinot Gris and Gewurztraminer are well suited to certain parts of Tasmania, too. Results with other grapes are still erratic but what is certain is the outstanding potential for high-acidity base wine for Champagne-method sparkling wine and most of the top sparkling wine houses on the mainland take grapes from here. For still reds and whites the only answer is to get out of the wind. North of Launceston, on the Tamar River, it is both sheltered enough and warm enough to be successful, near Freycinet on the east coast it is also warm and sheltered and the Coal River Valley in the south of the island can also ripen reds fairly consistently and tastily.

Tasmania's vineyards are concentrated in the eastern half of the island – east of Launceston, the Pipers River area overlooking the Bass Strait is appreciably cooler than the other main growing areas, and has developed a justified reputation for outstanding sparkling wine.

SPOTLIGHT ON
Tasmania

Late autumn sunshine can make a difference between a fine Tasmanian vintage and a merely quite good one. Pinot Noir, seen here at Moorilla Estate near Hobart, is by far the most important variety grown in Tasmania and thrives in the island's cool climate. The long, sunny autumn days and cool nights allow grapes to ripen slowly to their full flavour potential while maintaining a natural acid balance, a perfect recipe, in fact, for quality sparkling wine.

'TASMANIA – IT'S THE HOLY GRAIL.' This was about the fourth time I'd heard this on a recent trip to Australia. I'd heard it in Victoria, in South Australia, in New South Wales, and now here was a guy in Queensland saying exactly the same thing. So I raised the usual objections. Wasn't it too cold? Wasn't the weather too unpredictable, weren't rain, hail and frost all likely to turn up at the least helpful moments, like just after budburst or just as vintage started? And though I'd tasted enough of their reds over the years, were they ever going to get anything except Pinot Noir ripe on a regular basis? And the guy in Queensland, just like the other guys, said – they're getting there, and when they do, you'll be amazed.

Well, I wasn't convinced. I looked back at my tasting notes over the last few years, and even top Pinot Noirs weren't that easy to find. Good Cabernet and Merlots were very thin on the ground – even for a guy like me who enjoys tastes of mint and eucalyptus leaf, but wants a certain element of ripeness to go with it. Chardonnays and aromatic whites like Pinot Gris, Riesling and Gewurztraminer – yes I could find lovely examples of those. And fizz – well not only homegrown brands like Jansz and Pirie, but all the mainland producers who use Tassie for their top cuvées make a convincing case for great potential in the sparkling wine stakes. But sparkling wine has always been made out of acid wine – not acid wine from warm areas which has been picked really early – that just tastes green and mean – but acid wine made from grapes that have spent a long time on the vine in decidedly cool conditions creeping towards ripeness and usually not quite getting there.

Tasmania seems to do that brilliantly. As you tramp the chilly vineyards around the Tamar Valley or Pipers River in the north or the Derwent Valley in the south, you hear the phrase 'sparkling wine base' again and again. 'What's that over there?' Pause. 'Sparkling wine base.' 'And what's that?' Pause. 'Er... sparkling wine base.' And so it goes on, until you spot some lovely, protected, steep, north-facing slope – and before you can ask, the grower is bubbling over with excitement – this precious little parcel makes his top Chardonnay, or Pinot Noir, or whatever. Great sparkling wine and great still wine rarely come from the same place. Can Tasmania do what almost nowhere else in the world has managed?

Well, it's worth listening to what Dr Andrew Pirie says. He is one of Australia's most influential and thoughtful wine pioneers and as far as Tasmania is concerned, no-one knows it better than he does since he founded the trailblazing Pipers Brook winery in 1974 in the north-east of the island based on sound scientific principles.

He had always felt that one of Australia's likely problems was that it was too easy to ripen the fruit on the vine and consequently the subtleties of perfume and style that made the European classics so fascinating would not be obtainable under such cosy conditions. He'd toured Europe in the early 1970s – I'd met him as a student and we travelled together for a bit – and had noted that especially in some of France's classic wine areas such as Bordeaux and Burgundy and Champagne – the soils were poor, the vines were savagely pruned and packed close together to encourage competition, there was a fair amount of rain and rarely enough sun, and you never really knew whether your grapes had ripened enough until the moment you picked. But he loved the wines produced in these marginal conditions and wanted to emulate them back home in Australia. There were cool areas in the mainland – the highlands around Canberra, for instance, the New England Tablelands stretching up through New South Wales to Queensland – but although they might be cool, the air was usually dry and the sunlight was strong and plentiful. One place, however, looked as though it might provide humidity allied to gentle sunlight conditions – the cool, damp slopes and valleys of

WINE REGIONS

1. North-West
2. Tamar Valley
3. North-East
4. East Coast
5. Coal River Valley
6. Derwent Valley
7. Huon Valley/Channel

▬▬ VINEYARD AREAS

▢ OVER 200M

▢ OVER 500M

Not all of Australia is hot. You can almost feel the chill in the still air at the St Matthias Vineyard on the banks of the river Tamar near Launceston. But then, you can taste the cool in the wines as well – that's why in the warm climate world of Australia, Tasmania and its cool climate fruit is so special.

Tasmania, where the humidity is much the same as in Bordeaux and temperatures during the growing season are actually lower – more like those of Burgundy.

This wasn't bad going in the generally warm world of Australia. And there was something else. Even though Tasmania is one of the most southerly vineyard areas in the world, it still only straddles latitudes 41° to 43° South. In European terms, that puts you bang in the middle of the broiling plains of central Spain. Bordeaux and Burgundy are between 45° and 47° North. But Bordeaux on the western coast of France is warmed by the currents of the Gulf Stream. Tasmania compensates for its technically hotter latitude by being surrounded by cold Antarctic currents. And this could make all the difference. That latitude of between 41° and 43° South gives you a larger ripening period – a week longer than Bordeaux and as many as two weeks longer than the Mosel in Germany, Europe's most northerly quality wine region. Yet the humidity and the Antarctic influences are going to keep the temperature low.

And I must say – I suspect that frequently those temperatures are just a bit too low for fully ripe Bordeaux and Burgundy red wine styles, whilst being magic for fizz and lighter white styles. But then you come across protected patches of the Tamar Valley growing Cabernet and Merlot, you taste exciting scented Pinot and even Cabernets on the east coast at Freycinet or way south at Domaine A in the Coal Valley near Hobart – and you think – well, it took the French 2000 years to work out where the best patches of land were for their vines. Clearly there are patches of land all over the north, east and south of the island that could be really special. Does Tasmania have the will and the patience to search them out?

Between Hobart and the Tasman Peninsula in southern Tasmania, the Coal River Valley enjoys spectacular coastal landscapes and is one of Tasmania's warmest spots for vines. Even Cabernet Sauvignon and Merlot ripen fairly successfully here. However, wind from the sea is a particular problem for some of these coastal vineyards.

Some people clearly do, but I think it will be a long slow process. One of the things which will help is tourism. Tasmania is a beautiful, calm, frequently verdant island, sparsely populated, but with a whole raft of leisure attractions, led by the great National Parks and rainforests to the west. Tasmanian fish, seafood, game, fruit and veg, and cheese are also outstanding. So local wine, and the accompanying tourism, is an absolute natural, which will ensure people keep planting vineyards, but it doesn't ensure quality – nice tourists – me among them – are often happy to drink anything, so long as it's local.

And there have been Tasmanian wines for a long time; the first vineyards were planted in 1823, before those of either South Australia or Victoria – but Tasmania had few settlers and most of those were 'involved' with the penal colonies and so the vineyards had gone by 1850. When a Frenchman and an Italian had another go in the 1950s, local resentment at these foreigners and their dangerous product, wine, as well as a government that wouldn't license a winery to sell its own products and, anyway, told you Tasmania was too cold and you should be growing apples – meant that the revival was very fitful and didn't take off until Andrew Pirie's momentous decision to plant vines at Pipers Brook in 1974.

Pipers Brook is not an easy place to ripen vines, being situated to the east of the Tamar Valley with views across towards the Bass Strait – and winds to go with the view. But it's good for sparkling wine, often ripening two weeks later than the more sheltered Tamar sites. Nearby Clover Hill – another top sparkling site – ripens four weeks after the Tamar, which is only 20 kilometres west, but whose wide estuary and varied soils and aspects provide a warmth and a protection from wind that allows reds to ripen. Indeed, it is one of the few places in Tasmania where you can coax Cabernet Sauvignon to ripeness. Not every year, but often enough to make an impression.

Eastern Tasmania, especially between Swansea and Bicheno, is a supreme example of how local conditions can throw up fine vineyards seemingly from nothing. Opposite the Freycinet Peninsula there's a bluff that creates a protective amphitheatre with consequently so little rain that they often have to irrigate, and far more sunlight hours than you get just north or south of the bluff. Add to that the lack of harsh winds and it allows Freycinet Vineyard to create wonderful Pinot Noir and fine Cabernet. But they can't just plant the whole area. They've got a long piece of west-facing land that gets all the benefits of the warm afternoon sun, and then has all that advantage wiped out because it has lost the protection against the wind. So it looks like a beautiful site, but it remains unplanted.

In the South, the Coal River Valley again defies common sense. Here we are, heading south, almost to the icy Tasman Sea, and suddenly there's this valley that can ripen Pinot Noir and Cabernet to great effect. How? Why? Well, the valley is in a rainshadow – which means little rain, therefore few clouds, therefore loads of sun. And that'll ripen your grapes in the same way as the vineyards of Central Otago at the southern end of New Zealand's South Island have shown. One guy has even ripened Zinfandel here. You can usually hold off harvest until May – the excellent Domaine A starts on its Bordeaux varieties like Merlot in mid-April and always gets its Petit Verdot ripe by mid-May. There are quite a few vineyards now in Coal River Valley, and I'm not surprised.

Well, I *am* surprised, really. But it's merely my continued delighted astonishment at the beautiful vagaries of nature that the rains and winds that flow over the South of Tasmania somehow get deflected from the Coal River Valley. And from the Huon Valley too. This is an area actually south of Hobart. Some years the frosts and the roaring forties kill the vintage, but most years amazingly good Chardonnays and Pinot Noirs appear. Which leaves the Derwent River Valley inland from Hobart where the Italian Claudio Alcorso set out his stall in 1958. Well, places like the heavenly Moorilla Estate realized they're the first to pick in the whole of Tasmania! And winter doesn't arrive here until July. Further up the Derwent, the summers are hotter, but the winters close in much faster. Which is better? You tell me. Different, but exciting, conditions, right on the edge of the winemaking world. And the first Tasmanian wine I ever tasted was a Cabernet from Moorilla Estate – with Andrew Pirie in the 1970s, as we sat and ate pasta in Sydney – when he told me that Tasmania was Australia's Holy Grail.

Quick guide ◆ Tasmania

Location Tasmania is the most southerly, and coolest part of Australia. That said, however, there are patches of land like around Freycinet on the east coast and further south in the Coal River Valley where the local climate can get positively warm. The Tamar Valley and the North-East vineyards account for nearly 80 per cent of the island's production.

Grapes The island's unpredictable weather means that wineries spread their bets by growing a wide range of varieties.
※ Pinot Noir accounts for nearly 44 per cent of Tasmania's vineyards, with some Cabernet Sauvignon and a little Merlot and Pinot Meunier. In warmer spots there are plots of Shiraz, and even Petit Verdot, which is even more late ripening than Cabernet Sauvignon.
※ Chardonnay is the most popular white, followed by Riesling and Sauvignon Blanc. But Pinot Gris and Gewurztraminer can give delicious results.

Climate Temperatures are lower and rainfall higher than in most other Australian wine regions. However, most of Tasmania's rain comes when the vines are dormant and the ripening period is one of Australia's driest. Windbreaks on seaward slopes are necessary for protection from the wind.

Soil In the north, rich, moisture-retentive clays predominate, and in the south, peaty, alluvial soils.

Aspect Strong, westerly winds tend to restrict vineyards to east-facing slopes.

Do regions or vintages matter? Vintages are more important here than in most Australian wine regions. Sometimes a combination of wet and cold conditions mean that it is difficult to ripen anything except sparkling wine grapes.

Organization Tasmania is an island of smallholders with over 150 vineyards, most of them less than 5ha, but only 13 major wineries.

A few facts 1144ha of vineyards, 0.6% of Australia total plantings; 0.4% per cent of total production. Current number of wineries is 28.

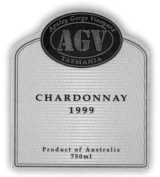

Apsley Gorge
Careful site selection is all important in Tasmania and as befits its name, Apsley Gorge's vineyard is located in a narrow, east-facing valley inland of Bicheno on Tasmania's East Coast.

APSLEY GORGE

East Coast
❄ *Pinot Noir*
🍇 *Chardonnay*

Former abalone diver and crayfisherman, Brian Franklin makes superb Pinot Noir and excellent Chardonnay in a converted fish factory at Bicheno on Tasmania's East Coast. The early wines were made under contract by Andrew Hood (see WELLINGTON page 149) but Franklin became so fascinated by the notion of making great Pinot Noir that he decided to take the next step and increase production enough to justify establishing a winery. The oldest vines on his tiny vineyard (planted in 1988) are now mature enough to allow him to seek complexity in his wines. The Chardonnay is in the cool, white peach, nectarine spectrum with a thick viscous texture while the fragrant Apsley Gorge Pinot Noir has vibrant dark berry flavours, silky texture and powerful, fine tannins.
Best years: (Pinot Noir) 2002, '01, '00, '99, '95.

BAY OF FIRES

North-East
❄ *Pinot Noir*
🍇 *Chardonnay, Sauvignon Blanc, Riesling, Pinot Gris*

The HARDY WINE COMPANY first showed interest in Tasmania in the mid-1990s as part of their search for new cool climate fruit sources for their premium sparkling

Bay of Fires
Bay of Fires Pinot Gris, first released in 2001, was the first time the large Hardy company had worked with this classic white variety.

wine, Arras. This led to the 2001 acquisition of the Rochecombe winery and vineyard from Pipers Brook. It is now home to Bay of Fires, its second label, Tigress, and the Arras bubbly. The vineyard (planted in the late 1980s) supplies about 25 per cent of the fruit for the 10,000 cases produced under these labels. There are sparkling wines at three price points, Pinots under both labels and a range of whites suited to the cool climate: Riesling, Chardonnay, Sauvignon Blanc and Pinot Gris. Best from Bay of Fires have been the bold, tightly structured Riesling and the floral, lean, intense Pinot Gris.
Best years: (Riesling) 2002, '01.

Freycinet
Wine Glass Bay is a beautiful bay on the Freycinet Peninsula and is the name used by the Freycinet winery for its export labels.

FREYCINET

East Coast
❄ *Pinot Noir, Cabernet Sauvignon, Merlot*
🍇 *Chardonnay, Riesling, Schonburger*

This small, 4500-case winery was established by Geoff and Susan Bull in 1980 and is now run by their daughter, Lindy, and her husband, Claudio Radenti, both trained winemakers, although Claudio proves his versatility by also brewing a very decent pint of beer, Hazards Ale, down in Hobart at the Wineglass Bay Brewing. The 9-ha vineyard is situated on an ideal site for ripening grapes: on valley slopes just off the Tasman Highway, not far from the town of Bicheno. Two of their wines are among Australia's best: the ethereal, savoury Pinot Noir and the complex, powerful, voluptuous Radenti sparkling wine. Both are produced in tiny volumes. They do make a little Cabernet and Merlot and in warmer years these, too, are exceptional. The floral, lemon drop Riesling, with its delicious pear and peach fruit flavour, and the high acid but oatmeally and decidedly Burgundian Chardonnay are also excellent. Freycinet achieved unwanted notoriety when the giant Spanish sparkling wine producer Freixenet stopped them using their own name abroad, for fear of confusing the wines. High quality Tasmanian Pinot Noir likely to be confused with mass production cheap Spanish fizz? I don't think so.
Best years (Pinot Noir): 2002, '01, '00, '99, '98.

Stefano Lubiana
Stefano Lubiana has established a high reputation for sparkling wines made in the traditional method from Pinot Noir and Chardonnay.

STEFANO LUBIANA

Derwent Valley
❄ *Pinot Noir, Merlot*
🍇 *Chardonnay, Sauvignon Blanc, Riesling, Pinot Gris*

Mario Lubiana was the quintessential successful immigrant: a displaced person who arrived in Melbourne in 1950 and worked hard for years so that he could establish a profitable family winery at Moorook in the Riverland. When he sold up in 1990, his son Steve and wife Monique decided to move to Tasmania to make premium wines in a cooler area. To help them establish their own vineyard and label, they set up a contract winemaking facility on a 170-ha property at Granton on the banks of the Derwent about 20km from Hobart. There are now 19ha under vines (about half of which is Chardonnay and Pinot Noir) and about 9000 cases are produced annually. Stefano Lubiana is best known for its sparkling wines: the vintage and non-vintage are among the best made in Australia. Both the Chardonnay and Pinot Noir are complex wines with impressive weight and concentration of flavour. Like FREYCINET, Lubiana also fell foul of a European fizz producer – this time Veuve Clicquot Champagne – for having an orange label just like Clicquot does. So someone can copyright the colour orange all of a sudden?
Best years (Vintage Brut): 1998, '95.

PIPERS BROOK VINEYARD

North-East
❄ *Pinot Noir, Cabernet Sauvignon, Merlot*
🍇 *Chardonnay, Riesling, Pinot Gris, Gewurztraminer*

In 1972 Andrew Pirie identified the cool Pipers Brook region of northern Tasmania as most likely to produce European style wines. And he went on, until his departure in 2003 following the purchase of the company by Kreglinger, to produce some of the most refined wines in Australia despite a continual battle against what, for Australia, is a very marginal climate for ripening grapes. In vintages such as 2000 and '98 the red wines come into their own, with an added dimension of fruit and a perfumed, Burgundian style that is lacking in

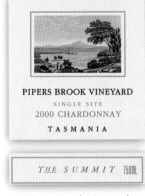

Pipers Brook Vineyard
The classic label image is based on a lithograph of St Paul's Dome, near Fingal, Tasmania, by the 19th-century convict artist, Joseph Lycett, who became famous for his topographical views of Australia. The Summit is the winery's top Chardonnay and comes from old vines at the top of the exposed Pipers Brook Vineyard hill.

cooler years – when the aromatic whites often excel, particularly Riesling, Pinot Gris and Gewurztraminer.

Pipers Brook has been decidedly aggressive in its expansion activities, first acquiring the important Rebecca Vineyard on the Tamar River (now renamed the Strathlynn Vineyard), and then buying the Heemskerk Wine Group, which included the Rochecombe winery, making it by far the biggest wine company in Tasmania.

These are keenly sought wines combining highish prices, clever marketing and skilled winemaking. Steely Riesling, classically reserved Chardonnay (Estate, Reserve and Summit), fragrant Gewurztraminer and refreshing Pinot Gris are some of the highlights, as well as increasingly good Pinot Noir (Estate, Reserve and Lyre). Its traditional method sparkling wine, called Pirie until the 1998 vintage and now Kreglinger Vintage, is especially good and with a little extra aging is outstanding. Andrew Pirie now runs PARKER ESTATE in Coonawarra. Second label Ninth Island is a reliable source of Tasmanian Pinot Noir and Chardonnay.
Best years: (Chardonnay) 2003, '02, '01, '00, '99, '98, '97, '95, '94, '93, '92, '91, '90.

PROVIDENCE

North-East
✴ *Pinot Noir*
⚜ *Chardonnay, Semillon, Riesling*
The revival of commercial viticulture in Tasmania began in the 1950s on this tiny vineyard at Lalla about 25km from Launceston. Jean Miguet, whose family had been making wine in Provence for five generations, came to Tasmania with the

Hydro-Electric Commission and worked the vineyard he called La Provence for 20 years. In 1980, it was purchased by Stuart and Brenda Bryce who quadrupled its size to 2 ha. A further 8ha of Pinot are being planted. The name was changed in 1996 following an unsuccessful court case brought by the French authorities. Although Stuart Bryce is a qualified winemaker, the wines have been made under contract by Andrew Hood (see WELLINGTON) since 1993. The Pinot Noir is outstanding – complex with savoury, minerally characters and silky texture – as is the 'Miguet', made only in the best vintages.
Best years: (Pinot Noir) 2002, '01, '00, '99, '96, '94.

Providence
Providence is Tasmania's oldest established vineyard and produces superb, award-winning Pinot Noir. Miguet is the reserve blend.

TAMAR RIDGE

Tamar Valley
✴ *Pinot Noir, Merlot, Cabernet Sauvignon*
⚜ *Riesling, Chardonnay, Sauvignon Blanc, Gewurztraminer, Pinot Gris*
Tamar Ridge was conceived by founder, Joe Chromy, on a grand scale seen locally only at PIPERS BROOK. Chromy sold his previous ventures into the wine industry, Heemskerk, Jansz and Rochecombe to Pipers Brook Vineyard in 1998 shortly before the Tamar Ridge wines appeared on the market. In 2003, Chromy sold Tamar Ridge to the timber company, Gunns, who have quickly moved into

Tamar Ridge
In just a decade Tamar Ridge has established a reputation for good quality, cool-climate wines and good value, too.

expansion mode. With the country's best-known viticulturist, Dr Richard Smart, on board, Gunns are planting a further 100ha of vines. As well as the Tamar Ridge varietals, there are some cheaper Devil's Corner wines and a Josef Chromy sticky and bubbly, as well as a Tamar Ridge bubbly. The latter is among the best traditional-method sparkling wines made in Australia. The Riesling, Gewurztraminer and Pinot Noir are all impressive and well-priced.
Best years: (Riesling) 2002, '01, '00, '99.

Wellington
The fruit for the Wellington/Hood Wines is purchased from different regions of Tasmania, mainly in the warmer south-east.

WELLINGTON/HOOD WINES

Coal Valley
Former scientist and university lecturer in wine science, Andrew Hood, moved to Tasmania in 1990 to establish a contract winemaking service. It soon became evident that there were opportunities to barter winemaking for fruit and so Hood's own brand, Wellington, came into being from the 1990 vintage. In 1994 Andrew Hood built his own winery which has expanded slowly to a 500-tonne capacity. Andrew Hood's winemaking skills have made a noteworthy contribution to the Tasmanian wine industry. At present, Wellington produces about 7500 cases – a quarter of the total volume that goes through the winery. The range includes excellent Riesling, Chardonnay, Pinot Noir and an Iced Riesling – one of Australia's best dessert wines. From 2004, there will also be Reserve and quaffing (under the Roaring 40s label) Chardonnay and Pinot Noir and a sweet, low-alcohol Riesling.
Best years: (Iced Riesling) 2001, '99, '98, '97.

Quick guide ◆ Best producers

Apsley Gorge, Bay of Fires (Hardys), Clover Hill, Coombend, Domaine A, Elsewhere Vineyard, Freycinet, Jansz, Stefano Lubiana, Moorilla, Notley Gorge, Pipers Brook Vineyard, Providence, Spring Vale, Tamar Ridge, Wellington/Hood Wines.

QUEENSLAND and NORTHERN TERRITORY

IUSED TO THINK that Queensland was easy to classify as a wine region. 'Too hot', I'd proclaim. 'Too tropical'. It's the Sunshine State, after all. It's sugar cane, and pineapples, mile upon mile of cotton plantations, even more miles upon miles of Australia's hottest and most crowded beaches. Sunshine Coast, Gold Coast, Surfer's Paradise. That sort of said it all.

But when I made an effort to actually taste the wines, it was perfectly clear that the Chardonnays and Cabernets and Shirazes I was enjoying couldn't possibly have come from broiling tropical conditions. And when I finally climbed into my hire car and headed off from Brisbane into the wine regions, I soon realised that Queensland's vineyard conditions are extremely diverse. If you want hot – Queensland has it. Roma is Australia's hottest vineyard area with the exception of Alice Springs in the middle of the real hot Outback. If you want tropical, well, Mount Tamborine's vineyards just south of Brisbane sit right next to a patch of rainforest. And if you want cold? Head for the Granite Belt. And take a sweater. The days may seem sunny enough, but the vineyards are anywhere between 800 and more than 1000 metres above sea level. Some of them are the highest in Australia. And the higher you go, whether the sun's out or not, the cooler you get.

None of Queensland's myriad climate conditions are exactly a viticultural paradise. There's a lot of summer rain and you see hail nets all over Queensland. And being 1000 metres high does cool you down, as does the frost that may catch you springtime or autumn and play havoc with your grapes. Yet there are now over 1300 hectares of vines in Queensland, and some very determined and talented people dead set on creating a quality wine industry.

Preston Peak's steep sloping vineyards south of Toowoomba are over 650 metres above sea level. The beautiful mountains in the background run for hundreds of kilometres south into New South Wales and provide numerous excellent sites for vineyards on their granite, silica and quartz-dominated slopes.

SPOTLIGHT ON
Queensland and Northern Territory

The Granite Belt region certainly lives up to its name: extraordinary granite boulders are strewn throughout the vineyards. These ones are in the Devil's Lair Vineyard belonging to Preston Peak. The soil itself is full of silica and quartz granules and decomposed granite. These help to hold heat in the soil, yet their lack of organic matter restricts yield and improves quality.

THEY TELL ME THAT STANTHORPE in the Granite Belt is the coldest place in Queensland. And I can easily believe it. Earlier this year, in late summer as I headed for bed around midnight, the shrill scream of the cicadas outside suggested it should be warm and balmy. But it wasn't. I was wishing I'd brought a sweater instead of just a T-shirt. When I woke early to check out the local vineyards, the dawn light was pale and cold, the grass was heavy with dew, the gum tree leaves were glistening silvery and wet like the sequins on a flapper's dance hall glad rags. Chilly too. And the vineyards that meandered randomly into the hollows and side valleys of the area lay folded in mist until well after breakfast time.

I shouldn't have been surprised. That word 'granite' should have warned me. It's a cold word. It's a cold stone. It conjures up pictures of wild Scottish peaks racked by wind and rain. The Granite City is Aberdeen, a gaunt and defiant outpost on Scotland's harsh east coast. Granite says tough. Granite says struggle. Which is exactly why the wines that come out of this high-altitude haven hidden from Queensland's hot holiday seaside to the east by the ferocious but beautiful Great Dividing Range have so much potential. The grape vine likes to struggle. Toughen up the growing conditions and you'll get much better fruit. Locate poor, infertile soils and you'll get much smaller but much tastier crops of grapes.

Well, you won't get much tougher soil than most of the stuff around Stanthorpe and the south to Wallangarra and the New South Wales border. Granite is everywhere. Angry granite rock faces spill out from the forest hillsides. Mighty boulders are strewn among the fields and by the kerb. The vineyard tracks are littered with rock. And stray off the paved roads into the wooded hinterland and the thin gum trees struggling among the stones show that this is tough country. But that's how the serious winemakers like it and why the Granite Belt, after a long but undistinguished history as a grape-growing area producing primarily table grapes, is now on track to being a serious contender among Australia's smaller wine regions.

Quick guide ◆ Queensland

Location Most of the vineyards are in the south-eastern corner of the state, along the border with New South Wales.

Grapes Shiraz is the principal red grape, with significant plantings of Cabernet Sauvignon and Merlot. Some Petit Verdot has shown promise. Chardonnay and Semillon are the most important quality white grape varieties but Verdelho is also making waves.

Climate Well known as the Sunshine State, Queensland is, not surprisingly, relatively hot but growing conditions in the Granite Belt are mild due to the high altitudes and cool night-time temperatures. In fact, it has a similar temperature range to central Victoria and can even experience snow. South Burnett is more humid and sub-tropical and both rain and hail can be a problem at harvest time. Inland Roma is hot and dry.

Soil The soils are generally slightly acid. They can be granitic and sandy grey, or brown-grey soils over a subsoil of white sand and clay. Around Roma the soil is a rich, sandy, alluvial loam.

Aspect The Granite Belt vineyards are at 750–1000m in the hilly area around Stanthorpe. These are the highest vineyards in Queensland, and some of the highest in Australia. South Burnett is a less daunting terrain, and its rolling landscape used to be covered with dairy farms. The vines have almost all appeared since the 1990s.

Do vintages matter? They certainly do around Stanthorpe where cool conditions can hinder reds' ripening. Nearer the coast you have to keep a weather eye open for possible cyclones at vintage time.

Organization Most Queensland wine is sold at the cellar door. However, a few of the larger producers are now selling wholesale and on the export market.

A few facts 2186ha of vineyards, 1 per cent of Australia's total plantings; less than 1 per cent of total production; currently 101 wineries with less than 30 just 10 years ago.

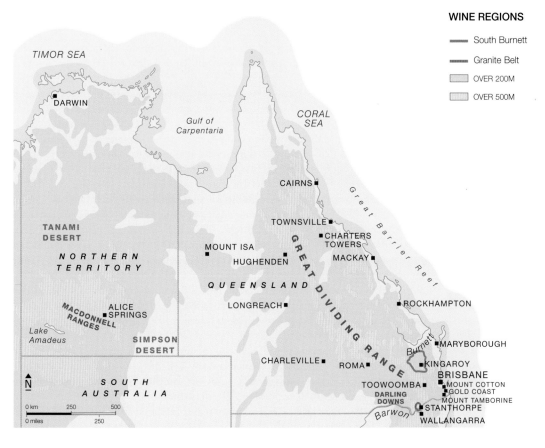

WINE REGIONS
— South Burnett
— Granite Belt
☐ OVER 200M
☐ OVER 500M

This is largely because the Granite Belt has been discovered by a new generation whose ambitions have been influenced by the astonishing nationwide growth in Australian wine since the mid-1990s. There was always good wine being made here before the influx of new blood. Angelo Puglisi who planted the first noble grape variety – Shiraz – on his Ballandean Estate in 1961 has made some lovely wines, including a surprisingly delicious Sylvaner. (What on earth persuaded him to plant such an unlikely and unheralded German variety as Silvaner in the first place?) Another pioneering family winery in the Granite Belt, Robinsons Family Vineyards were making good wine as far back as the 1980s – indeed their's was the first Queensland wine I tasted. But it is the new generation that is making the difference today.

Either, as with the Robinsons, when the eager, college-trained son takes over; or as in the inspiring offerings from Preston Peak or Boireann when a new generation starts from scratch and continually questions and probes and isn't prepared to take old truths at face value without putting them to the test. Their wines made with varieties like Petit Verdot and Viognier are proof of this. Or, indeed, when lifestyle seekers like lawyer Robert Channon get turned on to wine and immediately decide second best won't do.

And there's big business. Sirromet is a grand, tourism-focused group from Mount Cotton near Brisbane. Drive south from the wine town of Ballandean and you'll see their vast Seven Scenes development stretching away to your left, the vineyards threading their way between volcanic cones and National Park Forest, and first tastings of their young vine wines looking extremely promising.

The reason the Granite Belt stays cool is because it is high up. Over on the west side of the mountains most of the vineyards are on high plateau land between 700 and 1000 metres above sea level, though there are some like Symphony Hill hugging the mountain slope at more than 1000 metres. The land drops gently inland away to the west until suddenly the road is dropping faster and that's where the great hot heart of

Every visitor to Australia wants to see and if possible hug a koala bear. At Sirromet at Mount Cotton they have a sign at the entrance that tells you how many sightings of koalas there have been during the month. I visited early in March and the numbers were already in double figures. That's pretty good because koalas are fairly shy creatures and you can go for years in Australia without seeing one. Sirromet is in what is called a 'koala corridor', and they've made good use of this as part of their wine tourism attraction. Luckily the koala doesn't eat grapes – only gum leaves. But don't get me going on wallabies. There are loads of them around too – and they do like grapes.

Australia starts to make itself felt, and the vineyards end. If you're simply adding up hours of heat and sunshine, you'll get quite a big total but where the Granite Belt scores is that it hardly ever really bakes. Grapes like the temperature to stay below 30°C on the whole. Typically during the ripening season the Granite Belt wineries experience six days a month with heat spikes at more than 30°C. Even a supposedly super-cool area like the Yarra Valley near Melbourne often gets 25 days a month when the heat tops 30°C. This means that in the Granite Belt the grapes have a good chance of steady ripening, producing ripe but not overblown flavours from relatively low crops – given that the soils are generally pretty short on organic matter and pretty packed with slivers of quartz and silica that you can see shimmering among the rows of vines.

But there are hardships for the vines to endure here, too. For a start – when you're driving around the Granite Belt you'll see great spreads of black netting. This isn't to stop the birds eating the crop – though there is a bird problem: there always is when you put an alien crop like grape vines in the middle of gum forests that have been there since time immemorial. No. These are hail nets. There is a serious ever-present hail threat, particularly early in the growing season, and particularly if you're close to the mountains in the east. Ask any of the apple farmers around Applethorpe in the north of the Granite Belt about hail. It can wipe out your crop in a minute. Interestingly hail nets have another advantage too. The sun's radiation here is the strongest of any agricultural area in Australia. Hail nets can cut this radiation by anything from 10 to 40 per cent, thereby slowing down ripening. Some early-ripening varieties like Chardonnay or Merlot taste much better if you slow down their ripening process.

But there's a risk here too. Frost comes to the high vineyards not only in springtime but also at the end of the ripening season in April. You can wake up and find your crop of late-ripening Cabernet Sauvignon just got too late this year – frosted before you picked. Rain is also a problem. Most of Australia's vineyard regions are extremely dry in the summer. But the Granite Belt receives two-thirds of its 800mm annual rainfall during the grape-growing season. Usually this rain is in the form of violent storms that don't do much harm unless they arrive when the vine is trying to flower, or is finishing off its ripening.

OTHER REGIONS

Although the Granite Belt is the best known of Queensland's vineyard regions, and, I suspect, the one with the greatest quality potential, there are various other growing regions, and quite a few wineries. Some wineries, particularly on the Gold Coast and Sunshine Coast, either don't grow grapes, or buy in grapes or wine from further inland, because it is fairly subtropical out on the coast. But remember – Queensland has 18 million tourists a year and wine tourism is one of the best ways to sell your wine for a decent price.

South Burnett is the second most important region – sometimes producing more wine than the Granite Belt, though when I visited in 2004 they'd just lost 1000 tonnes of fruit in a vicious hail storm. This is an area centred on Kingaroy about 150 kilometres north-west of Brisbane that was largely planted after a Government Report in 1994 recommended grapes as a good crop. It's pretty hot up here – during the dry, hot spells of summer, water stress can be dangerous for the vines, though vineyards that push up into the Bunya Mountains in the south are decidedly cooler, and none of the grapes are contract grown, though wineries like Barambah Ridge and, way south, Rimfire, have had some success.

Toowoomba, directly west of Brisbane, also grows good grapes, particularly reds like Shiraz and Petit Verdot, and Inglewood has some decent vineyards just north-west of the Granite Belt. Then there are occasional 'tourist' area vineyards like Mount Tamborine and Albert River south of Brisbane.

And, if you feel really intrepid, Roma, 300 kilometres out into the broiling west, was the site of Queensland's first winery – Bassett's – which was founded in 1863 and it's still there, now called Romavilla – and still making a range of fortifieds.

NORTHERN TERRITORY

When some intrepid friend told me they'd just sampled the local brew at Alice Springs on the way back from a visit to Uluru (Ayers Rock) I presumed they were taking the mickey. I mean, the centre of Australia is just this great baking red desert, isn't it? It has certainly looked like that whenever I've flown over it. Golden Rule time. Never underestimate the ingenuity of an Australian winemaker when it comes to turning a quid.

Yes, the centre of Australia is an arid, fly-blown desert. And yes, there is a vineyard there, Chateau Hornsby – about 11 kilometres south of Alice Springs. And there are vines too. Just over 2 hectares are planted with a motley selection of Cabernet, Shiraz, Grenache, Chardonnay, Riesling and Semillon. Drip irrigation is hard at it right through the growing season, fed by a couple of deep boreholes, and the winery itself is underground to try to keep things cool. The owner is always eager to proclaim the first vintage in Australia. Indeed, his top seller is Early Red, a Shiraz he starts to pick as the clock strikes midnight each New Year's Eve. I'm surprised that anyone in Australia is sober enough at that time to tell a grape from a coconut, but there you go.

South Burnett, in the rolling plains north-west of Brisbane, is Queensland's second most important wine region and new plantings are a common sight. Indeed, since the 1990s this is the area that has seen most vineyard growth in Queensland with hundreds of new hectares being planted on land that used to support dairy farms.
Indications are that the quality is pretty good – and the conditions are much easier than up in the Granite Belt. The vineyards are interspersed with peanut farms, the area's most important crop. The vintage here starts very early, in mid-January, and South Burnett's white grapes are often the first to ripen in Australia.

ALBERT RIVER

🎇 *Shiraz, Cabernet Sauvignon, Merlot*
🍃 *Chardonnay, Viognier*

Situated in the rainshadow of Tamborine Mountain on the historic Tamborine House property in the Queensland Gold Coast hinterland (about 45 minutes' drive from Brisbane, although I approached it from the other side covered in dust after a hairy drive over the unsealed Mount Lindsay Highway), this is one of Australia's great winery tourism destinations. David and Janette Bladin have vast experience in hospitality and it shows. A magnificent Brisbane landmark, Auchenflower House has been relocated and by that, I mean they actually moved the whole house, lock stock and barrel. It serves as a grand cellar door. It's early days for the wines (vines were planted in 1998) but they are being supervised by Peter Scudamore-Smith MW and show promise.

Albert River
This is just the sort of full-bodied, big wine to enjoy with your kangaroo steak. Grand Masters' Wine Series Shiraz benefits from 15 months of aging in new French and American oak.

BARAMBAH RIDGE

South Burnett
🎇 *Cabernet Sauvignon, Shiraz*
🍃 *Chardonnay, Semillon, Verdelho*

Having had four winemakers in the first four years, the group of investors who established Barambah Ridge in 1996 have been fortunate to secure the service of Stuart Pierce as his five years with the company have given it stability. Pierce's wines are clean and well-made but show an idiosyncratic flair. This is crucial because the world doesn't need more blandly correct wines, so more power to Stuart's elbow. The judges at the 2003 Queensland Wine Awards commented on this in awarding a gold medal to his Verdelho. At present, about half of Barambah Ridge's production (6000 cases) comes from its own vineyards.

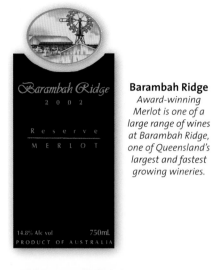

Barambah Ridge
Award-winning Merlot is one of a large range of wines at Barambah Ridge, one of Queensland's largest and fastest growing wineries.

BOIREANN

Granite Belt
🎇 *Cabernet Sauvignon, Merlot, Shiraz, Grenache, Petit Verdot, Cabernet Franc, Mourvedre, Nebbiolo, Barbera*
🍃 *Viognier*

After working for a bank in Rockhampton, Peter Stark was looking for a change in lifestyle when he and his wife Therese bought this 10-ha property in 1994. The vineyard was planted from 1997 onwards as an adjunct to their first enterprise, bed and breakfast accommodation.

Winemaking has now taken over and the vineyard has been expanded to 1.4ha. The amount of each variety is tiny: 400 Cabernet Sauvignon vines, 300 Merlot, 200 Grenache, and also minute amounts of grapes like Petit Verdot, Cabernet Franc and Viognier, which should all excel. Considering the young age of the vines, these wines already have remarkable richness and concentration of power. They are some of the best reds produced in Queensland, but unfortunately in minuscule quantities.

Boireann
James Halliday recently praised this Shiraz wine, co-fermented with 7 per cent Viognier, as Queensland's best red. I agree.

ROBERT CHANNON WINES

Granite Belt
🎇 *Cabernet Sauvignon, Merlot, Shiraz*
🍃 *Verdelho, Chardonnay*

The threat of a lawsuit from the largest Champagne house when it wanted to use the name Channon Estates (Channon, Chandon. Geddit?) provided the fledgling winery with the kind of publicity of which one only dreams. It's early days yet, as planting of the vines, located at 950m in what is close to being a cool climate area, only began in 1998, but the seriousness of the operation can be seen in Robert Channon's decision to net the entire vineyard permanently as protection against the birds. The smart, efficient winery was completed in 2002 and is supervised by one of Queensland's best winemakers, Mark Ravenscroft. At this stage, the Verdelho is the top wine: floral, intense, taut with attractive tropical fruit flavours and it has won the Best White Wine trophy at the past three Queensland Wine Awards. But the quality of Reserve Cabernet and Merlot from new plantings and from nearby Glen Aplin show this isn't just a white wine operation.

Robert Channon Wines
Tangy, aromatic Verdelho is one of the best wines at Robert Channon with a citrous peel freshness and a lovely waxy texture.

CLOVELY ESTATE

South Burnett
🎇 *Shiraz, Cabernet Sauvignon, Merlot, Sangiovese, Barbera, Nebbiolo, Grenache, Mourvedre, Petit Verdot, Chambourcin*
🍃 *Chardonnay, Semillon, Verdelho*

As a result of the Queensland Government's Macarthur Report (1994) into the viability of the South Burnett for viticulture, Clovely was established as an unlisted public company in 1998. It has 175ha of estate vineyards (in two blocks) near Murgon from which all the Clovely wines are sourced. There are also 40,000 olive trees on the

Clovely

Clovely's colourful labels for their Queensland range of wines are designed to reflect Queensland's bright, fresh and relaxed lifestyle. The Chardonnay depicts the Southern, Orange-Eyed Tree Frog.

property. There are three ranges of wines – the quaffable Queensland, the medium-priced Left Field and the premium Reserve Chardonnay and Reserve Shiraz Cabernet.

HERITAGE ESTATE

Granite Belt
❋ *Merlot, Shiraz, Cabernet Sauvignon*
❋ *Chardonnay*

Argentinian winemaker, Paolo Cadenzas-Rhymer, has had an immediate impact at Heritage. Their wines have improved dramatically: so, too, have those which are made under contract. Their vineyard is now 10 years old and this shows through in wines such as their Reserve Merlot and Reserve Shiraz. Best of all has been the Botrytis Chardonnay – fine, intensely sweet though with refreshing natural acidity to provide balance.

Heritage Estate

This fine, intensely sweet Botrytis Chardonnay still has enough refreshing natural acidity to provide balance. It will benefit from 5–10 years of aging.

JIMBOUR STATION

❋ *Merlot, Petit Verdot, Shiraz, Cabernet Sauvignon*
❋ *Chardonnay, Verdelho, Viognier*

This 21-ha vineyard (established in 2000) lies on a gentle slope in a secluded part of this Darling Downs property not far from the station homestead. This is the Australian Outback: Crocodile Dundee meets Hugh Johnson. Jimbour was settled in 1841 and its magnificent homestead was built from 1874 to 1877. Originally a vast sheep station, it is now a modest 2150ha – which pays its way by growing grain and fodder, running a Charolais cattle stud and commercial breeding herd and viticulture. The wine business is in the capable hands of the ubiquitous Peter Scudamore-Smith MW who is sourcing fruit at present from the Granite Belt and South Burnett. In 2003, 7000 cases were produced under the Jimbour Station label though this will increase when the the vineyard comes into full production in 2006. At present, the Reserve Chardonnay and the Shiraz are the most promising wines. And it will be fascinating to see what styles emerge from their home-grown grapes.

Jimbour

This Reserve Chardonnay was released in 2002 to commemorate the 160th anniversary of the explorer Ludwig Leichhardt's pioneering crossing from Jimbour across the Outback to the tip of the Northern Territory.

PRESTON PEAK

Granite Belt
❋ *Shiraz, Cabernet Sauvignon, Merlot, Petit Verdot, Pinot Noir, Nebbiolo*
❋ *Chardonnay, White Muscat, Viognier*

The first of the two Preston Peak vineyards, the 8-ha Devil's Elbow, was established in 1994 on an old farming property in the Granite Belt where the winery is situated. There are 1.5ha of vines and a cellar door on the Preston property close to Toowomba where the Preston Peak's owners, Ashley Smith and Kym Thumpkin, work as dentists. Three price points are represented by the Wildflower Series, Leaf Series and the Reserve

Preston Peak

The high altitude and thin soil of the Devil's Elbow Vineyard contributes to this austere Chardonnay, with excellent length.

ranges. Two wines that stand out are the Leaf Series Verdelho – a fragrant white with tropical fruit flavours – and the Reserve Shiraz – approachable, soft and satisfyingly fleshy.

SIRROMET

❋ *Cabernet Sauvignon, Shiraz, Merlot, Cabernet Franc, Petit Verdot, Nebbiolo, Pinot Noir, Mataro*
❋ *Chardonnay, Sauvignon Blanc, Semillon, Pinot Gris, Viognier, Colombard, Verdelho, Marsanne*

Sirromet is Queensland's largest wine producer and represents a massive investment by its owner, Terry Morris. The winery and tourism complex at Mount Cotton is located halfway between Brisbane and the Gold Coast and attracts significant numbers of locals and tourists. Sirromet has two major vineyards in the Granite Belt: Seven Scenes (101ha under vine) and St Jude's (17ha) and there are 11ha of Chambourcin at Mount Cotton.

Sirromet

Sirromet's top Chardonnay comes from the Seven Scenes Vineyard at Ballandean in the heart of the Granite Belt region. The Special Release T M Chardonny – named after the owner – is also classy.

Quick guide ◆ Best producers

Albert River, Bald Mountain, Ballandean, Boireann, Casley Mount Hutton, Robert Channon, Clovely Estate, Cody's, Kominos, Preston Peak, Robinsons Family, Sirromet, Symphony Hill, Wild Soul, Windermere.

Wine Vintages

'IF YOU WANT TO DRINK REALLY OLD WINES, don't drink Australian wine'. The poor, deluded soul who came out with this particular bon mot has obviously never had the privilege of sitting down to a very long lunch in the heart of Australian wine country and sampling 30-year-old Rieslings, 20-year-old Shirazes and Cabernets and even 90- (yes, 90) year-old fortifieds that are all stunning examples of their type and positive proof that, although much Australian wine is made with early drinking in mind, there are plenty of examples that can and do age extremely well (and often need to).

Unfortunately, most of us don't get such sampling opportunities either, and finding older Australian wines outside of the country itself is no easy task. But it is far from impossible. Auctions are they key – try the main London salerooms in Europe, or two Australian houses. Langtons is the leading seller and expert on older Australian wines; indeed, it produces a highly respected classification of Australia's 'first growth' wines, a wine guide and has a very informative website, as well as actually selling the stuff. The other good source is Oddbins – not the UK High Street version, but Oddbins Auctions of Adelaide. Look them up (see page 164), then take great care with the credit card!

As to what wines age well – well, not surprisingly this varies. Australia is an enormous continent with widely varying climatic conditions. It is more meaningful to talk about wine regions than states because states are huge with a great diversity of wine styles, quality and aging ability, and vintages can be markedly different even within a state. So, Barossa Shiraz is quite different from Hunter Valley Shiraz, as Coonawarra Cabernet differs from Margaret River Cabernet; Clare might have a terrific vintage, Padthaway might get rained away.

Australian winemakers are used to good ripening conditions. Barossa Valley Shiraz, for instance, needs its alcohol levels of 13–14 per cent to give the wines scope to add complexity as they age. Hunter Valley Semillon is picked early and is lower in alcohol, yet it can age for 20 years or more. Coonawarra Cabernet comes in two guises: super-concentrated wine needing substantial bottle age or wine which is drinkable after four years. Margaret River Cabernet has fine tannins and fruit, which shows well after five years and will keep much longer. Clare and Eden Valley Rieslings have purity of fruit and good acidity for aging; the best live for 30 years or more. Australian Chardonnay is generally good to drink on release, but wines from cool climates can age 10 years. Heard enough? Start exploring, storing and enjoying the benefits of a few older Australians.

The private cellar at Brand's of Coonawarra contains more than 1000 bottles of Brand's wines dating back to the early 1950s. Top examples of Shiraz and Cabernet Sauvignon from the Coonawarra region are some of Australia's longest-lived wines.

VINTAGE CHART

	03	02	01	00	99	98	97	96	95
South Australia									
Barossa/Clare Shiraz	7○	10○	9○	8○	8○	10○	8□	10□	7○
Coonawarra Cabernet	8○	9○	9○	6○	8○	10○	7□	9□	5●
Clare/Eden Valley Riesling	9○	10○	9□	7□	8○	10○	10□	8□	8□
Adelaide Hills Chardonnay	8□	7□	8□	7□	7●	9●	9●	8✳	8✳
New South Wales									
Hunter Valley Semillon (premium unoaked)	7○	8○	5○	9○	8○	10○	8□	9□	7○
Hunter Valley Shiraz	9○	8○	6●	9□	7●	9□	7✳	9●	7✳
Victoria									
Yarra Valley Pinot Noir	8□	9□	8□	9□	8●	9✳	10●	7✳	7✳
Cabernet Sauvignon	8○	9○	9□	8●	7□	9□	9□	5●	7●
Chardonnay	8□	9□	7□	8●	7✳	9●	9●	7✳	7✳
Shiraz	8□	7○	9□	8□	7●	8□	10●	6✳	9●
Western Australia									
Margaret River Cabernet Sauvignon	7○	10○	8○	10○	8○	7○	9○	10□	9●
Chardonnay	8□	8□	9□	7●	8●	7●	8●	9✳	9✳
Sauvignon Blanc/Semillon blends	9□	9●	8●	8●	6✳	7✳	8✳	8✳	9✳
Great Southern Riesling	8□	9□	8□	6●	7●	8●	8●	8●	9✳
Shiraz	9○	8○	9□	7□	7○	6□	7●	9□	8●
Tasmania									
Pinot Noir	8□	9□	7□	9□	9●	9✳	9●	4✳	7✳
Chardonnay	8□	9□	7□	8□	8□	10●	9●	5✳	6✳

Key ○= needs more time　□ = ready but will improve　●= at peak　✳= fading or tired

SOUTH AUSTRALIA

Only the south-east corner of this largely desert state is suitable for viticulture, but it still covers a wide area, from north to south especially, and the range of climate and terrain is broad.

The more established regions – Clare Valley, Barossa, McLaren Vale, Coonawarra and Langhorne Creek – tend to specialize in full-bodied reds from Shiraz, Cabernet Sauvignon and, increasingly, Grenache-based blends. The top examples are capable of a good 15-20 years' aging, and in the best vintages, will keep for up to 25 years or more, although many wines will be drinking well after only about four years. The lighter Grenaches should be drunk young.

The younger – and cooler – regions, like Adelaide Hills, Eden Valley, and Padthaway, are producing more elegant table wines, especially from Chardonnay, Riesling and Sauvignon Blanc. The better Chardonnays show every sign of aging gracefully for up to 10 years; some very fine Rieslings will age for even longer – those from Clare and Eden Valley are great keepers: most years, the wines are lovely at five to seven years and many age well for much longer. Adelaide Hills Pinot Noir could surprise us in the future, but most current examples are best drunk within five years.

Annual Vintage Reports

2004

Welcome, dam-filling winter rains returned most of South Australia to relative normality after the previous year's water shortfalls, and this was followed by a warm, wet spring, which the vines loved. December was hot, causing some concern, but January was the mildest in more than a decade and a bumper crop of grapes thrived. February was then scorching, leading to some losses, but March was kinder again, with cool ripening conditions. Vintage was late and long and quality is top

Coonawarra Cabernet Sauvignon

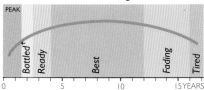

Most Aussie Cabs are excellent at around five years but Coonawarra is one of the world's classic regions for Cabernet and Cabernet changes so much in bottle that it would be a shame to forget the pleasures of mature wine. The top Coonawarra wines in good vintages are best around 10 years of age.

notch in virtually all varieties, though April rains in Coonawarra caused a few late disease problems.

2003

Drought, intense heat, then rain during vintage – 2003 was definitely what the winemakers call 'challenging'. But it was one of those years where, even though the rains came at just the wrong time, they still did more good than harm. Not surprisingly, the reds performed better than the whites, and Shiraz was the star performer overall, especially from Langhorne Creek and the Clare and Barossa Valleys. Riesling did well, as usual, in Eden Valley and Clare, however, and there was some good Chardonnay and Sauvignon Blanc from the cooler climes of the Adelaide Hills.

2002

After the intense heat of 2001, conditions went the opposite way in 2002 with an uncharacteristically cool summer across the board. This has resulted in some outstanding, if atypical wines from all areas. There is some amazing Shiraz coming out of Barossa, Clare, McLaren Vale and Langhorne Creek, as well as superior Semillon and Chardonnay. Riesling from Clare and Eden Valley is exceptionally good, and there are some very fine reds and whites from the Limestone Coast in the far south-east of the state, too. The normally baking Riverland region thrived and produced some great grapes and wines. Fruit struggled to ripen in the Adelaide Hills, however.

2001

A seriously hot summer, even by South Australian standards, put the pressure on in the warmer regions, and white grape varieties suffered from the intense heat in the Barossa and McLaren Vale in particular. The reds, however, stood up to the onslaught much better, with some classically good Shiraz from Clare, Barossa and McLaren Vale and promising Cabernet Sauvignon from further south in Langhorne Creek and Coonawarra. In the Adelaide Hills Pinot Noir didn't enjoy the heat, but other varieties there fared better. There were some intense Rieslings from the Eden and Clare Valleys.

2000

South Australia, like most of the country's wine regions in 2000, experienced an early budburst. During the spring, cool, windy and, in some places, frosty conditions soon reminded everyone that Mother Nature is fickle and that computer weather predictions are not 100 per cent reliable.

Top Clare Valley Riesling

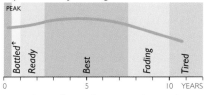

Most Clare Valley Rieslings are at their peak within their first five years. A few, however, are meant for longer aging and will go on improving beyond that time, the lime zest freshness deepening to a memorable buttered toast and honey richness.

The Barossa had its third dry winter in succession, but then unseasonable spring rain and cold affected the flowering and thus reduced the crop by up to 40 per cent. Shiraz was hardest hit of all, yet the fruit quality was very high. It was worse in the Clare Valley, where yields were down significantly (although there was plenty of good quality Riesling), and the McLaren Vale (where the reds are quite elegant as a result of slow, cool ripening).

The cool Adelaide Hills seemed to enjoy it more than other regions; reds and whites did well. Coonawarra escaped the February rains and started and finished vintage early; while Cabernet Sauvignon yields were low, the fruit quality was high. Premium red and white wines across the state showed intense flavours.

1999

The state had one of the most difficult vintages in recent years and the wine quality was very mixed. Those producers with the most healthy, balanced vineyards were quite successful but others had a terrible year. In the Barossa, a dry winter and spring led to lower than usual yields but rain during vintage caused mould

Adelaide Hills Chardonnay

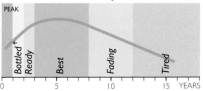

Adelaide Hills is now emerging as one of the country's classic wine regions. Most Australian Chardonnay is made for drinking on release at two years old or so but good Adelaide Hills examples although certainly attractive to drink on release have the structure and acidity to age for a decade, and they positively need five years' aging to really show what they're made of.

problems and generally low sugar levels. Reds were lighter-bodied and for early drinking. Langhorne Creek fared worst with the wet and mouldy conditions, Shiraz in particular; McLaren Vale also suffered but less drastically, the results varying from good to not-so-good, while Clare also had a difficult year and strict selection of grapes was needed; Riesling was very good, particularly if the fruit had been picked before the vintage rain. The Riverland was only fair. By contrast, the later-ripening Coonawarra had a very good vintage, Petaluma's Brian Croser saying that it was as though someone had held an umbrella over the district.

1998

In South Australia quality was more variable than in eastern parts of the country. The harvest started later in Clare and McLaren Vale as producers had to wait for the grapes to ripen. Although there were widespread conditions of drought, overall summer temperatures swung less from the norm than in the east. Clare Riesling looks set to rival the outstanding 1997s, while quality in the regions was generally very good.

1997

A February heatwave with temperatures over 40°C for a week caused some damage to vines but not to wine quality. Generally another cool summer and late harvest, but a late burst of warmth in Coonawarra gave excellent reds. Clare has exceptional Riesling and very good reds; McLaren Vale was also excellent across the board, and Padthaway produced first-class whites. Whites in hotter areas such as the Riverland, especially Chardonnay, were excellent, meaning that the large-volume commercial white wines were outstanding. Sauvignon Blanc was generally below par, lacking much needed acidity.

Barossa Valley Old Vine Shiraz

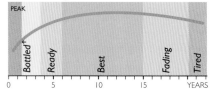

Styles here vary, but the most intense wines can combine early drinkability with the ability to age beautifully for a couple of decades or more. Mature examples can often show a meaty, Christmas cake-like character and spectacular richness on the palate.

1996

Excellent for both quality and quantity throughout the warmer regions, especially Clare, McLaren Vale and the Barossa, despite the stop-start ripening period with its hot and cold spells of weather. Spring frost cut some Chardonnay yields in Coonawarra.

1995

Like Australia's eastern seaboard, South Australia suffered a severe drought in the winter of 1994, followed by frost in the Barossa which cut the crop. Heavy spring rains helped, but even so the Barossa and Clare valleys were 36 per cent down on 1994's quantities. With the exception of Coonawarra, quality was good, and in the case of McLaren Vale Shiraz, very good.

Other good years: For red, Shiraz or Cabernet 1990, '85, '84 and '82 could still yield some fine bottles. 1991, '90 and '86 were exceptionally good for Coonawarra Cabernet. 1980, '81, '86, '90 and '91 also produced fine reds in Barossa. For Penfolds Grange, Australia's longest-living red, 1994, '92, '91, '90, '88, '86, '84, '83, '80, '76, '71, '67, '66, '63, '62, '55, '53, and '52 were all very good. For Clare or Eden Valley Riesling, 1990 and '86 were excellent.

NEW SOUTH WALES

The great aging dry white of New South Wales is Hunter Valley unwooded Semillon made in a low-alcohol, early-harvested, early-bottled, delicate, bone-dry style. This is capable of 20 years' aging, but can also be drunk very young. Riper, oak-aged Semillons are shorter-lived.

Cabernet Sauvignon, Shiraz and Cabernet blends from Mudgee, the Hunter Valley and the Canberra District are capable of 15 years, occasionally longer. The same is likely to apply to reds from emerging areas such as Orange, Hilltops and Cowra. Most of these wines, however, are best enjoyed at five to 10 years. The hotter regions, Riverina and Murray-Darling produce wines that are best drunk as young as possible, although a few reds are capable of aging.

Annual Vintage Reports
2004

Good spring rains and a long, dry ripening period meant that a huge crop was on the cards, but the by now almost traditional heavy downpours in the Hunter Valley mid-vintage curbed any excesses somewhat. Semillon and Verdelho are looking good, Chardonnay less so, while reds that were harvested before the deluge are said to be outstanding. Yields were still well up on last year's drought-affected figures.

2003

The Hunter had a rare rain-free vintage, and it was its earliest ever, but yields were well down due to the drought that affected most of the country. Quality was excellent, however, particularly for Chardonnay and Shiraz, with some good Semillon and Verdelho as well. Mudgee, Cowra and Canberra also produced good Chardonnay, though some Mudgee reds were affected by heavy rains during harvest.

2002

While much of the rest of the country was enjoying an almost perfect vintage, the Hunter got a couple of characteristic vintage time downpours, resulting in Chardonnay and Semillon being the only real standout wines. Cowra also copped a bit of late season rain, but other regions were more fortunate, with Mudgee making some benchmark reds and good Semillon, and the Riverina enjoying one of its best ever years.

2001

After a good, wet spring and a hot January, the Hunter once again fell victim to heavy vintage rainfall. Some excellent Semillon and Chardonnay escaped the deluge, but the reds suffered, especially in the Lower Hunter. Mudgee, Orange and Cowra had a better season, though each with its own challenges, with whites again performing best. Some Mudgee Cabernet was also good.

2000

New South Wales felt the wrath of the rain gods early on, and things became more difficult and testing as the season progressed. Warmer, drier conditions arrived in February to save the vintage. The sun finally shone on the Hunter and some parcels of Semillon, Chardonnay and Shiraz

Hunter Valley Semillon (premium unoaked)

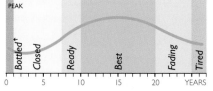

Passionate wine enthusiasts love this style, one of Australia's classics. The traditional way of making it is to bottle it young and green and lemony, and then not touch for perhaps 5 to 10 years. During the aging process these wines develop remarkably, acquiring a complex, honeyed, straw-like bouquet, waxy texture and a unique flavour of custardy biscuits and lime.

were very good, both in quality and volume; indeed, 2000 turned out much better than expected. Mudgee and Orange saw lower crop levels and some disease, but the vineyards dried out and quality was fair to good. Riverina produced average quality wine, but plenty of it, much to the relief of wine companies faced with such heavily reduced crops in the higher quality regions. Good fruit selection was once again all- important.

1999

The Hunter Valley had rain at the wrong times and, while early-picked Semillon should be up to par, it wasn't a memorable year for red varieties. Chardonnay was probably the best variety. Orange and Mudgee also had a wet vintage and rot was a big problem. As in other areas, good wines were made by those producers with less vigorous vineyards and modest yields, and who selected their grapes carefully.

1998

Quality was above average to excellent. Drought conditions resulting from El Niño contributed to a reduction in yield with reduced fruit set leading to ideally ripened small berries. The wine regions of New South Wales were very dry and harvested very early with abnormally high mid-summer temperatures accelerating development. High sugar levels were attained and, surprisingly, acids were also high, promising wines of excellent potential longevity. The Hunter Valley in particular had its best year since 1991: the usual rainy conditions at harvest stayed away.

1997

A vintage that the Hunter Valley would like to forget for early varieties: repeated rain and rot wrecked most of the white grapes, especially in the damper Broke Fordwich area. But a drier end of vintage saw some good reds made. Although some producers did not bottle any '97 Semillon, others were very happy with classic 'wet-year' Semillon styles with good acidity levels. Cowra and Mudgee also had an indifferent year and their common problem of overcropping and lack of ripeness was shared by the Riverina.

1996

A successful year, with yields good and quality average to good, although Chardonnay in the Riverina and Cowra suffered from spring frost. As in 1991, this was a very good vintage for Hunter red wines.

1995

A smaller vintage than expected here, as elsewhere in Australia, with the Hunter being 46 per cent down on 1994. Quality of the reds was good but most should have been drunk by now.

VICTORIA

Victoria has many red wines which age gracefully, mostly Cabernet Sauvignon and Shiraz-based wines from Grampians, North-East Victoria, Bendigo, Heathcote, the Pyrenees and Yarra Valley. The top examples keep for 15 to 20 years.

Pinot Noir from the more southerly regions (e.g. Mornington Peninsula and Geelong) is best drunk within two to five years, but those from the best producers in the best vintages can last well for as many as eight years. Chardonnay from Yarra Valley, Geelong and Mornington Peninsula is capable of improving over five years or more in good vintages. Riesling is far less common in Victoria, but the best from the high country of Victoria's Great Dividing Range including King Valley, Strathbogie Ranges, Goulburn Valley and Mansfield age for many years, as do those from Grampians and Drumborg.

Annual Vintage Reports

2004

In common with the rest of Australia, Victoria had an unusually lengthy vintage. Despite some meteorological challenges – hail in the Yarra, frosts in Rutherglen, extreme heat in the north and west of the state – yields were well above average in virtually all areas. Whites fared better than reds, generally, with Chardonnay and cool climate aromatics doing particularly well. There was some good Shiraz and Cabernet as well.

2003

The drought was as much a factor for Victoria as for anywhere else in Australia, resulting in an early vintage and reduced yields, but some excitingly intense fruit, too. The southern regions in particular – Yarra Valley, Mornington Peninsula and Macedon – enjoyed an almost ideal growing season and made some great wines. In the very hot North-East, some wines were affected by smoke taint from bushfires.

2002

The cool spring and summer which so benefited warmer regions, created big problems for Victoria's cool climate regions, where yields were slashed to the point that some producers had no fruit at all. That said, the quality was good for Pinot Noir

and aromatic whites. Further north, Central Victoria, the North-East and Murray Darling all benefited from the weather, producing elegant wines capable of great aging.

2001

Most of Victoria had a great start to the season, with good rains and mild weather until late in the year. However, by Christmas a serious heatwave was setting in, putting great stress on vines. This was compounded by heavy rains in March. Yarra Valley Cabernet and Merlot seemed to suffer least, with Great Western Shiraz also looking good. Pinot Gris and Chardonnay from Mornington Peninsula did well.

2000

In the north the Murray Darling dropped crop levels by perhaps 15 per cent, thanks to the cool conditions and outbreaks of disease; quality, however, was very good. The King Valley was particularly good with full, deep reds and fruity whites. The southern regions and wine regions around Melbourne all started harvesting early and crop levels were fair; white varieties and Pinot Noir did well in the Yarra Valley. Some of the better growers in the Mornington Peninsula claimed 2000 as one of the region's best vintages for many years. Generally, Victorian wines were more restrained and concentrated.

1999

The warmer, drier sites in the Yarra Valley had a reasonably good year as did those with excellent vineyard management; some Chardonnay and Sauvignon Blanc were good. The Mornington Peninsula had a wet, humid summer; a dry, mild autumn ripened a small crop well, but it is variable. Geelong enjoyed a warm and dry summer and autumn; Pinot Noir and Cabernet Sauvignon look long-lived. Yields at Great Western were severely cut by late spring frost but at least the harvest was dry and the premium Shiraz is excellent, yet again.

North-East Victoria Muscat (Rutherglen)

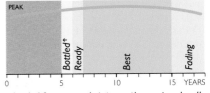

Blended from several vintages these wines hardly change in bottle. Dark, sticky and super-raisiny, they may lose some perfume but otherwise they will stay much as they are for a couple of decades or more.

1998

Wines of above average quality were produced throughout. Drought conditions resulting from El Niño have contributed to a reduction in yield with reduced fruit set leading to ideally ripened small berries. Victoria was very dry and harvested very early with abnormally high mid-summer temperatures accelerating development. High sugar levels were attained and, surprisingly, acids are also high, promising wines of excellent potential longevity. The harvest was conducted in ideal conditions with autumnal rain arriving after the crop was in.

1997

A very dry, hot season with the same February heatwave that hit South Australia. Yields were down and reds in the Yarra Valley and Grampians are exceptional dark and concentrated, especially Pinot Noir. A superb vintage in all regions: high quality, low quantity.

1996

A great vintage in Rutherglen and the warmer regions, but the Mornington Peninsula, the Yarra Valley and Geelong had rain at picking time and some mould problems. Yields were up everywhere. Not a vintage for keeping. Some decent whites and Pinot Noirs.

1995

There was a smaller-than-usual crop here, as elsewhere in Australia. Most of the wines will be past their best now.

Other good years: Care should be taken with older vintages, as most of the wines will be past their best – 1994, '91, '90, '88, '86 and '84 are the years to look for. Old bottlings of Liqueur Muscat or Tokay, or port-style wines, can also be excellent.

WESTERN AUSTRALIA

In Western Australia, only the south-west coastal areas are suitable for winemaking. It is 260km from the Swan Valley to Great Southern – the former is hot and dry, the latter cooler and suited to finer table wines.

The wines suitable for aging are confined to the far south-west, particularly Margaret River, the state's leading wine region where fuller-bodied reds made from Cabernet Sauvignon, Merlot and Shiraz can be cellared for up to 20 years.

Pinot Noir is best drunk within five years of release, as is Semillon, Sauvignon Blanc and dry white blends, while Mount Barker Riesling is a 15-year proposition and the Chardonnay, especially from Margaret River, is among the longest-lived in Australia: up to 10 years from the best producers in the best vintages.

Annual Vintage Reports

2004

Like much of the rest of the country, Western Australia enjoyed reasonable winter rains and ideal spring conditions for fruit-set, resulting in a bumper crop. Unfortunately, storage and over-supply issues meant that a significant amount of red grapes were left unpicked. The only real hiccup was in the Great Southern region, which had a very grey summer, which led to reds taking their time ripening and a very long vintage, but quality all round is excellent.

2003

Drought, then rain, and not always at the right time, made the Western Australian vintage a very challenging mixed bag. Margaret River did well with Cabernet Sauvignon, Semillon and Sauvignon Blanc, while Shiraz and Riesling were a success in the Great Southern. The normally hot Swan Valley and Perth Hills experienced a good season.

2002

A cool year and a dry one, which resulted in some fantastic whites, though some reds struggled to achieve optimum ripeness levels. Margaret River Chardonnay, Riesling from the Great Southern and Sauvignon Blanc from both regions excelled, with intense fruit characters. Merlot performed well, particularly from Manjimup and Pemberton where the variety seems to thrive, but Cabernet and Pinot Noir tended to struggle.

2001

Although the western summer was long and dry, it was nothing like as hot as in many eastern areas, and cooled off considerably in time for vintage, giving the

Margaret River Cabernet Sauvignon

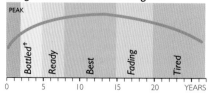

Cabernet Sauvignon is one of Margaret River's success stories – the wines have structure and backbone and despite a considerable depth of black cherry and black olive fruit, they usually need up to 10 years to open out.

state an excellent vintage overall, with some first class wines. It was a classic year for Margaret River Cabernet Sauvignon, Shiraz and Chardonnay and also for Great Southern Shiraz, Riesling and Sauvignon Blanc, which show excellent varietal character here.

2000

Western Australia enjoyed very good weather conditions in 2000, with a slow start followed by hot, dry days and cool nights throughout the summer period. Margaret River reds are deep and long, with excellent flavour. White wines generally are intense and well weighted, although some disease in the vineyards (such as a spot of downy mildew) will guarantee lower yields, not that this will bother the better-managed vineyards anyway. As if to counterbalance the lower volume of fruit, native flowers had a right time of it which meant the greedy local birds had something better to do than damage expensive vine fruit. Late-season rains from Margaret River across to Mount Barker saw some botrytis creep in where it wasn't welcome, but the vintage was, overall, another good one. The better reds are jam-packed with deep colour and pure fruit flavour.

1999

Western Australia bore the brunt of a mid-vintage cyclone. Nevertheless some good wine was made despite the inclement weather, especially Chardonnays and other whites picked before the rain, but it was not a year for reds for long-term cellaring. Cabernet Sauvignon and Merlot are the pick of the bunch.

1998

In Western Australia the vintage was more variable than in other regions. The summer was warm and relatively dry and in the Swan Valley mild temperatures during harvest resulted in a good, ideally ripened crop. Mid-harvest rain further south in Margaret River and Great Southern resulted in wines of varying quality, lacking the excitement of other states.

1997

Western Australia avoided the heatwave of the eastern states but experienced ripening problems, especially in Margaret River where there was a bunchrot outbreak, unusual in such a dry climate. Despite these problems excellent whites were made, especially Riesling, with some fine Semillon-Sauvignon Blanc blends and decent, if lighter-bodied Chardonnay.

Cabernet Sauvignon was as good as the excellent '96s.

1996
A hot summer brought high degrees of ripeness. Quality, especially in Margaret River, was excellent with yields back to normal. A great year for Cabernet Sauvignon and Chardonnay.

1995
The crop shortfall here was less than elsewhere, partly because the state did not suffer the winter drought that affected the eastern vineyards. Quality was high, with some outstanding reds and whites.

Other good years: 1994, '92, '90, '85, '84, '82, '81 and '80, but buy only Cabernet-based reds and full-bodied Shirazes. Little else is likely to have lasted.

TASMANIA

The cool southern isle produces the grapes that go into Australia's finest sparkling wines and the best of these will age and improve for five to 10 years. Tasmania's other strong suit is Pinot Noir, many of which are a delight to drink young, but some can be laid down for up to a decade. Aromatic whites also thrive here, and Riesling will develop for 10 to 15 years. Tasmanian Chardonnay tends to be finer and more elegant than some mainland examples and it, too, can be kept with confidence for up to 10 years.

Annual Vintage Reports
2004
Excellent fruit set was followed by an almost non-existent summer – dry but cool – then heavy rains fell towards the end of another long vintage. As a result, wines tend towards the lean, with aromatic whites and Pinot Noir performing best.

2003
Everything was going swimmingly in Tassie until the heavens opened during vintage, causing some disease problems. However, early-picked Chardonnay and Pinot Noir (and the resulting sparkling wine) was very good.

2002
Yields were slashed after a cold, wet spring resulted in poor fruit-set. However, quality was excellent, thanks to a warm, dry autumn. Pinot Noir and aromatic whites are worth seeking out and keeping.

2001
An unusually warm spring and summer

resulted in a huge crop of good quality fruit, although a drop of late rain caused a few problems for some reds. Pinot Noir was excellent, as was Chardonnay, and there was some good Cabernet.

2000
Pinot Noir has won wide acclaim, with some claiming it as the best vintage yet. A warm, dry growing season saw increased yields and decidedly low acid levels, resulting in soft, approachable wines that are probably best drunk young.

1999
Tasmania enjoyed good spring rain and a sunny late season with cold nights; red wines have depth and the wine intended for sparkling bases is very intense.

1998
Wines of above average quality were produced throughout Tasmania. Drought conditions resulting from El Niño contributed to a reduction in yield with reduced fruit set leading to ideally ripened small berries.

1997
A superb vintage: high quality, low quantity. Tasmania had the best year since 1994 with excellent ripeness and depth of flavour; a godsend following its *annus horribilis* of 1996.

1996
Tasmania had rain at picking time and some mould problems. Yields were up. Not a vintage for keeping. Some decent whites and Pinot Noirs.

1995
Tasmanian whites were better than first anticipated and the Pinot Noir was light but attractive. Most of the wines are past their best by now.

QUEENSLAND

Queensland's wine industry has expanded rapidly in recent years and its production is now on a par with Tasmania's. Most wineries are small and rely heavily on cellar door sales. Shiraz is the outstanding variety and most of it can be cellared for five years. Some fine Cabernets and early-drinking styles, mainly from Shiraz and Merlot, are also made.

Annual Vintage Reports
2004
After an encouragingly benevolent spring and early summer, Queensland was struck by unusually intense heat followed by rains

and widespread botrytis. Early-picked aromatic whites and Cabernet Sauvignon did well, however.

2003
As in New South Wales, the drought was an issue and resulted in a very early vintage and much-reduced yields, but quality was extremely high, particularly in South Burnett.

2002
After a reasonable spring, conditions in the vineyard just got hotter and drier as the summer progressed, but where the vines weren't over-stressed, quality of the fruit was excellent, with Cabernet Sauvignon performing particularly well.

2001
Heavy falls of up to 300mm of rain during vintage took a considerable toll, with yields cut by anything up to 75 per cent in some varieties. Early-picked whites, especially Chardonnay and Semillon, did well, however, and some Cabernet was good.

2000
Perfect growing season, complete with rain when it was wanted, generally mild conditions and no typical mid-summer heat blast. Cabernet Sauvignon and Shiraz did particularly well, though whites were also good.

Visiting the Wine Regions

GENERAL

Australian Tourist Commission (ATC)
www.australia.com

NEW SOUTH WALES

Visit New South Wales
foodandwine.visitnsw.com.au

Langton's Fine Wine Auctions
www.langtons.com.au
Tel: +61 (0)2 9310 4231

Canberra District
Canberra Tourism
www.canberratourism.com.au
Tel: +61 (0)2 6205 0044

Canberra District Wine Industry
Association (including
information for tourists)
www.canberrawines.com.au
Tel: +61 (0)438 028 335

Yass Visitor Information Centre
Tel: +61 (0)2 6226 2557

Cowra
Cowra Tourism
www.cowratourism.com.au
Tel: +61 (0)2 6342 4333

Hunter Valley
Hunter Valley Wine Country
Tourism
www.winecountry.com.au
Tel: +61 (0)2 4990 4477

Mudgee
Mudgee-Gulgong Tourism
www.mudgee-gulgong.org
Tel: +61 (0)2 6372 1020

Mudgee Wine Grape Growers
Association Inc (including
information for tourists)
www.mudgeewine.com.au
Tel: +61 (0)2 6372 7409

Orange
Orange City Council (including
information for tourists)
www.orange.nsw.gov.au/visit_i
ndex.htm
Visitor Information Centre
Tel: +61 (0)2 6393 8226

Riverina
Griffith Visitors Information
Centre
griffith.nsw.gov.au/Griffith
VisitorsCentre.htm
Tel: +61 (0)2 6962 4145 or
Toll Free 1800 68 1141

Riverina Regional Tourism
www.riverinatourism.com.au
Tel: +61 (0)2 6921 1155

QUEENSLAND

Queensland Holidays
queenslandholidays.com.au

Granite Belt
Southern Downs Tourist
Association
qldsoutherndowns.org.au
Tel: + 61 (0)7 4661 2057

Tamborine Mountain
Tamborine Mountain Tourism
Association
tourismtamborine.com.au
Tel: 1300 881 164 (within
Australia)

South Burnett
Fraser Coast South Burnett
Regional Tourism Board Ltd
www.southburnettholidays.info

South Burnett Tourism
Association
tourism.southburnett.com.au
Tel: + 61 (0)7 4162 3199

SOUTH AUSTRALIA

National Wine Centre
www.wineaustralia.com.au
Tel: +61 (0)8 8222 9222

South Australia Tourism
Commission
www.southaustralia.com

Oddbins Wine Auctions
www.oddbins.com.au
Tel: +61 (0)8 8365 4722

Adelaide Hills
Adelaide Hills Wine Region Inc
www.adelaidehillswine.com.au
Tel: +61 (0)8 8370 8808

Barossa Valley
The Barossa Wine and Tourism
Association
www.barossa-region.org
Tel: +61 (0)8 8563 0600

Clare Valley
Clare Valley Visitor Information
www.clarevalley.com.au
Tel: +61 (0)8 8842 2131

Coonawarra
Coonawarra Vignerons
www.coonawarra.org
Tel: +61 (0)8 8737 2392

Fleurieu
Fleurieu Peninsula Tourism
www.fleurieupeninsula.com.au
Tel: +61 (0)8 8556 8766

Langhorne Creek
Wine Industry Council
www.langhornewine.com.au

Limestone Coast
Limestone Coast Tourism
www.thelimestonecoast.com
Tel: 1800 087 087 (within
Australia)

McLaren Vale
McLaren Vale and Fleurieu
Visitors Centre
Tel: +61 (0)8 8323 9944

Padthaway
Bordertown Visitor Centre
Tel: +61 (0)8 8752 0700

Riverland
Mildura Murray Outback
Tourism
www.visitmildura.com.au
Tel: +61 (0)3 5021 4424

TASMANIA

Discover Tasmania
www.discovertasmania.com.au

VICTORIA

Visit Victoria
www.visitvictoria.com

Langton's Fine Wine Auctions
www.langtons.com.au
Tel: +61 (0)3 9428 4499

Bendigo
The Bendigo & District
Winegrowers Association Inc.
www.bendigowine.org.au
Tel: 1300 656 650 (within
Australia)

Gippsland
www.winesofgippsland.com

Mornington Peninsula
Mornington Peninsula
Vignerons Association
(including information for
tourists)
www.mpva.com.au

Rutherglen
Rutherglen Visitors Information
Centre
www.visitrutherglen.com.au

Yarra Valley
Yarra Valley Tourism Association
www.yarravalleytourism.asn.au
Tel: +61 (0)3 5962 2600

WESTERN AUSTRALIA

Western Australian Tourism
www.westernaustralia.com

Great Southern
Mount Barker Tourist Bureau
www.mountbarkerwa.com
Tel: +61 (0)8 9851 1163

Margaret River
Augusta Margaret River
Tourism Association
www.margaretriverwa.com
Tel: +61 (0)8 9757 2911

Pemberton
Pemberton Tourist Centre
www.pembertontourist.com.au
Tel: 1800 671 133 (within
Australia)
Tel: +61 (0)8 9776 1133

Swan Valley
Swan Valley Tourist Information
www.swanvalley.info
Tel: +61 (0)8 9379 9400

Who owns What

The world's major drinks companies are getting bigger and as these vast wine conglomerates stride across continents, it seems highly likely that local traditions will – for purely business reasons – be pared away, along with individuality of flavour. It's not all bad news: in some cases wineries have benefited from the huge resources that come with corporate ownership, but I can't help feeling nervous knowing that the fate of a winery rests in the hands of distant institutional investors. Below I have listed some of the names that crop up again and again in the context of Australian wine – and will no doubt continue to do so, as they aggressively pursue their grasp of market share.

Other wine companies – which bottle wines under their own names – are gradually spreading their nets. Kendall-Jackson of California, for example, owns Yangarra Estate in McLaren Vale and also wineries in Chile, Argentina and Italy. Gallo, the second-biggest wine producer in the world, has a distribution agreement with McWilliam's of Australia. Cross-ownership is making it enormously difficult to know which companies remain independent, and the never-ending whirl of joint ventures, mergers and takeovers shows no signs of slowing down, which means that the following can only be a snapshot at the time of going to press.

BERINGER BLASS

The wine division of Foster's, the giant brewers, takes its name from California's Beringer and Australia's Mildara Blass (originally Wolf Blass) companies and owns wineries in California, Italy, New Zealand and, of course, Australia.

Australian brands include Annie's Lane, Baileys of Glenrowan, Black Opal, Andrew Garrett, Half Mile Creek, Ingoldby, Jamiesons Run, Maglieri, Mildara, Greg Norman Estates, Robertson's Well, The Rothbury Estate, St Huberts, Saltram (Mamre Brook, Metala, Pepperjack), T'Gallant, Wolf Blass, Yarra Ridge and Yellowglen.

CONSTELLATION WINES

The world's largest wine producer was created in 2003 by the merger of US-based wine, beer and spirits group Constellation Brands with Australia's BRL Hardy, now renamed as The Hardy Wine Company. California's Blackstone brand was the result of an earlier joint venture between the two giants.

The Hardy Company brands include Hardys (Annabella, Nottage Hill, Siegersdorf, Tintara), Banrock Station, Bay of Fires, Houghton (Moondah Brook, Crofters) Kamberra (Meeting Place), Leasingham, Reynell, Stonehaven (Stepping Stone) and Yarra Burn. Arras, Omni and Sir James are sparkling wine labels while Berri Estates, Renmano and Stanley are cask wine labels. The Hardy Wine Company owns 50% of each of Barossa Valley Estate, Brookland Valley and the Lane (formerly Ravenswood Lane) and owns 40% of New Zealand's Nobilo (Selaks, White Cloud). Hardy also distributes Starvedog Lane and Redmans.

FREIXENET

Spanish Cava producer making a bid for global market share, with some of Spain's biggest names and wine companies in Champagne, Bordeaux, California and Mexico. It also owns Australia's Wingara Wine Group (Deakin Estate, Katnook Estate and Riddoch Estate).

LION NATHAN

Australian-based brewery with operations in New Zealand and China which in 2001 branched out into wine, buying the premium Petaluma and Banksia groups. The former includes Petaluma (Bridgewater Mill, Croser, Sharefarmers), Mitchelton (Preece), Knappstein, Stonier and Smithbrook, while Banksia consisted of St Hallett, Tatachilla and Hillstowe.

There is some sharing of facilities within the Petaluma group though, with the exception of the Pemberton vineyard, Smithbrook, which has most of its wines made at the Knappstein winery in Clare from juice trucked across the Nullabor, the wineries operate more or less autonomously. All the wines of the Banksia group are now made at St Hallett in the Barossa.

LVMH

French luxury goods group Louis Vuitton-Moët Hennessy owns Champagne houses Moët & Chandon (including Dom Pérignon), Krug, Canard-Duchêne, Mercier, Ruinart and Veuve Clicquot, and has established Domaine Chandon sparkling wine companies in California, Australia, Argentina and Spain. The purchase of Ch. d'Yquem, the world-famous estate in Sauternes, Bordeaux, in 1999 was a major coup. It also owns Cape Mentelle and Mountadam in Australia, Cloudy Bay in New Zealand, Newton in California and Terrazas de los Andes in Argentina.

MCGUIGAN SIMEON

The 2002 merger of Brian McGuigan Wines (established in 1992) with Simeon Wines (established in 1994) and its huge vineyard holdings has created one of Australia's largest wine companies. This position has been strengthened by the takeover in 2003 of the Riverina-based Miranda winery, itself Australia's eighth largest company and enjoying a large foothold in the important cask sector, which accounts for 45% by volume of the Australian market. The company now has close to 6000 hectares of vineyards throughout Australia. Their brands include McGuigan, Tempus Two, Earth's Portrait and Miranda.

PERNOD RICARD

The French spirits giant owns Australia's Orlando-Wyndham Group, which includes Jacob's Creek, Carrington, Coolabah, Morris, Orlando, Poet's Corner, Richmond Grove, Russet Ridge and Wyndham Estate. Poet's Corner also has the Henry Lawson, Trilogy and Montrose labels and Orlando has Gramps, the Saints range (St Helga, St Hilary and St Hugo) and regional wines: Steingarten Riesling from the Eden Valley, Jacaranda Ridge Cabernet Sauvignon from Coonawarra, Lawson's Shiraz from Padthaway and Centenary Hill Shiraz from Barossa.

Pernod Ricard also owns Etchart (Argentina); Long Mountain (South Africa) and has interests in wineries in Georgia.

SOUTHCORP

Australia's biggest wine conglomerate, which merged with Rosemount in 2001. Southcorp's major Australian brands include Leo Buring, Coldstream Hills, Devil's Lair, Lindemans, Penfolds, Queen Adelaide, Rosemount Estate, Seppelt and Wynns. Minor brands include Blue Point, Edwards & Chaffey, Glass Mountain, Kaiser Stuhl, Killawarra, Matthew Lang, Minchinbury, Rouge Homme and Seaview. Southcorp has larger vineyard holdings (more than 8000 hectares) around Australia than any other wine group. These include prized vineyards in Coonawarra and the Barossa.

Glossary

Acidity Naturally present in grapes; gives red wine an appetizing 'grip' and whites a refreshing tang. Too much can make a wine seem sharp but too little and it will be flabby.

Aging Essential for fine wines and for softening many everyday reds. May take place in vat, barrel or bottle, and may last for months or years. It has a mellowing effect on a wine but too long in storage, though, and the wine may lose its fruit.

Alcohol Alcohol is found in all wines, but levels vary from as little as 7% for a Mosel Riesling and 10% for a Hunter Semillon to maybe 15% for a rich, ripe Shiraz – and higher for fortifieds. Alcohol balances other flavours in a wine, for example softening the attack of the acid, and makes the wine feel richer in your mouth. Without it you would just be downing a glass of grape juice.

Alcoholic content Alcoholic strength, sometimes expressed in degrees, equivalent to the percentage of alcohol in the total volume.

Alcoholic fermentation Biochemical process whereby yeasts, natural or added, convert the grape sugars into alcohol and carbon dioxide, transforming grape juice into wine. It normally stops when all the sugar has been converted or when the alcohol level reaches about 15%.

Amarone Italian term for wine, particularly Valpolicella or Soave from the North-East, made from grapes that have been dried on racks for two or three months to concentrate the sugar and acidity before fermentation. The wine is therefore usually sweet and usually high quality, particularly as the best producers select the best fruit for this style. If residual sugar is left in the wine it will be sweet. If it is fermented out to dryness it is called *amarone*.

Aromatic All wines have an aroma, but an aromatic wine is particularly pungent or spicy and is usually from an aromatic variety like Gewurztraminer.

Balance The relationship between all the elements in a wine – sweetness, acidity, tannin, alcohol, fruit and body. An unbalanced wine will taste as though it is lacking something – and it is.

Barrel aging Time spent maturing in wood, normally oak and normally 225-litre barrels (also known as barriques after their French name). The wine takes on vanilla and cinnamon flavours from the wood, becomes deeper in colour, is naturally clarified and its tannins softened. The process prepares a wine for bottle-aging where it will continue to gain complexity.

Barrel fermentation Oak barrels may be used for fermentation instead of stainless steel to give a rich, oaky flavour to the wine.

Basket press Traditional basket presses delicately extract the juice from the skins without breaking the grape seeds and overextracting the harsh tannins from the skins. With a basket press the winemaker has more control over extraction and can get better tannins. Basket presses are back in fashion and popping up in both large and small wineries, usually for small parcels of reds and not just from old vines. Whites are almost never put through basket presses. Key wineries using them are Wendouree, Rockford, Cape Mentelle, Reynell and Moss Wood.

Bin number System of numbering batches of wine for identification purposes, particularly used in Australia where certain successful bin numbers have now become wine brands in themselves. Penfolds, Lindemans, Wyndham, McGuigan and Leasingham in particular still use this system of wine labelling.

Biodynamics Based on the principles of Rudolf Steiner, biodynamics considers the sources of heat and light that a plant receives, as well as the soil and water. This includes a consideration of wider forces at work, taking into account lunar phases, planetary cycles, and even astrology. The aim is to re-establish the harmony and balance of the vineyard – both of plants and soil. While adherents of biodynamics do not reject the basic methods of organic farming, they further seek to restore the environment to its best state. This involves the application of mineral and vegetable preparations, in homeopathic amounts, at known propitious times of the day (or night) to encourage fertility in the soil. Dismissed by some, the growing number of top-flight producers around the world who are wholly committed to biodynamic practice is impressive. Leading proponents in Australia include Jasper Hill and Cullen. Michel Chapoutier continues to follow biodynamic principles at his vineyard in Mount Benson in the Limestone Coast and in his joint venture with Ron Laughton of Jasper Hill.

Blend A wine made from two or more varieties (many grapes need to have their weaknesses balanced by complementary varieties) or from several wines of the same variety to maintain a consistent style or increase quality. The wines can also be of different origin, styles or age. Almost all wines are blended: this can be either from vines in adjacent rows in a vineyard or from regions hundreds of miles apart. In the case of the best wines, the best lots are selected to reflect the quality of the vintage and the character of the vineyard.

Bold A wine with distinct, easily understood flavours.

Botrytis *Botrytis cinerea* fungus which, in warm autumn weather, attacks white grapes, shrivels them and concentrates the sugars to produce quality sweet wines, as in the Sauternes region of Bordeaux, France. Also called 'noble rot'. The Riverina produces world class, luscious sweet Semillon wines from botrytized grapes that can easily rival those of Sauternes.

Brut Term for 'dry', usually seen on Champagne labels and sparkling wines in the New World.

Budbreak/burst Period when the first shoots emerge from the vine buds in spring. Marks the end of the vine's dormant period during the winter.

Canopy management Adjustments to alter the exposure of a vine's fruit and leaves to the sun, to improve quality, increase yield and help to control disease. Simpler measures include leaf trimming, early fruit culling and more general pruning.

Cask Wooden (usually oak) barrel used for aging and storing wine. In Australia the term is also used, rather misleadingly, for wine packaged in boxes.

Champagne method Traditional way of making sparkling wine by inducing a second fermentation in the bottle in which the wine will be sold.

Chewy A wine with a lot of tannin and strong flavour, but which is not aggressive.

Claret English term for red Bordeaux wines, taken from the French word *clairet*, which was traditionally used to describe a lighter style of Bordeaux.

Clarification Term covering any winemaking process (such as filtering or fining) that involves the removal of solid matter either from the must or the wine.

Climate A critical influence on the style and quality of wine. Cool climate areas are at the coolest limits for grape ripening and are good for reserved, elegant styles. In warm climate areas vines ripen easily but often need to be irrigated. Warm climate wines are rich and high in alcohol. Red grapes generally need a warmer climate than white ones.

Clone Propagating vines by taking cuttings produces clones of the original plant. Vine nurseries now enable growers to order specific clones to suit conditions in their vineyards. Through this clonal selection it is possible to control yield, flavour and general quality.

Cold fermentation Long, slow fermentation at low temperature to extract maximum freshness from the grapes. Crucial for whites in hot climates.

Complex A wine that has layer upon layer of flavours.

Concentration The intensity and focus of flavour in a wine.

Crush Another word for vintage. It can also mean the quantity of grapes crushed. In Australia this is measured in tonnes per hectare.

Domaine A wine estate.

Dry farming Growing crops without the aid of irrigation. In countries such as Australia where irrigation is widely practised, fruit from dry farmed vines is often highly prized.

Dusty A dry, slightly earthy taste sometimes found in reds. Can be very attractive if combined with good fruit.

Earthy A smell and taste of damp earth – appealing in some red wines.

Enologist Wine scientist or technician. The role has become an increasingly high-profile one due to publicity afforded by flying winemakers.

Estate bottled A wine made and bottled by a single property, though this may encompass several different vineyards.

Fat A wine that is full-bodied and unctuous.

Fermentation See Alcoholic fermentation, Malolactic fermentation.

Filtering Removal of yeasts, solids and any impurities from a wine before bottling.

Flying winemaker Term coined in the late 1980s to describe enologists, many of them Australian or Australian-trained, brought in to underperforming regions, mainly in Europe and South America, to improve the quality, chiefly of bulk wines. Employing a range of New World vinification practices, the aim has been to produce clean, fruity wines at attractive prices. A number, among them Geoff Merrill and Jacques Lurton, produce their own labels in wine regions all around the world.

Fortified wine Wine which has high-alcohol grape spirit added, usually before the initial alcoholic fermentation is completed, thereby preserving sweetness. Among the best known are sherry, Madeira and Port from Europe and the Liqueur Muscats and Tokays produced at Rutherglen in North-East Victoria.

Fresh A young wine with lively fruit flavours and good acidity.

Fruit flavour In wine this comes from the grapes, yet wine seldom tastes of grapes. Instead, flavours can resemble plums, strawberries, gooseberries or many other fruits – or, indeed, nuts, coffee beans, green leaves or biscuits.

Garagiste French term coined recently to describe a Bordeaux winemaker who makes minuscule amounts of wine originally literally in a garage which are then sold for very high prices.

Geographical Indication (GI) Australian term to indicate the origin of a wine, i.e. the wine zones, regions and sub-regions.

Green harvest Green harvest, or crop-thinning, involves the removal of grape bunches during the growing season. When carried out before flowering the process promotes earlier ripening and reduces yield. The remaining bunches will compensate for the removal by setting better and growing larger. However, the increased size of individual berries may result in more compacted bunches, aggravating the risk of rot. Bunches may be removed later in the season, usually after fruit set when the berries change colour (veraison), when the technique will have a greater impact on reducing yield.

Hectolitre (hl) 100 litres; 22 imperial gallons or 133 standard 75-cl bottles.

Irrigation Application of water to vines in dry viticultural areas. Vines in arid climates can fail to ripen fruit fully, resulting in poor yields, and wines that are low in sugar, flavour and acidity. Methods include flood irrigation and sprinklers, but by far the most effective is drip irrigation where water is applied directly to the roots.

Late harvest Late-harvested grapes contain more sugar and concentrated flavours; the term is often used for sweetish New World wines, invariably for wines of lesser quality.

Lees Coarse sediment – dried yeasts, etc. – thrown by wine in a cask and left behind after racking. Some wines stay on the lees for as long as possible to take on extra flavour.

Length This is the flavour that persists in the mouth after swallowing or tasting. A flavour that continues or even improves for some time after the wine is gone is a mark of quality.

Lyre Trellis system for training vines with a split canopy, developed by Bordeaux, that gives both improved quality and yield by reduction of shade. It is now being adapted to vineyards in Australia, New Zealand, California and Chile. Both spur and cane pruning are possible.

Malolactic fermentation Secondary fermentation whereby sharp, appley malic acid is converted into mild lactic acid and carbon dioxide; occurs naturally after alcoholic fermentation. It is encouraged in red wines, softening them and reducing their acidity, but often prevented in whites to preserve a fresh taste, especially in wines made in warm regions, where natural acidity will be lower.

Maturation The beneficial aging of wine.

Melbourne 'Dress Circle' Term used to describe the wine regions in the immediate area around Melbourne, i.e. the Yarra Valley, Mornington Peninsula, Gippsland and Geelong.

Mesoclimate Describes the climate of a specified geographical area, be it one vineyard or several (or simply a hillside or valley). Often confused with Microclimate or Macroclimate.

Must The mixture of grape juice, skins, pips and pulp produced after crushing (but prior to completion of fermentation), which will eventually become wine.

Négociant French term for merchant or shipper who buys in wine from growers, then matures it, maybe blending it too, and bottles it for sale.

Noble rot See Botrytis.

Oak Traditional wood for wine casks. During aging or fermenting it gives flavours, such as vanilla and tannin, to the wines. The newer the wood, the greater its impact. French oak is often preferred for aging fine wine. American oak is cheaper but can give strong vanilla overtones. In Australia American oak is more common for Shiraz, especially in the Barossa, McLaren Vale and Langhorne Creek. French oak is increasingly being used for top quality Shiraz from cooler climates such as the Great Southern and the Grampians and is usually used for Cabernet Sauvignon and Merlot. European oak (meaning Eastern Europe and Russia) is being used increasingly. Oak is rarely used on white wines in Australia. There is an increasing mastery of the use of barrel maturation, bringing out the most apt qualities – be it flavour or structure – for the style of wine sought by the winemaker. Excessive oakiness is less commonly encountered than it was ten years ago, while the use of barriques has become even more widespread. The age and the size of the barrels used are crucial, as are the source of the wood and the amount of toasting (charring) it undergoes while being worked by the cooper. Whether the oak is American or French, suffers low-level or high toasting, and is new, one year old, two years old and so on, or simply a large inert vessel, it has a corresponding influence on the wine to be bottled. This influence rapidly diminishes as the barrel ages. Oak barrels are also often used as fermentation vessels, being almost mandatory for many top white classic Burgundies and Chardonnays as well as Sauternes. Those wines fermented as well as aged in oak have a much greater lifespan.

Old vines Old vines can give more concentrated, intensely flavoured wine. There are no legal definitions of how old a wine has to be to qualify, but the term is a fairly reliable indicator. A wine made from old vines should mean – but doesn't always – at least 20 years old, if not twice that. Australia has some of the oldest vines in the world, at over 150 years old.

Oxidation Over-exposure of wine to air, causing bacterial decay and loss of fruit and flavour. Often characterized by a rather sherry-like aroma.

Robert Parker Hugely influential American wine critic and author whose palate moves markets internationally and persuades winemakers to change the style of their wines (although none of them would ever admit it). His tasting notes and marks out of 100 (based on the US high school system of marking) can send prices soaring or plummeting.

Phylloxera Vine aphid (*Phylloxera vastatrix*) which devastated viticulture worldwide in the late 19th century. It reached Australia in 1877 (first being discovered near Geelong in Victoria). Since then, the superior but vulnerable European *Vitis vinifera* has been grafted on to phylloxera-resistant American rootstocks.

Phylloxera has never reached Chile nor large areas of Australia (South Australia, Western Australia, Tasmania and the Hunter Valley are prime examples), so vines there are ungrafted and can live up to twice as long. This is why South Australia has some of the oldest Shiraz and Grenache wines in the world.

Powerful A wine with plenty of everything, especially alcohol.

Premium Best quality, and therefore more expensive.

Producer The company that makes the wine and the most important consideration when choosing a wine.

Pruning Method of trimming the vine which takes place mainly in the dormant winter months. Also the primary means of controlling and improving yield (see Canopy management). Vines are either spur pruned or cane pruned, depending on the vine training system used. In its wild state the vine has a mechanism of self-regulation which prevents it from overcropping. In Australia, this has been harnessed to develop Minimal Pruning, a technique which is appropriate for warm, arid climates.

Racking Gradual clarification of a quality wine as part of the maturation process. The wine is transferred from one barrel to another, leaving the lees or sediment behind. Racking also produces aeration necessary for the aging process, softens tannins and helps develop further flavours.

Réserve The term should indicate the wine has been aged longer in oak but many New World producers use it freely on their wine labels to indicate different wine styles or a special selection rather than a better wine. It has no legal meaning. Other similar terms are Private Reserve and Special Selection.

Residual sugar Sugar left over in the wine after fermentation is complete. A perceptible level of residual sugar makes the wine taste sweet.

Ripe A wine made from well-ripened grapes has good fruit flavour. Unripe wines can taste green and stalky.

Ripening Process in the development of grapes prior to harvesting, when the grapes start to soften, gain colour and lose acidity. The length of ripening time before harvesting varies according to variety and can be influenced by vine diseases, environmental factors and excess yields.

Rootstock The root stump of the vine on to which the fruiting branches are grafted. Most rootstocks are from phylloxera-resistant American vines.

Sauternes A wine region in Bordeaux, France, famous for its sweet white wines made from botrytized grapes. See Botrytis.

Second fermentation A second alcoholic fermentation that is the integral part of all but the cheapest sparkling wine production.

Whether it takes place in bottle or tank, it involves the addition of yeast and sugar to give both a small increase in the alcohol level and enough carbon dioxide to create the all-important fizz.

Single-vineyard Wines with real individuality tend to be made using grapes from just one vineyard. Some of the best known Australian examples are Grosset's Polish Hill and Watervale Riesling wines, Petaluma's Tiers Vineyard Chardonnay, Lindemans' St George Cabernet Sauvignon and McWilliam's Lovedale Semillon.

Solera Blending system used for sherry and some other fortified wines, such as those from Rutherglen and Glenrowan in North-East Victoria. When mature wine is run off a cask for bottling, only a quarter or so of the volume is taken, and the space is filled with similar but younger wine from another cask, which in turn is topped up from an even younger cask, and so on.

Spicy Exotic fragrances and flavours common in Gewurztraminer; also the tastes of pepper, cinnamon or cloves in reds such as Australian Shiraz. Spiciness can be an effect of oak aging.

Structure 'Plenty of structure' refers to a wine with a well-developed backbone of acid and tannin, but enough fruit to stand up to it.

Sugar Naturally present in grapes. Transformed during fermentation into alcohol and carbon dioxide.

Tannin This is the stuff in red wines that stains your teeth and dries your mouth, but in the right amounts can do marvellous things to the flavour and texture of the wine. Derived from grape skins, pips, stems and from aging in oak barrels; softens with time and is essential for a wine's long-term aging.

Terra rossa When the calcium is leached out of limestone, it can form a reddish soil, the staining coming from dehydrated iron compounds. It is usually associated with Mediterranean climates, which have very dry summers and wet winters that enable the leaching and hydrating processes to occur. However its most famous manifestation is in the Coonawarra region, South Australia.

Terroir The concept that wine is an expression of where it comes from, rather than simply a product of the climate and grape variety. It has developed from the French term used to denote the combination of soil, climate and exposure to the sun – that is, the natural physical environment of the vine.

Toasty A flavour like buttered toast that results from maturing a wine in oak barrels.

Training Method of vine management using a permanent vine structure, either free-standing, up stakes, along wires or onto a trellis or training system (see Canopy management), which will determine the type of pruning. Methods vary from region to region according to soil, climate, variety and land availability, but are generally

determined by the vigour of the vineyard and the density of planting.

Varietal The character of wine derived from the grape; also wine made from, and named after, a single or dominant grape variety and in Australia containing at least 85 per cent of that variety. (The minimum percentage varies slightly between countries.) This is the simple, modern way to label wine rather than the traditional European system of appellations. A varietal character is one which shows the basic traits associated with a specific grape.

Veraison French term for the change of colour of grapes as they ripen.

Vigneron French term for winegrower.

Vinification The process of turning grapes into wine.

Vintage The year's grape harvest, also used to describe the wine of a single year.

Viticulture Vine-growing and vineyard management.

Weight or **body** Describes the different impressions of weight and size wines give in the mouth. This is what is referred to as full-, medium- and light-bodied.

Winemaker The person responsible for controlling the vinification process.

Yeast Organism which, in the wine process, causes grape juice to ferment. In the New World it is common to start fermentation with cultured yeasts, rather than rely on the natural yeasts present in the winery, known as ambient yeasts.

Yield Perhaps the most important factor in dertmining the quality of a wine. The yield is the amount of fruit, and ultimately wine, produced from a vineyard, generally ranging between 40 and 100 hectolitres per hectare – it varies according to soil, climate, grape variety and vine density as well as age, pruning and training. The lower the quantity of grapes each vine is allowed to produce, the more intense the juice in the grapes and the flavours in the wine will be. The classic European appellation system is based on the premise that low yield equals high quality, but balance of the vineyard is the real key. Only in the world's top vineyards with naturally low vigour is it feasible to reduce yield and balance the vine.

Zone As part of the classification system for Australian wine many of its traditional wine areas have been incorporated into zones, regions and sub-regions.

Index of Main Wines

Illustration captions are indexed in *italic*.

General Index

Main references are indexed in **bold**. Illustration captions are indexed in *italic*.

Acknowledgements

Oz Clarke and Websters International Publishers would like to thank the many organisations, wineries and individuals who have given invaluable help with the preparation of this book, in particular the following:

IN THE UK
Paul Henry and Linda Simpson of the Australian Wine Bureau, Austravel, Hazel Murphy, Craig Smith.

IN AUSTRALIA
AWEC (Australian Wine Exporting Council) and the following:
Tim Adams, Anna Aldridge, Max Arney, John Angove, Doug Balnaves, Peter Barry, Susanne Bell, Ross Brown, Andrew Buller, Justin Byrne, Colin Campbell, Bailey Carrodus, Larry Cherubino, Greg Clayfield, Brian Croser, Vanya Cullen, Peter Dawson, Darren De Bortoli, Stephen Doyle, Pam Dunsford, Peter Fuller, Gordon Gebbie, James Halliday, Philippa Hambleton, Andrew Hardy, Ken Helm, Stephen and Prue Henschke, Toby Hill, Michael Hill-Smith, Rob Hill-Smith, Richard Howden, John Innes, Lian Jaensch, Tony Jordan, Tim Knappstein, Rick Kinzbrunner, Max Lake, David Lance, Ron Laughton, Michelle Lawler, Peter Lehmann, Peter Leske, Bob McLean, Rod McPherson, Sally Marden, Charlie Melton, Geoff Merrill, Barry Morey, Mick Morris, Robert O'Callaghan, Chester Osborn, Stephen Pannell, Chris Pfeiffer, Dave Powell, Ros Ritchie, Craig Rutledge, Jonathan Scott, Philip Shaw, Stephen Shelmerdine, Michael Sinclair, Craig Smith, Bruce Tyrrell, Mark Walpole, Adam Wynn.

PHOTO CREDITS
Angove's 30, 40; Bleasdale Winery 27 (below); Adam Bruzzone, Adelaide 1, 2-3, 34, 176; Domaine Chandon 33; Len Evans 31; Hardy Wine Company 25 (below), 96; Nigel James 6; Peter Lehmann 31; Lindemans 3; McWilliam's 4, 12, 29, 92, 158; Orlando-Wyndham 20, 28; Howard Park and Madfish Wines (F22 Photography) 128; Preston Peak 152; Romavilla Winery 25 (above); Philip Shaw/Aldridge Wine Consulting 31; Sirromet 154; Tourism Queensland 150, 155; Tyrrell's 31.
All other photographs supplied by Cephas Picture Library. All Cephas photographs by Mick Rock except:
Andy Christodolo/Cephas 46, 52, 78, 84, 102, 110, 126, 129; Jeffery Drewitz/Cephas 86, 97, 103; Kevin Judd/Cephas 7, 8, 9, 10, 14, 15, 16, 19, 24, 26, 31, 41, 43, 50, 57, 69, 108, 122, 135, 142, 146; Clay McLachlan/Cephas 13; Steven Morris/Cephas 100; Howard Shearing/Cephas 145; Phil Winter/Cephas 16.